*Software
Measurement
and Estimation*

Software Measurement and Estimation

A Practical Approach

Linda M. Laird
M. Carol Brennan

IEEE COMPUTER SOCIETY

WILEY-INTERSCIENCE

A John Wiley & Sons, Inc., Publication

Published by John Wiley & Sons, Inc., Hoboken, New Jersey.
Published simultaneously in Canada.

For general information on our other products and services or for technical support, please contact our Customer Care Department within the United States at (800) 762-2974, outside the United States at (317) 572-3993 or fax (317) 572-4002.

Wiley also publishes its books in a variety of electronic formats. Some content that appears in print may not be available in electronic formats. For more information about Wiley products, visit our web site at www.wiley.com.

Library of Congress Cataloging-in-Publication Data:

Laird, Linda M., 1952-
  Software measurement and estimation: a practical approach / Linda M. Laird, M. Carol Brennan.
    p.cm
  Includes bibliographical references and index.
  ISBN 0-471-67622-5 (cloth)
  1. Software measurement. 2. Software engineering.   I. Brennan, M. Carol, 1954-   II. Title.
  QA76.76.S65L35 2006
  005.1′4- -dc22   2005028945

Printed in the United States of America

10   9   8   7   6   5   4   3   2   1

For my Mom and Dad—LML

To my family, JB, Jackie, Colleen, Claire, and Spikey—your support has always been beyond measure. And to my mother, who I'm sure is smiling down at her "mathematical" daughter.—MCB

Contents

Acknowledgments   **xv**

1. Introduction   **1**

   1.1 Objective / 1
   1.2 Approach / 2
   1.3 Motivation / 3
   1.4 Summary / 5
   References / 6

2. What to Measure   **7**

   2.1 Method 1: The Goal Question Metrics Approach / 9
   2.2 Method 2: Decision Maker Model / 10
   2.3 Method 3: Standards Driven Metrics / 10
   2.4 Extension to GQM: Metrics Mechanism / 11
   2.5 What to Measure Is a Function of Time / 12
   2.6 Summary / 12
   Problems / 13
   Project / 13
   References / 13

3.   Measurement Fundamentals   **15**

3.1   Initial Measurement Exercise / 15

3.2   The Challenge of Measurement / 16

3.3   Measurement Models / 16

    3.3.1   Text Models / 16

    3.3.2   Diagrammatic Models / 18

    3.3.3   Algorithmic Models / 18

    3.3.4   Model Examples: Response Time / 18

    3.3.5   The Pantometric Paradigm: How to
    Measure Anything / 19

3.4   Meta-Model for Metrics / 20

3.5   The Power of Measurement / 21

3.6   Measurement Theory / 22

    3.6.1   Introduction to Measurement Theory / 22

    3.6.2   Measurement Scales / 23

    3.6.3   Measures of Central Tendency and Variability / 24

        3.6.3.1   Measures of Central Tendency / 25

        3.6.3.2   Measures of Variability / 25

    3.6.4   Validity and Reliability of Measurement / 27

    3.6.5   Measurement Error / 28

3.7   Accuracy Versus Precision and the Limits of
Software Metrics / 30

3.8   Summary / 31

Problems / 31

Projects / 33

References / 33

4.   Measuring Size   **34**

4.1   Physical Measurements of Software / 34

    4.1.1   Measuring Lines of Code / 35

    4.1.2   Language Productivity Factor / 35

    4.1.3   Counting Reused and Refactored Code / 37

    4.1.4   Counting Nonprocedural Code Length / 39

    4.1.5   Measuring the Length of Specifications and Design / 39

4.2   Measuring Functionality / 40

    4.2.1   Function Points / 41

        4.2.1.1   Counting Function Points / 41

        4.2.1.2   Function Point Example / 45

    4.2.1.3   Converting Function Points to Physical Size / 47
    4.2.1.4   Converting Function Points to Effort / 47
    4.2.1.5   Other Function Point Engineering Rules / 48
    4.2.1.6   Function Point Pros and Cons / 49
  4.2.2   Feature Points / 50
4.3   Summary / 51
Problems / 51
Project / 52
References / 53

5.   Measuring Complexity   **54**

5.1   Structural Complexity / 55
  5.1.1   Size as a Complexity Measure / 55
    5.1.1.1   System Size and Complexity / 55
    5.1.1.2   Module Size and Complexity / 56
  5.1.2   Cyclomatic Complexity / 58
  5.1.3   Halstead's Metrics / 63
  5.1.4   Information Flow Metrics / 65
  5.1.5   System Complexity / 67
    5.1.5.1   Maintainability Index / 67
    5.1.5.2   The Agresti–Card System
              Complexity Metric / 69
  5.1.6   Object-Oriented Design Metrics / 71
  5.1.7   Structural Complexity Summary / 73
5.2   Conceptual Complexity / 73
5.3   Computational Complexity / 74
5.4   Summary / 75
Problems / 75
Projects / 77
References / 78

6.   Estimating Effort   **79**

6.1   Effort Estimation: Where Are We? / 80
6.2   Software Estimation Methodologies and Models / 81
  6.2.1   Expert Estimation / 82
    6.2.1.1   Work and Activity Decomposition / 82
    6.2.1.2   System Decomposition / 83
    6.2.1.3   The Delphi Methods / 84

6.2.2   Using Benchmark Size Data / 85

    6.2.2.1   Lines of Code Benchmark Data / 85

    6.2.2.2   Function Point Benchmark Data / 87

6.2.3   Estimation by Analogy / 88

    6.2.3.1   Traditional Analogy Approach / 89

    6.2.3.2   Analogy Summary / 91

6.2.4   Proxy Point Estimation Methods / 91

    6.2.4.1   Meta-Model for Effort Estimation / 91

    6.2.4.2   Function Points / 92

    6.2.4.3   Object Points / 94

    6.2.4.4   Use Case Sizing Methodologies / 95

6.2.5   Custom Models / 101

6.2.6   Algorithmic Models / 103

    6.2.6.1   Manual Models / 103

    6.2.6.2   Estimating Project Duration / 105

    6.2.6.3   Tool-Based Models / 105

6.3   Combining Estimates / 107

6.4   Estimating Issues / 108

    6.4.1   Targets Versus Estimates / 108

    6.4.2   The Limitations of Estimation: Why? / 109

    6.4.3   Estimate Uncertainties / 109

6.5   Estimating Early and Often / 112

6.6   Summary / 113

Problems / 114

Projects / 116

References / 116

7.   In Praise of Defects: Defects and Defect Metrics   **118**

7.1   Why Study and Measure Defects? / 118

7.2   Faults Versus Failures / 119

7.3   Defect Dynamics and Behaviors / 120

    7.3.1   Defect Arrival Rates / 120

    7.3.2   Defects Versus Effort / 120

    7.3.3   Defects Versus Staffing / 120

    7.3.4   Defect Arrival Rates Versus Code Production Rate / 121

    7.3.5   Defect Density Versus Module Complexity / 122

    7.3.6   Defect Density Versus System Size / 122

7.4   Defect Projection Techniques and Models / 123

    7.4.1   Dynamic Defect Models / 123

        7.4.1.1   Rayleigh Models / 124

        7.4.1.2   Exponential and S-Curves Arrival
        Distribution Models / 127

        7.4.1.3   Empirical Data and Recommendations for
        Dynamic Models / 128

    7.4.2   Static Defect Models / 129

        7.4.2.1   Defect Insertion and Removal Model / 129

        7.4.2.2   Defect Removal Efficiency:
        A Key Metric / 130

        7.4.2.3   Static Defect Model Tools / 132

7.5   Additional Defect Benchmark Data / 133

    7.5.1   Defect Data by Application Domain / 133

    7.5.2   Cumulative Defect Removal Efficiency
    (DRE) Benchmark / 134

    7.5.3   SEI Levels and Defect Relationships / 134

    7.5.4   Latent Defects / 135

    7.5.5   A Few Recommendations / 135

7.6   Cost Effectiveness of Defect Removal by Phase / 136

7.7   Defining and Using Simple Defect Metrics:
    An Example / 136

7.8   Some Paradoxical Patterns for Customer
    Reported Defects / 139

7.9   Answers to the Initial Questions / 140

7.10 Summary / 140

Problems / 141

Projects / 142

References / 142

8. Software Reliability Measurement and Prediction   **144**

8.1   Why Study and Measure Software Reliability? / 144

8.2   What Is Reliability? / 144

8.3   Faults and Failures / 145

8.4   Failure Severity Classes / 145

8.5   Failure Intensity / 146

8.6   The Cost of Reliability / 147

8.7   Software Reliability Theory / 148

    8.7.1   Uniform and Random Distributions / 148

  8.7.2 The Probability of Failure During
       a Time Interval / 150
  8.7.3 $F(t)$: The Probability of Failure by Time T / 151
  8.7.4 $R(t)$: The Reliability Function / 151
  8.7.5 Reliability Theory Summarized / 152
 8.8 Reliability Models / 152
  8.8.1 Types of Models / 152
  8.8.2 Predicting Number of Defects Remaining / 154
 8.9 Failure Arrival Rates / 155
  8.9.1 Predicting Failure Arrival Rates Using
       Historical Data / 155
  8.9.2 Engineering Rules for MTTF / 156
  8.9.3 Musa's Algorithm / 157
  8.9.4 Operational Profile Testing / 158
  8.9.5 Predicting Reliability Summary / 161
 8.10 But When Do I Ship? / 161
 8.11 System Configurations: Probability and Reliability / 161
 8.12 Answers to Initial Question / 163
 8.13 Summary / 164
 Problems / 164
 Project / 165
 References / 166

9. Response Time and Availability   **167**

 9.1 Response Time Measurements / 168
 9.2 Availability / 170
  9.2.1 Availability Factors / 172
  9.2.2 Outage Scope / 173
  9.2.3 Complexities in Measuring Availability / 173
  9.2.4 Software Rejuvenation / 174
       9.2.4.1 Software Aging / 175
       9.2.4.2 Classification of Faults / 175
       9.2.4.3 Software Rejuvenation Techniques / 175
       9.2.4.4 Impact of Rejuvenation on Availability / 176
 9.3 Summary / 177
 Problems / 178
 Project / 179
 References / 180

10. Measuring Progress   **181**

    10.1   Project Milestones / 182

    10.2   Code Integration / 185

    10.3   Testing Progress / 187

    10.4   Defects Discovery and Closure / 188

         10.4.1   Defect Discovery / 189

         10.4.2   Defect Closure / 190

    10.5   Process Effectiveness / 192

    10.6   Summary / 194

    Problems / 195

    Project / 196

    References / 196

11. Outsourcing   **197**

    11.1   The "O" Word / 197

    11.2   Defining Outsourcing / 198

    11.3   Risk Management and Outsourcing / 201

    11.4   Metrics and the Contract / 203

    11.5   Summary / 206

    Problems / 206

    Projects / 207

    References / 207

12. Financial Measures for the Software Engineer   **208**

    12.1   It's All About the Green / 208

    12.2   Financial Concepts / 209

    12.3   Building the Business Case / 209

         12.3.1   Understanding Costs / 210

               12.3.1.1   Salaries / 210

               12.3.1.2   Overhead costs / 210

               12.3.1.3   Risk Costs / 211

               12.3.1.4   Capital Versus Expense / 213

         12.3.2   Understanding Benefits / 216

         12.3.3   Business Case Metrics / 218

               12.3.3.1   Return on Investment / 218

               12.3.3.2   Payback Period / 219

               12.3.3.3   Cost/Benefit Ratio / 220

               12.3.3.4   Profit and Loss Statement / 221

12.3.3.5   Cash Flow / 222

12.3.3.6   Expected Value / 223

12.4   Living the Business Case / 224

12.5   Summary / 224

Problems / 227

Projects / 228

References / 230

13.   Benchmarking   **231**

13.1   What Is Benchmarking? / 231

13.2   Why Benchmark? / 232

13.3   What to Benchmark / 232

13.4   Identifying and Obtaining a Benchmark / 233

13.5   Collecting Actual Data / 233

13.6   Taking Action / 234

13.7   Current Benchmarks / 234

13.8   Summary / 236

Problems / 236

Projects / 236

References / 237

14.   Presenting Metrics Effectively to Management   **238**

14.1   Decide on the Metrics / 239

14.2   Draw the Picture / 240

14.3   Create a Dashboard / 243

14.4   Drilling for Information / 243

14.5   Example for the Big Cheese / 247

14.6   Evolving Metrics / 249

14.7   Summary / 250

Problems / 250

Project / 251

Reference / 251

Index   **252**

Acknowledgments

First and foremost, we acknowledge and thank Larry Bernstein. Your ideas, suggestions, enthusiasm, and support are boundless. Without you, this textbook would not exist.

Second, we thank and recognize all of you whose work has been included. Our mission is to teach and explain, and although this text contains some of our own original concepts, the majority of the ideas came from others. Our job is to select, compile, and explain ideas and research results so they are easily understood and used. To all of you whom we reference—thank you, you have given us shoulders to stand on.

In addition, special thanks to Capers Jones and Barry Boehm, the fathers of software measurement and estimation. They graciously have allowed us to use their benchmarking data and models, as have the David Consulting Group, Quantitative Software Management Corporation, David Longstreet and Don Reifer. Thank you all. Our gratitude also to Vic Basili for his review and blessing of our take on his GQM model. To the folks at Simula Research Laboratories—we love your work on estimation—thank you so very much, especially Benta Anda and Magne Jørgensen. David Pitts—thank you for your ideas on the challenge of measurement. John Musa—your work and ideas in Software Reliability are the cornerstone. Thanks also go to Liz Iversen for graciously sharing her wealth of experience with effective metrics presentation.

We also thank all of our talented colleagues who provided review and input to this text. This includes Beverly Reilly, Cathy Timko, Beth Rennicks, David Carmen, and John Russell—your generosity is truly appreciated. A very special thank you goes out to our favorite CFO, Colleen Brennan. She knows how to make financials understandable to us "techies." Our gratitude also to our "quality sisters," Claire Kennedy and Jackie Hughes, for their review and input. To Carolyn Goff, thank you for ideas, opinions, reviews, and support. We rely on them. And thanks to the great people we have had the pleasure to work with and learn from over our many years in the software industry; you all made this book possible.

Finally, we would like to say thank you to our students. Your feedback has been invaluable.

1

Introduction

You cannot predict nor control what you cannot measure.
—*Fenton and Pfleeger* [1]

When you can measure what you are speaking about, and express it in numbers, you know
something about it, but when you cannot measure it, when you cannot express it in numbers,
your knowledge is of a meager and unsatisfactory kind.
—*Lord Kelvin, 1900*

1.1 OBJECTIVE

Suppose you are a software manager responsible for building a new system. You need to tell the sales team how much effort it is going to take and how soon it can be ready. You have relatively good requirements (25 use cases). You have a highly motivated team of five young engineers. They tell you they can have it ready to ship in four months. What do you say? Do you accept their estimate or not?

Suppose you are responsible for making a go/no-go decision on releasing a different new system. You have looked at the data. It tells you that there are approximately eight defects per thousand lines of code left in the system. Should you say yea or nay?

So how did you do at answering the questions? Were you confident in your decisions?

The purpose of this textbook is to give you the tools, data, and knowledge to make these kinds of decisions. Between the two of us, we have practiced software development for over fifty years. This book contains both what we learned during those fifty years, and what we wished we had known. All too often, we were faced with situations where we could rely only on our intuition and gut feelings, rather than managing by the numbers. We hope this book will spare our readers the stress and sometimes poor outcomes that result from those types of situations.

We will provide our readers, both students and software industry colleagues, with practical techniques for the estimation and quantitative measurement of software projects. Software engineering has long been in practice both an art and a science. The challenge has been allowing for creativity while at the same time bringing strong engineering principles to bear. The software industry has not always been successful at finding the right balance between the two. We are giving you the foundation to "manage by the numbers." You can then use all of your creativity to build on that foundation.

1.2   APPROACH

This book is primarily intended to be used in a senior or graduate metrics and estimation course. It is based on a successful course in the Quantitative Software Engineering Program within the Computer Science Department at Stevens Institute of Technology. This course, which teaches measurement, metrics, and estimation, is a cornerstone of the program. Over the past few years, we have had hundreds of students, both full-time and part-time from industry, who have told us how useful it was, how they immediately were able to use it in their work and/or school projects, and who helped shape the course with their feedback. One consistent feedback was the importance of exercises, problems, and projects in learning the material. We have included all of these in our text.

We believe that the projects are extremely useful: you learn by doing. Some of the projects can be quite time consuming. We found that teams of three or four students, working together, were extremely effective. Not only did students share the work load and learn from one another, but also team projects more closely simulated a real work environment, where much of the work is done in teams. For many of the projects, having the teams present their approaches to each other was a learning experience as well. As you will find, there frequently is no one right answer. Many of the projects are based on a hypothetical system for reserving theater tickets. It is introduced in an early chapter and carried throughout the text.

Although primarily intended as a textbook, we believe our colleagues in the software industry will also find this book useful. The material we have included will provide sound guidance for both establishing and evolving a software metrics program in your business. We have pulled from many sources and areas of research and boiled the information down into what we hope is an easy to read, practical reference book.

The text tackles our objectives by first providing a motivation for focusing on estimation and metrics in software engineering (Chapter 1). We then talk about how to decide what to measure (Chapter 2) and provide the reader with an overview of the fundamentals of measurement theory (Chapter 3). With that as a foundation, we identify two common areas of measurements in software: size (Chapter 4) and complexity (Chapter 5).

A key task in software engineering is the ability to estimate the effort and schedule effectively, so we also provide a foundation in estimation theory and a multitude of estimation techniques (Chapter 6).

We then introduce three additional areas of measurement: defects, reliability, and availability (Chapters 7, 8, and 9, respectively). For each area, we discuss what the area entails and the typical metrics used and provide tools and techniques for predicting and monitoring (Chapter 10) those key measures. Real-world examples are used throughout to demonstrate how theory can indeed be transformed into actual practice.

Software development is a team sport. Engineers, developers, testers, and project managers, to name just a few, all take part in the design, development, and delivery of software. The team often includes third parties from outside the primary company. This could be for hardware procurement, packaged software inclusion, or actual development of portions of the software. This last area has been growing in importance over the last decade[1] and is, therefore, deserving of a chapter (Chapter 11) on how to include these efforts in a sound software metrics program.

Knowing what and how to estimate and measure is not the end of the story. The software engineer must also be able to effectively communicate the information derived from this data to software project team members, software managers, senior business managers, and customers. This means we need to tie software-specific measures to the business' financial measures (Chapter 12), set appropriate targets for our chosen metrics through benchmarking (Chapter 13), and, finally, be able to present the metrics in an understandable and powerful manner (Chapter 14).

Throughout the book we provide examples, exercises, problems, and projects to illustrate the concepts and techniques discussed.

1.3   MOTIVATION

Why should you care about estimation and measurement in software and why would you want to study these topics in great detail?

Software today is playing an ever increasing role in our daily lives, from running our cars to ensuring safe air travel, from allowing us to complete a phone call to enabling NASA to communicate with the Mars rover, from providing us with up-to-the-minute weather reports to predicting the path of a deadly hurricane; from helping us manage our personal finances to enabling world commerce. Software is often the key component of a new product or the linchpin in a company's plans to decrease operational costs and increase profit. The ability to deliver software on time, within budget, and with the expected functionality is critical to all software customers, who either directly or indirectly are all of us.

---

[1]Just do an Internet search on "software outsourcing" to get a feel for the large role this plays in the software industry today. Our search came back with over 5 million hits! Better yet, mention outsourcing to a commercial software developer and have your tape recorder running.

When we look at the track record for the software industry, although it has improved over the last ten years, a disappointing picture still emerges [2].

- A full 23% of all software projects are canceled before completion.
- Of those projects completed, only 28% were delivered on time, within budget, and with all originally specified features.
- The average software project overran the budget by 45%.

Clearly, we need to change what we are doing. Over the last ten years, a great deal of work has been done to provide strong project and quality management frameworks for use in software development. Software process standards such the Capability Maturity Model® Integration developed by the Software Engineering Institute [3] have been adopted by many software providers to enable them to more predictably deliver quality software products on time and within budget. Companies are pursuing such disciplines for two reasons. First and foremost, their customers are demanding it. Customers can no longer let their success be dependent on the kind of poor performance the above statistics reflect. Businesses of all shapes and sizes are demanding proof that their software suppliers can deliver what they need when they need it. This customer demand often takes the form of an explicit requirement or competitive differentiator in supplier selection criteria. In other words, having a certified software development process is table stakes for selling software products in many markets. Second, software companies are pursuing these standards because their profitability is tied directly to their ability to meet schedule and budget commitments and drive inefficiencies out of their operations. At the heart of software process standards are clear estimation processes and a well-defined metrics program.

Even more important than being able to meet the standards, managing your software by the numbers, rather than by the seat of your pants, enables you to have repeatable results and continuous improvement. Yes, there will be less excitement and less unpaid overtime, since you will not end up as often with the "shortest schedule I can't absolutely prove I won't make." We think you can learn to live with that.

Unquestionably, software engineers need to be skilled in estimation and measurement, which means:

- Understanding the activities and risks involved in software development
- Predicting and controlling the activities
- Managing the risks
- Delivering reliably
- Managing proactively to avoid crises

Bottom line: You must be able to satisfy your customer and know what you will spend doing it.

To predict and control effectively you must be able to measure. To understand development progress, you must be able to measure. To understand and evaluate quality, you must be able to measure.

Unfortunately, measurement, particularly in software, is not always easy. How do you predict how long it will take to build a system using tools and techniques you've never used before? Just envisioning the software that will be developed to meet a set of requirements may be difficult, let alone trying to determine the building blocks and how they will be mortared together. Many characteristics of the software seem difficult to measure. How do you measure quality or robustness? How do you measure the level of complexity?

Let us look at something that seems easy to measure: time. Like software, time is abstract with nothing concrete to touch. On the surface, measuring time is quite straightforward—simply look at your watch. In actuality, this manner of measuring time is not scientifically accurate. Clock time does not take into account irregularities in the earth's orbit, which cause deviations of up to fifteen minutes, nor does it take into account Einstein's theory of relativity. Our measurement of time has evolved based on practical needs, such as British railroads using Greenwich Standard Time beginning in 1880 and the introduction of Daylight Savings Time. Simply looking at your watch, although scientifically inaccurate, is a practical way to measure time and suits our purposes quite well [4].

For software then, like time, we want measures that are practical and that we expect will evolve over time to meet the "needs of the day." To determine what these measures might be, we will first lay a foundation in measurement and estimation theory and then build on that based on the practical needs of those involved in software development.

1.4 SUMMARY

This textbook will provide you with practical techniques for the estimation and quantitative measurement of software projects. It will provide a solid foundation in measurement and estimation methods, define metrics commonly used to manage software projects, illustrate how to effectively communicate your metrics, and provide problems and projects to strengthen your understanding of the methods and techniques. Our intent is to arm you with what you will need to effectively "manage by the numbers" and better ensure the success of your software projects.

ESTIMATION AND METRICS IN THE CMMI®

The Capability Maturity Model® Integration (CMMI) is a framework for identifying the level of maturity of an organization's processes. It is the current framework supported by the Software Engineering Institute and resulted from the integration and evolution of several earlier capability maturity models. There are two approaches supported by CMMI—the continuous representation and the staged representation. Both provide a valid methodology for assessing and improving processes (see Reference 3 for details on each approach) and define levels of capability and maturity. For example, the staged approach defines five levels of organizational maturity:

1. Initial
2. Managed
3. Defined
4. Quantitatively managed
5. Optimizing

As organizations mature, they move up to higher levels of the framework. Except for Level 1, which is basically ad hoc software development, each level is made up of process areas (PAs). These PAs identify what activities must be addressed to meet the goals of that level of maturity. Software estimation and metrics indeed play a part in an organization reaching increasing levels of maturity. For example, Level 2 contains a PA called Project Planning. To fulfill this PA, the organization must develop reasonable plans based on realistic estimates for the work to be performed. The software planning process must include steps to estimate the size of the software work products and the resources needed. Another PA at Level 2 is Project Monitoring and Control. For this PA, the organization must have adequate visibility into actual progress and be able to see if this progress differs significantly from the plan so that action can be taken. In other words, there must be some way to measure progress and compare it to planned performance. At Level 4, the PAs focus on establishing a quantitative view of both the software process and the software project/product. Level 4 is all about measurement, to drive and control the process and to produce project/product consistency and quality. The goal is to use metrics to achieve a process that remains stable and predictable and to produce a product that meets the quality goals of the organization and customer. At Level 5, the focus is on continuous measurable improvement. This means that organization must set measurable goals for improvement that meet the needs of the business and track the organization's performance over time.

Clearly, a well-defined approach to estimation and measurement is essential for any software organization to move beyond the ad hoc, chaotic practices of Level 1 maturity.

REFERENCES

[1] N. Fenton and S. Pfleeger, *Software Metrics*, 2nd ed., PWS Publishing, Boston, 1997.

[2] The Standish Group, "Extreme Chaos," 2001; www.standishgroup.com/sample_research.

[3] M. B. Chrissis, M. Konrad, and S. Shrum, *CMMI Guidance for Process Integration and Product Improvement*, SEI Series in Software Engineering, Addison-Wesley, Boston, 2003.

[4] D. Pitts, "Why is software measurement hard?" [online] 1999. Available from http://www.stickyminds.com. Accessed Jan. 6, 2005.

2

What to Measure

There are many characteristics of software and software projects that can be measured, such as size, complexity, reliability, quality, adherence to process, and profitability. Through the course of this book, we will cover a superset of the most practical and useful of these measures. For any particular software project or organization, however, you will need to define the specific software measurements program to be used. This defined program will be successful only if it is clearly aligned with project and organizational goals. In this chapter, we will provide several approaches for defining such a metrics program.

Fundamentally, to define an appropriate measurements program you need to answer the following questions:

- Who is the customer for the metrics?
- What are their goals with respect to the product, process, or resource under measurement?
- What metrics, when collected, will demonstrate whether or not the goal has been or is being met?

As you might guess, to define an aligned metrics program, it is critical to engage your "customer" as well as project/organizational staff who are knowledgeable in the object to be measured. So no matter which approach is used, identifying your

Software Measurement and Estimation, by Linda M. Laird and M. Carol Brennan
Copyright © 2006 John Wiley & Sons, Inc.

The Importance of Understanding What Is Being Measured. NON SEQUITUR © 2004 Wiley Miller. Dist. By UNIVERSAL PRESS SYNDICATE. Reprinted with permission. All rights reserved.

customer and getting the affected stakeholders involved will be a common element.[1]

2.1 METHOD 1: THE GOAL QUESTION METRICS APPROACH

The Goal Question Metric (GQM) approach, defined by Basili et al. [2], is a valuable, structured, and widely accepted method for answering the question of what to measure. Briefly, the GQM drives the definition of a metrics program from the top down:

1. Identify the Goal for the product/process/resource. This is the goal that your metrics "customer" is trying to achieve.
2. Determine the Question(s) that will characterize the way achievement of the goal is going to be assessed.
3. Define the Metric(s) that will provide a quantitative answer to each question. Metrics can be objective (based solely on the object being measured) or subjective (based on the viewpoint taken as well as the object measured).

For example, let's look at a software product delivery. The product/project manager may have the following goal for the product:

Goal: Deliver a software product that meets the customer's expectation for functionality.

One question that could help characterize the achievement of this goal would be:

Question: How much does the software, as delivered to the customer, deviate from the customer requirements?

One metric that could be used to answer this question would be:

Metric: Number of field software defects encountered. Typically, there will be a contractual agreement on what constitutes a defect, often based on software performance that deviates from mutually agreed upon requirements. The more specific the requirements, the more objective this metric becomes.

Another metric that could be used to address this question is:

Metric: Customer satisfaction level as indicated on some form of survey. This is a subjective metric, based solely on the viewpoint of the customer.

---

[1]A common misstep is to select the metrics based on what data is available or what is of most interest to the metrics engineer. These metrics efforts tend to be doomed before they begin. It costs money and time to collect metrics. The metrics need to be valuable to whomever is asking for the work to be done—that is, the customer. Always begin with an understanding of who the customer is.

This approach can be taken for any and all goals and stakeholders to define an aligned metrics program. For example, it can be used as the structured approach behind Method 2 once the decision makers have been identified.

2.2   METHOD 2: DECISION MAKER MODEL

Another method for selecting metrics is to focus on project decision making. The decision maker is the customer for the metric, with metrics produced to facilitate informed decision making. In this method, you need to determine what the needs of the decision maker are, recognizing that these will change over time [3]. This method is entirely consistent with the GQM method, with a focus on decisions that must be made. Figure 2.1 illustrates this concept.

Understanding the decisions that must be made will naturally lead to the project measures that must be put in place to support this decision making. For example, a software project manager will need to make resource allocation decisions based on current status versus planned progress. To be able to make these decisions, he/she will need measures of both time and effort during the development life cycle. A test manager will need to determine if the quality of the software is at a level acceptable for shipment to the customer. To be able to make this decision, he/she will need to have a measure of current quality of the software and perhaps a view of how that has changed over time.

With this method, look to the needs of the decision makers to define the metrics to be used.

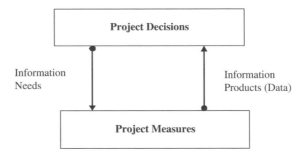

Figure 2.1. Decision maker model.

2.3   METHOD 3: STANDARDS DRIVEN METRICS

There are generic software engineering standards for sets of metrics to be collected and, frequently, industry specific ones as well. Some organizations use these to drive their metrics programs. For example, the Software Engineering Institute software maturity model requires the measurement of system size, project time, level of effort, and software defects. SEI integrates these measures with the required processes in support of Project Management and Continuous Improvement. We consider the SEI set, along with productivity, to be the minimal set for any organization. To reiterate, we consider the minimal set to be:

System size
Project duration
Effort
Defects
Productivity

Different industries may have their own standards for metrics, reliability, and safety. For example, in the telecommunications industry, the TL9000 standard defines a lengthy set of metrics that software suppliers must produce and make available to their customers and, in anonymous form, to the telecommunications industry. In the nuclear power industry, EIC 60880:1986-09 defines standards and metrics for "Software for Computers in Safety Systems in Nuclear Power Stations."

With this method, look for both industry and generic standards that are aligned with your business goals for an indication of metrics to be used.

2.4 EXTENSION TO GQM: METRICS MECHANISM

There is an important addition to all of the above approaches that must be considered. The mechanism for collecting the metrics data must be well understood and agreed to before implementing the program. So, with a nod to Basili and company, let's add Mechanism to the GQM approach, giving us GQM^2:

1. Goal
2. Question
3. Metric
4. Mechanism: This includes identifying *who* will be responsible for ensuring the collection and reporting of valid data, *how frequently* the data will be *collected*, *how frequently* the data will be *reported*, and *what infrastructure* (e.g., tools, staff resources) will be needed to collect and report the data.

Failing to understand and gain agreement on this last "M" can lead to numerous failures of the metrics program:

- Data is incomplete or invalid because no one has ensured that it is entered in a timely and correct manner.

- Data is "stale" and not useful for current decision making.
- Data is unavailable when needed.
- Project budgets are overrun due to the cost of the metrics program infrastructure.
- Project schedules are overrun due to unplanned staff time for data entry and validation.

So, let's expand our earlier product delivery example by adding our final M:

Mechanism for defect metric: Owner = Customer Service Manager; Frequency Collected = as defects occur; Frequency Reported = Monthly; Infrastructure = Existing customer defect entry tool + 0.25 clerical staff.

Mechanism for customer satisfaction metric: Owner = Product Manager; Frequency Collected = after each major software delivery; Frequency Reported = Quarterly; Infrastructure = Existing Customer Survey sent with each release + 0.1 Product Manager.

2.5 WHAT TO MEASURE IS A FUNCTION OF TIME

One characteristic of any metrics program is that it is a function of time in three ways. First, what to measure certainly varies based on the current position in the software development and software product lifecycles. For example, code inspection metrics are collected and monitored during the code development time in the lifecycle. During the testing phase, development time to deliver a fix may be what that same decision maker needs to know. Reliability of the software may need to be measured in the early stages of product delivery and deployment, while cost to maintain might be the area of interest when a product is near the end of its life.

Second, business needs change over time and the metrics program must change to remain in alignment. For example, if customer surveys show dissatisfaction with product reliability, a system availability metric may need to be created and monitored. If competitors are beating our products to market with similar functionality, we may need to establish development process measures that will allow us to focus on the most time consuming areas in order to drive improvement.

Third, metrics, especially when used as a factor in recognition and/or compensation, can lose their efficacy over time. Focus can become fixated on the metric itself and how to "manage the metric" rather than on the ultimate goal the project is trying to achieve. This may necessitate selecting a different metric that supports the goal or changing the way the existing metric is calculated.

2.6 SUMMARY

Each software project and organization is faced with the question of what to measure. To answer this question, you must know your customers and their goals and use that to drive the appropriate definition of a measurement program. Standards and approaches such as the decision maker model, GQM, and GQM^2 provide ways to answer that question. Regardless of the approach chosen, defining the metrics program should be part of the initial project planning process. Gaining agreement from all stakeholders at the start will ensure that the metrics needed to make decisions and assess goal attainment are available when and where they are needed. Every metrics program should be revisited regularly to ensure continuing alignment with changing business and project needs.

PROBLEMS

2.1   What is the first step in defining a metrics program?

2.2   Assume you are the manager in charge of user training on Product A. If your goal is to provide effective user training with each release of the product, define one metric that would be useful to produce.

2.3   Once you have defined an effective metrics program for your organization, how frequently should you change it?

2.4   You are given the job of creating metrics for a project. You read everything you can, speak with your friends, figure out the cost effectiveness of various metrics, and, finally, define a set of 25 metrics. All of your friends, including your boss, think they look great. You present them to your director. She is not thrilled. What might have gone wrong?

2.5   Your boss wants you to define and collect metrics for him. He is responsible for system testing. What decisions might he need to make? What might be some reasonable metrics?

PROJECT

2.1   You are the new CIO of your university or business, and you are appalled at the lack of data being used in decision making within your organization. You decide to start with your own job and lead by example. Use the GQM^2 methodology for your own position to define the metrics you need.

REFERENCES

[1]   R.S. Kaplan and D.P. Norton, "The balanced scorecard—measures that drive performance," *The Harvard Business Review*, 1992.

[2]   V.R. Basili, G. Caldiera, H.D. Rombach, and R. van Solingen, "Goal Question Metric (GQM) approach," *Encyclopedia of Software Engineering*, John Wiley & Sons, Hoboken, New Jersey, 2002.

[3]   J. McGary, D. Card, C. Jones, B. Layman, W. Clark, J. Dean, and F. Hall. *Practical Software Measurement, Objective Information for Decision Makers*, Addison-Wesley, Boston, 2002.

3

Measurement Fundamentals

Measurement is the process by which numbers or symbols are assigned to attributes of entities in the real world in such a way as to describe them according to clearly defined rules.

—Fenton and Pfleeger [1]

3.1 INITIAL MEASUREMENT EXERCISE

What is so hard about measuring software, you may think? OK, so why don't you try counting the number of lines of strncat.

```
/* Strncat() appends up to count characters from string
src to string dest, and then appends a terminating null
character. If copying takes place between objects that
overlap, the behavior is undefined. */
char *strncat (char *dest, const char *src, size_t count)
  {
     char *temp=dest;
     if (count) {
           while (*dest)
                 dest++;
           while ((*dest++ =*src++)) {
                 if (--count == 0) {
                       *dest='\0';
                       break;
                       }
           }
           } return temp;
  }
```

Software Measurement and Estimation, by Linda M. Laird and M. Carol Brennan
Copyright © 2006 John Wiley & Sons, Inc.

What number did you come up with? What rules did you decide to use? In experiments with students, the answers range from 11 to 19, with occasional counts over 100 if the data definitions are included. As with most everything, it depends on how you count and what the rules are. Did you count comment lines? Did you count lines with just a "}"? If instead, we have a well-specified model that tells us "the rules," then, counting lines becomes simple, and the students all arrive at the same answer.

3.2   THE CHALLENGE OF MEASUREMENT

In software, the issue is that so many things that we want to measure seem so "unmeasurable." How do you measure the complexity of a program? What does complexity even mean? How do you measure productivity? If someone can write 100 lines of code in two hours to program a function, but the software has five bugs in it, is it reasonable productivity? And what is that productivity? Better yet, if someone else can program the same function in one line of code, in one hour, what is their productivity? Whose productivity is better?

Software measurement is difficult—it is abstract and difficult to visualize and touch. It is also a relatively new discipline: we still are learning.

3.3   MEASUREMENT MODELS

The key to "making the unmeasurable measurable" is *models*. A model is an abstraction, which strips away unnecessary details and views an entity or concept from a particular perspective. Models allow us to focus on the important parts, ignore those that are irrelevant, and hypothesize and reason about an entity. Models make measurement possible.

We must have models of whatever we want to measure. For example, say we want to know how much of the total system development effort is testing. To determine that, we need a model of both the overall development process and the testing process, which specifies when testing starts and when it ends, what is included, and the number of people involved. If our model starts with unit test by the programmer, it is a different model and will give different results than one that includes only system test.

There are three types of models you can use—*text*, *diagrammatic*, and *algorithmic*—that is, words, pictures, and numbers.

3.3.1   Text Models

Text models tend to be the least effective, but the most common. It is difficult to adequately describe complex situations and dynamics using just words.

Here is a text model for software development [2]:

Effort: The time required to develop a product, expressed as increments of staff development time (e.g., staff months/hours). In general, effort is a function of size and results in cost.

Features: The requirements of the product to be developed.

Size: The magnitude of the product to be developed. In general, size is a function of features.

Defects: The incompleteness of the product. In general, defects are a function of size and schedule.

Schedule: The total development time; completion times for principal milestones. In general, schedule is a function of effort and resources.

Resources: The number of developers applied to the product development.

This text model has advantages and disadvantages. Each item is clearly defined and easy to understand, but the relationships between items may be difficult to visualize. But notice that this text model describes software development in such a way that we can discuss it, measure it, and predict it: if the size changes, the number of defects will change. This text model gives structure to the abstract concept of "software development."

We frequently use metaphors and heuristics to provide insight into the software development environment dynamics. These tend to work well, due to the breadth of meaning we associate with metaphors. The downside is that these models can limit, as all models, our creative thinking as they structure it [2]. Some examples of text model metaphors for software development are:

- The Wild, Wild West
- Agile Development (both a metaphor and a name)
- Death March
- Software Factory

Notice how each metaphor evokes a different mental image and response. You probably can envision the environment, the types of people, and processes from just the few words.

Some examples of heuristics models are:

- "Adding additional staff to late projects makes them later" F.P. Brooks [3]
- "Prototyping cuts the work to produce a system by 40%" L. Bernstein

EXERCISE: (a) What is a metaphor for the software development that you do? (b) Do you have a heuristic for the percentage of effort spent in coding versus system testing? What is it?

3.3.2 Diagrammatic Models

Diagrammatic models can be extremely powerful. There are many techniques for diagrammatic modeling, two of which are Weinberg's [4] and Senge's [5]. They allow you to model the entities, the relationships between them, and their dynamics. Use one of the formal diagram modeling techniques if you will be doing extensive modeling. Otherwise, simplistic flow diagrams (annotated circles and arrows) should suffice. Figure 3.1 is a simple diagrammatic model of software development, which matches the text model above.

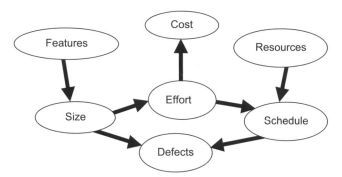

Figure 3.1. Diagrammatic model of software development.

EXERCISE: Consider creating a diagram model of one of the software metaphors from above. What would it look like?

You may find this difficult, which is due to the connotations that we unconsciously associate with the metaphors. Although a picture may be worth a thousand words, sometimes using the right words is best.

3.3.3 Algorithmic Models

Algorithmic models are also called parametric models. In the right situations, they can be extremely powerful, as they can clearly describe the relationship between entities. Some examples of algorithmic models for software development are:

- Effort = Schedule * Resource.
- % Defects Found During One Test Cycle = 30% of defects remaining in product.
- Effort = $A *$ (Size-of-Program^{B}) $+ C$, where A, B, and C are all empirically derived constants.

3.3.4 Model Examples: Response Time

The three different types of models—text, diagrammatic, and algorithmic—can be used together or separately, as dictated by the situation. As a final model example, consider response time.

Text: The response time (RT) is measured from the return key to the first response on the screen. The metric is the average RT within a typical hour.

Diagrammatic: See Figure 3.2.

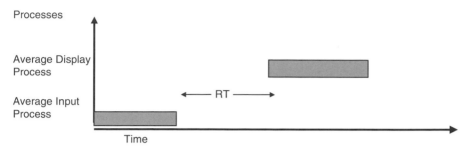

Figure 3.2. *Response time model.*

Algorithmic: RT = Average (beginning of response – end of input) over a typical hour.

We must have a model of whatever we are measuring. Models document entities within a system and their interactions in a consistent manner. We cannot interpret data without reference to an underlying model, nor can we really reason about a system without an underlying model. Models allow us to consider improvement strategies and predict the expected results.

3.3.5 The Pantometric Paradigm: How to Measure Anything

You may be concerned about how to create a model. The Pantometric Paradigm [6] is a simple method to produce a purely visual and quantitative model of anything within the material world. You can use it to create an initial model that can evolve to meet your needs. The simple process is:

1. Reduce what you are trying to model to the minimum required by its definition. Strip away all extraneous information.
2. Visualize it on a piece of paper or in your head.
3. Divide it in fact or in your imagination into equal parts.
4. Then measure it (e.g., count the parts).

Now you have a quantitative representation (model) of your subject which matches your definition. You can now manipulate it, reason about it, experiment with it, and evolve it.

EXERCISE: How would you model a college metrics class?

Answer: It depends on how you want to define the class, and what is important to you. One model could be the lectures. Another might be the students taking the class. If it were the lecture, the model could be a list of the lectures by week. We could then measure the number of lectures and the number of lectures by topic.

3.4   META-MODEL FOR METRICS

Another method for creating models that takes abstract concepts to empirical measurements is from Kan [7], and is depicted in Figure 3.3. You begin with an abstract concept, define it, create an operational definition, and then specify a real-world measurement. An example of this methodology, using the same response time example, is shown in Figure 3.4.

There are attributes of software that we can define and measure directly, such as the number of modules in a system or the number of people assigned to a project. These are called "direct measures." However, many of the attributes we want to measure are calculated, such as number of defects per thousand lines of code

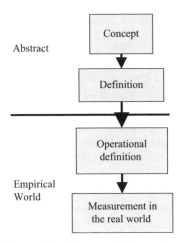

Figure 3.3. *Meta-model for metrics.*

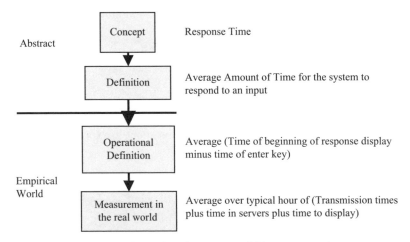

Figure 3.4. *Example using meta-model for response time.*

(KLOC) or average number of lines of code (LOC) produced per week. These are called "indirect measures."

EXERCISE: Define a four-level model for software reliability using the metrics meta-model.

3.5 THE POWER OF MEASUREMENT

Measurement is extraordinarily powerful, more so than a young professional ever suspects. What you measure is what you get. Or more accurately, it is what you get people to do. Measurement typically causes people to focus on whatever it takes to score well on that measurement. It is a specific expression of what is valued. You can easily cause unproductive behavior as people try to look the best on the wrong metrics. If you measure people by the number of lines of code they produce, they will create a larger system. If you measure people by the number of defects they create, the volume of defects will somehow start to decrease.

We both worked on a large project (400+ people) that measured field defects, which were reported to top management. One department within the project felt vulnerable and, although they had many satisfied customers, felt that they could not "afford" high-priority defect reports. Consequently, customers learned to call to talk about a problem if they wanted it fixed. If, instead, the customers filed an official defect report, it might take months (rather than days) to get the problem fixed.[1]

In the 44th Dilbert newsletter [8], we have an excellent example of measurement gone awry.

> I worked as an accountant in a paper mill where my boss decided that it would improve motivation to split a bonus between the two shifts based on what percentage of the total production each one accomplished.

> The workers quickly realized that it was easier to sabotage the next shift than to make more paper. Co-workers put glue in locks, loosened nuts on equipment so it would fall apart, you name it. The bonus scheme was abandoned after about ten days, to avoid all-out civil war.

Extensive productivity research was done between 1927 and 1932 at the AT&T Hawthorne plant in Cicero, Illinois. They studied manufacturing and believed that if the environment was changed in certain ways (such as more light), it would improve productivity. And they were right. Productivity improved. Then they changed another factor and measured the result. Productivity improved. Then they changed it back to the original state. Productivity improved. What was the conclusion? Whatever management paid attention to and measured improved. The difference was not the changes. It was the attention and measurement. This result is called "The Hawthorne Effect." What you pay attention to, and measure, will improve.

---

[1]We do not condone or recommend this type of behavior. We only report that it occurs.

You need to believe in and remember the power of measurement. It drives behavior. If you ever question it, remember that when your 5th grade teacher told you that you had to write neatly to get an A, you did your best to write neatly.

3.6 MEASUREMENT THEORY

3.6.1 Introduction to Measurement Theory

Measurement theory allows us to validly define measurements and metrics and to use statistical analysis on our metrics data.

Measurement theory is a branch of applied mathematics. The specific theory we use is called the Representational Theory of Measurement. It formalizes our intuition about the way the world actually works. In this theory, intuition is the starting point for all measurement [1]. Any data manipulation of the measurements must preserve the relationships that we observe between the real-world entities that we are measuring.

Measurement theory allows us to *validly* analyze and manipulate our measurement data.

As an example, consider a customer satisfaction survey. Your users were asked what they thought of your customer support. The possible answers were:

1—Excellent
2—Good
3—Average
4—Inadequate
5—Poor

The result was that you ended up with a score of 3. So, you have average support, and it means you just need to improve a bit, right? Well, maybe. Or maybe not. When you looked at the data, you found out that your scores were 50% Excellent and 50% Poor. No one thought your customer support was average. Measurement theory dicates that taking the average of this kind of data is invalid and can give misleading results.

Measurement theory allows us to use statistics and probability to understand quantitatively the possible variances, ranges, and types of errors in the data.

Assume that you are responsible for estimating the effort and schedule for a new project. You use a prediction model for development effort, and it predicts that, on average, the effort will be 10 staff years with a duration of 1 year. What would you then tell your boss as your estimate? Maybe you would pad it by one staff year, just to be safe. What if you knew that the standard deviation is 2 staff years? A standard deviation of 2 means that 68% of the time, you expect the result to be between 8 and 12 staff years. This means that ∼16% of the time it will be over 12 staff years. Now what would you estimate? 12 staff years? 13? Or 10? What if, instead, you knew that the standard deviation was 4 months? Then what would you estimate? 10.5 staff years? (By the way, if we were the boss, we would prefer an answer that included the range with probabilities. We would want the additional information to better trade-off the risks and the rewards.)

3.6.2 Measurement Scales

Consider two different types of scales that measure weight: one is a balance scale, the other is a bathroom scale. What is the difference? Which is better?

The balance scale is a relative scale. It compares the weights of objects. The bathroom scale is an absolute scale that gives you an absolute number. Initially, you may think the second scale is better. It does give you an answer. However, as you think more about it, you realize the first may have less error. Bathroom scales frequently are inaccurate. And as you think more and more about it, you probably reach the conclusion that the scales are neither better nor worse, just different ways of measuring.

In measurement theory, we have five types of scales: *nominal, ordinal, interval, ratio,* and *absolute.*

A *nominal scale* is an unordered set of named categories, such that the only comparisons that are valid are "belongs to." For example, you could have a nominal scale for the type of project, and the possible values would be "commercial," "military," or "MIS." The purpose of a nominal scale is to create a mapping from the real world into a set of categories that has some meaning in terms of how you will use it. For example, military projects are consistent in that the number of lines of code produced per staff hour tends to be less than an MIS project. Alternatively, you may wish to count the number of the different types of projects in your data sample. However, with nominal scales, there is no sense of ordering between different types, based on the categories. A project that is "commercial" may be larger or smaller than a "military" project. Using the nominal scale, you do not know how they compare. You need additional relationships and attributes, such as size and complexity, to make comparisons.

The *ordinal scale* is a linearly ordered set of categories, such that comparisons such as "bigger than" or "better than" make sense. An example would be the criticality of trouble reports (TRs). It could have the values of "critical," "major," and "minor." You know that one critical TR is worse than one major TR is worse than one minor TR. However, you do not know if two major TRs are worse than four minor TRs.

The *interval scale* is an ordinal scale with consistent intervals between points on the scale, such that addition and subtraction make sense, but not multiplication and division. Examples are the Fahrenheit and Centigrade temperature scales, where it does make sense to say that if it is 80° in Miami and 10° in Buffalo, then it is 70° warmer in Miami, but it makes no sense to say that it is 8 times hotter in Miami. Interval scales are rarely used in software measurement.

The *ratio scale* is an ordered, interval scale, where the intervals between the points are constant, and all arithmetic operations are valid. With temperature, the traditional example is the Kelvin scale, where there is an absolute 0, and 70°K really is 7 times hotter than at 10°K. With software measurement, examples abound, such as defects per module or lines of code developed per staff month.

The *absolute scale* is a ratio scale that is a count of the number of occurrences, such as the number of errors detected. The only valid values are zero and positive integers.

EXERCISE: Figure 3.5 is a "pain scale," which is a series of six faces, each of which shows progressively more pain and distress. You are at the doctor's office and you are asked to pick the face that best matches how you feel. What kind of scale is the face scale?

| 0 | 1 | 2 | 3 | 4 | 5 |
| NO HURT | HURTS LITTLE BIT | HURTS LITTLE MORE | HURTS EVEN MORE | HURTS WHOLE LOT | HURTS WORST |

Figure 3.5. FACES Pain Scale [9].

Answer: Ordinal. It is an ordered scale, but the intervals between items are not necessarily consistent.

EXERCISE: If you have five critical errors, two major errors, and five minor errors, what is the average error?

Answer: It does not make sense to have an "average" error in this case. You could talk about the median, or that you have a bimodal distribution, but the "average" error is not major.

Scales can be subjective or objective. Two familiar subjective scales are the Likert Scale and the Verbal Frequency Scale. For example:

Likert Scale: This program is very reliable. Do you
• Strongly agree, agree, neither agree nor disagree, disagree, strongly disagree
Verbal Frequency Scale: How often does this program fail?
• Always, often, sometimes, seldom, never

These subjective scales are ordinal scales; there is an implied order and relationship. Averages or ratios are *not valid* (although frequently used).

3.6.3 Measures of Central Tendency and Variability

With measurement, you have data that you need to analyze, understand, and turn into information. The most basic analysis is to understand the data's central tendencies and variability. This section reviews basic statistics that can and should be part of every software engineer's repertoire.

3.6.3.1 *Measures of Central Tendency*   The *central tendency* is the middle, or center, of a data set, be it the mean, median, and/or mode. Recall the following definitions:

> Mean is the sum of all the occurrences, divided by the number of occurrences.
> Median is the middle occurrence in an ordered set.
> Mode is the most frequent occurrence.

For the *nominal scale*, only mode makes sense, since there is no ordering.

For *ordinal scales*, mode and median apply, but mean is irrelevant. For example, if you used a Likert Scale (e.g., a 5 point scale ranging from 5 for strongly agree through 1 for strongly disagree) and asked baseball fans to indicate their agreement/disagreement with the statement "I love the New York Yankees," you might get a distribution that had 40% strongly agreeing, 40% strongly disagreeing, and the remaining 20% evenly spread throughout the other three categories. It would be meaningless (and wrong) to then conclude that the average fan's response was neutral, even though the mean was 3. The most meaningful statements you could make would speak to the bimodal distribution.

For *interval*, *ratio*, and *absolute scales*, mean, mode, and median are all meaningful and relevant.

3.6.3.2 *Measures of Variability*   The measures of central tendency indicate the center of the data. Not only do we need to describe the sameness, but we also need to describe the differences and variability.

The standard and simplest measures of variability are *range*, *deviation*, *variance*, *standard deviation*, and *index of variation*. Even without a statistics background, these measures are simple and useful enough that they can and should be part of every software engineer's knowledge base.

- *Range*: The range of values for the mapping of the data that is calculated by subtracting the smallest from the largest. For example, assume you have three modules—A, B, and C—which have sizes of 10 KLOC, 24 KLOC, and 50 KLOC, respectively. Then the range of KLOC per module would be from 10 to 50 KLOC or 40 KLOC.
- *Deviation*: The distance away from the mean of the measurement. In our example, the average size of a module $= 84/3 = 28$ KLOC. Then the deviations for our modules A, B, and C are 18, 4, and 22, respectively.
- *Variance*: A measurement of spread, which is calculated differently if it is for a full population or a sample of a population.
  For a full population, where N is the number of data points,
  Variance $= \Sigma(\text{Deviations}^2)/N$.

For a sample population,

Variance $= \Sigma(\text{Deviations}^2)/(N - 1)$.

In our example, the variance (module size) $= (324 + 16 + 484)/3 = 275$. To pick the right SD formula, you need to decide if your data is a complete population or a sample of that population. In this example, we assume that the data is for a complete population, that is, there are only three modules to consider. If instead the three were "a representative sample" of a larger set of modules, then we would divide by two rather than three.

- *Standard Deviation (SD)*: The "typical" distance from the mean. SD $= \sqrt{\text{variance}}$. In our example, the standard deviation $= 16.6$.
- *Index of Variation (IV)*: An index that indicates the reliability of the measurement. IV $=$ SD/mean. In our example, IV $= 16.6/28 = 0.59$. This metric normalizes standard deviation by dividing it by the mean. A SD of 1 with a mean of 250 is entirely different from a SD of 1 with a mean of 2. The lower the index of variation, the less the variation.

Figure 3.6 illustrates lower and higher variance. With low variance, the values cluster around the mean. With higher variance, they spread farther out.

Standard deviation is the classic measurement of variation. As the variance increases, so does the standard deviation. It has additional significance for normal (e.g., bell-shaped) distributions, in that the standard deviation intervals define a certain distribution. The interval contained within 1 standard deviation (SD or σ) of the mean is $\sim 68\%$ of the population. The interval within 2 SD is $\sim 95\%$ of the population, within 3 SD is $\sim 99.73\%$ of the population, and within 6 SD is $\sim 99.9999988\%$. The standard deviation percentages (68%, 95%, 99.7%) are numbers you should know.

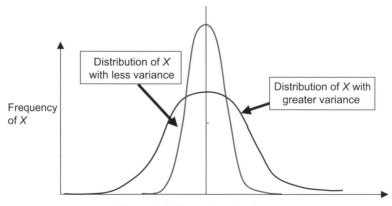

Figure 3.6. Examples of variance.

3.6.4 Validity and Reliability of Measurement

If you had to choose between a valid measurement and a reliable measurement, which would you choose? Which *should* you choose? And what exactly is the difference?

The question of valid and reliable refers to the transformation of the abstract concept of a metric into the operational definition (recall the meta-model from Section 3.4). Is the operational definition a valid and/or reliable transformation of what we want to measure?

Valid measurements measure *what* we intend to measure. Completely valid measurements for complex concepts such as quality, productivity, and complexity are difficult, if not impossible, due to the difficulty of creating an operational definition that matches the breadth of the concept. If you define your quality metric to be the total number of defects per KLOC (i.e., the defect density) of a module, then how do you account for factors such as ease of use and elegance? If you define productivity as "the number of tested lines of code produced per day," how do you compare the productivity of one person who can code a feature in one line versus a person who codes the same feature in 100 lines?

A reliable measure is one that is consistent. Assume that you have a tool that counts defects, but it only counts the defects discovered during system and acceptance testing. This is a reliable measure. The tool will consistently count the defects. It is not totally valid as a count of all defects in a project, but it is reliable and useful. Another example is a watch. Some people set their watch five minutes ahead of time. This is a reliable measure of time, but not valid.

The index of variation is one measure of the reliability of a measurement: the smaller the IV, the more reliable the metric.

Theoretically, there are three types of metric validity [1]: construct, criterion-related, and content.

Construct validity refers to whether the metric is constructed correctly. For example, an invalid construct would be one that uses the mean as a measure of central tendency for a metric that has an ordinal scale. So far within this chapter, we have been discussing construct validity.

Criterion-related validity refers to the ability to use the operational definition to predict the behavior of the abstract concept, which is extremely important. Predictive measures consist of both mathematical models and predictive procedures. For example:

- Function points can predict lines of code (LOC) (based on language).
- Lines of code can predict effort, where the mathematical model is Effort $= A * LOC^B + C$. The predictive procedures are the method for determining A, B, and C.

Predictive procedures need to be validated to understand their inherent accuracy. The validation is done by comparing empirical data with the outcomes predicted by the predictive models.

Content validity refers to the ability of the operational definition and measurement method to capture the full range of meanings associated with the abstract concept. Productivity measures based on functionality produced rather than lines of code produced have higher content validity.

There is a natural conflict between reliability and validity in measurement. Reliable measurements tend to be tightly and narrowly defined. Valid measurements tend to be broadly defined and composites of other metrics (such as a quality metric defined as a function of defect, ease-of-use, and ease-of-maintenance measures).

The traditional belief is that valid metrics are somehow better than reliable ones, if you have to choose. Both do serve their purposes, and in many cases, the reliability of a measurement that is invalid (think of the scale that always underweighs by 10 pounds) can be attenuated (by always adding 10 pounds to the result).

3.6.5   Measurement Error

What kind of errors might you make with the kind of foot measuring stick [10] shown in Figure 3.7? You might measure the wrong part of a foot and always get the wrong measurement. Or you might make an error in reading the measurement, reading a little too high or a little too low.

Figure 3.7. *Foot measuring stick [10].*

The first type of error is a *systematic* error, meaning it is an error in the measurement system. It will show up every time. It affects the validity of the measurement. It is the "bias" with a measurement. The second type of error is a *random* error, meaning it is an error in the measurement itself, which will appear "at random." It affects the reliability of the measurement. It is the "noise" within a measurement.

In software development, if you were recording and calculating defects found during code inspections, a systematic error would occur if no one compared the code to the requirements, so those defects were never found or counted. Random errors would be errors that the inspector made in recording the number and types of defects found.

Figure 3.8 is a graph of random error. Random errors increase the variance but do not change the mean.

Figure 3.9 is a graph of systematic error. Systematic errors change the mean but not the variance.

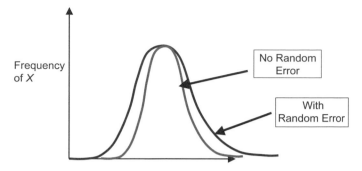

Figure 3.8. *Distributions of X with and without random error.*

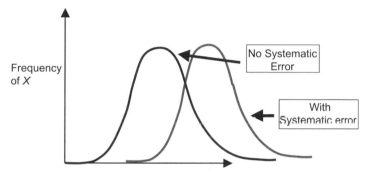

Figure 3.9. *Distributions of X with and without systematic error.*

Valid measurements can have random errors. Reliable measurements can have systematic errors.

You can reduce and manage measurement errors by:

1. Attenuating the measurement for systematic errors. Once you realize Mary always underestimates by 25%, increase her estimates.
2. Test pilot your measurements, looking for both systematic errors and sources of random errors. If you know that 10 defects were found in testing the last week, and the official measurements only show 8, find out what went wrong.
3. *Triangulate* your metrics. Use different measurements and measurement processes without the same systematic errors. All effort estimation methods have high variance. Use at least three methods, and look at the mean and standard deviations of the results.
4. Use statistics to determine and adjust for random errors.

Figure 3.10 is one final look at measurement error. If reality is the vertical line on the left, then the distance from the actual mean to reality is the bias, or systematic error. The clustering/variation around the mean is the random error.

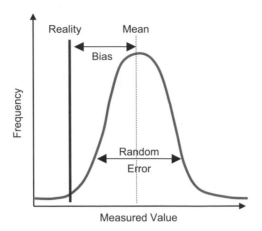

Figure 3.10. *Measurement error.*

3.7 ACCURACY VERSUS PRECISION AND THE LIMITS OF SOFTWARE METRICS

It is the mark of an instructed mind to rest satisfied with the degree of precision which the nature of a subject admits, and not to seek exactness when only an approximation of the truth is possible

—Aristotle, 330 B.C.

The accuracy of a measurement is the degree to which a measurement reflects reality. Precision of a measurement represents the size of differentiation possible with a measurement. In software engineering, we measure our processes and our products, and use those measures to control, predict, monitor, and understand. Many of these measures have inherent variations, making highly precise measurements impossible or irrelevant. Consider counting the size of the code. There isn't one standard way of counting, which would make it easy to compare your size measurements with another company's.

Estimation is not precise by its very nature, and software estimation is no exception. You will find that size estimates are considered excellent if they are within 10%. This lack of precision means that reporting an estimate to be 1253 LOC is misleading. It implies that you actually believe this estimate is a better estimate than 1254 LOC, which is highly doubtful. Instead, if your accuracy is $\pm10\%$, then report the estimate to be 1250 LOC. Better yet, estimate 1250 LOC$\pm10\%$, which is more accurate, although less precise. Also, recall and use what you learned about significant digits in grade school. If you are calculating an indirect metric, it should not have more significant digits than the factors going into it.

3.8 SUMMARY

Measurement can be a challenge, especially in software, due to its abstract nature. An entity and the measurement of it are not equivalent. For example, aspects of the quality of software can be measured by using defect data, or defect data and performance data, but these are only certain aspects, not the whole story.

For each concept we want to measure, such as quality or complexity, we need to decide which aspects are the most relevant and important to us and use those aspects to create a model of the concept. There are different techniques to take these abstract concepts and create real-world metrics that measure them. The underlying key is *models*—you need to have models to allow you to create the specific definitions of abstract concepts.

Measurement theory and statistics are tools that allow us to validly analyze and compare the metrics data. This chapter contains an introduction to both, including measurement scales, measures of central tendencies and variation, and measurement error. These concepts are the basic building blocks of measurement and metrics.

PROBLEMS

3.1 If the definition of quality was the defect density of a software release, what would be (a) an operational definition and (b) a measurement in the real world?

3.2 You decide to measure productivity by lines of code produced per month, but you do not count comments. What do you think will happen?

3.3 True or False: You can measure anything in the material world.

3.4 True or False: Models are nice to have but not crucial to software measurement.

3.5 True or False: Algorithmic models are preferred because they are the most precise.

3.6 Suppose we take a sample of the number of defects in different modules. We get the following data: 10, 20, 15, 18, and 22. Calculate the mean, SD, and IV for the number of defects per module.

3.7 True or False: The mean is a valid measure of central tendencies for a metric using the ordinal scale.

3.8 You are trying to understand customer satisfaction with your reliability, so you survey and ask the following: How satisfied are you with the reliability of the release?

    1 = Extremely
    2 = Very Satisfied

3 = Average Satisfaction
4 = Not Satisfied
5 = Very Disappointed

Three of your customers chose #1, two chose #2, and one chose #5. What would be the valid way to report the central tendency of the answers to this survey question?

3.9 True or False: A higher IV indicates a more reliable metric.

3.10 True or False: If there is random error in a measurement, the standard deviation will be greater than that of the true values being measured.

3.11 True or False: Precision is more important than accuracy in a metric.

3.12 Suppose I want to evaluate which programmer is the best programmer. I've decided that I will look at two criteria—quality and productivity. Quality is defined as the number of bugs found per month and productivity is defined as the number of lines of code written per month. What conclusions can I draw from the following table?

Programmer	Quality	Productivity
A	2	2500
B	5	500
C	25	200
D	35	1000

3.13 I also define a Good Programmer Index (n) = Productivity (n) / Quality (n). What conclusions can I now draw from the previous data? What is the scale of this index? Is it a reliable measure? Why or why not?

3.14 True or False: For a normal distribution, one σ (one standard deviation, above and below the mean) includes $\sim$80% of the population.

3.15 Your officemate decides to measure his code quality by the percentage of comments in his code. You tell him it is an invalid metric. To which *type* of metric (in)validity are you referring: construct, criterion, or content? Is this metric reliable?

3.16 What is a metric which has predictive procedures, other than effort estimation? How would you validate it?

3.17 Why do you think variance is defined differently for samples of populations compared to complete populations?

PROJECTS

3.1 Consider the concept of productivity. Define it with (a) a text model, (b) a diagrammatic model, and (c) an algorithmic model.

3.2 Define your own metric for programmer productivity. Then evaluate it. Is it valid? Reliable? Precise? What type of systematic errors would you expect to encounter? What type of random errors do you expect? How difficult will it be to obtain the data?

3.3 If you work on a project, find out how quality is measured. Evaluate the metric for reliability, validity, and cost.

REFERENCES

[1] N. Fenton and S. Pfleeger, *Software Metrics*, 2nd ed., PWS Publishing Company, Boston, 1997.

[2] D. Pitts, "Why is software measurement hard?" [online] 1999. Available from http://www.stickyminds.com. Accessed Jan. 6, 2005.

[3] F.P. Brooks, *The Mythical Man Month*, Addison-Wesley, Reading, Mass., 1974.

[4] G. Weinberg, *Quality Software Management, Volume 2: First-Order Measurement*, Dorset House Publishing, New York, 1993.

[5] P. Senge, *The Fifth Discipline*, Doubleday, New York, 1990.

[6] A.W. Crosby, *The Measure of Reality*, Cambridge University Press, Cambridge, United Kingdom, 1997.

[7] S. Kan, *Metrics and Models in Software Quality Engineering*, 2nd ed., Addison-Wesley, Boston, 2003.

[8] Dilbert newsletter. Available from http://www.unitedmedia.com/comics/dilbert/dnrc/html/newsletter44.html. Accessed Jan. 6, 2005.

[9] M.J. Hockenberry, D. Wilson, and M.L. Winkelstein, *Wong's Essentials of Pediatric Nursing*, 7th ed., Mosby, St. Louis, 2005.

[10] Photograph available from http://www.howcool.com/pleasersshoes/Measuring-Stick.jpg. Accessed Jan. 10, 2005.

4

Measuring the Size of Software

How big is it? Well . . . it depends on how you count.

Size is one of the most basic attributes of software. Some of the key questions people want to know about a project involve size. For example:

- How big is the software? How big is it compared to other projects?
- How much effort is it going to take to build the software?
- How does our quality compare to other projects?
- How productive are we compared to other projects?

Size is fundamental to all of these metrics. In order to answer the questions, we need to be able to measure size in a standardized way that allows us to compare ourselves against other projects and external benchmarks.

In this chapter, we examine size in both the physical and functional sense. Both views are important in effort prediction and in normalization of other important metrics such as productivity and quality.

4.1 PHYSICAL MEASUREMENTS OF SOFTWARE

The traditional measure for software size is the number of lines of code (LOC). It is a simple measure, but it easily encourages undesirable behavior when used

Software Measurement and Estimation, by Linda M. Laird and M. Carol Brennan
Copyright © 2006 John Wiley & Sons, Inc.

inappropriately. If productivity is measured based on LOC/programmer day, the more lines you write, whether or not they do something useful, the more productive you are. It also seems overly simplistic. Although "a rose is a rose is a rose," a line of code can be a blank, a comment, or a ";", or it can be calculating a missile trajectory.

So how should we measure size? The LOC measure is frequently rejected because it does not seem to adequately address the functionality, complexity, and technology involved and may cause the wrong organizational behavior. However, consider an analogy to buildings. A building has a size, typically in square feet. It is an extremely useful measurement. Two thousand square feet means something to us all. However, size is not the only way to describe a building. It could be a home or an office building. It could be an executive seaside retreat or a cabin in the woods. Size is a major cost factor in buildings, but it is just one factor. One would expect the cost per square foot of a self-storage building to be less than a state-of-the-art data center, with raised floors, dual power supplies, and optical networking. However, one also would expect that the construction cost per square foot of a data center built in Montana and one built in New Hampshire would be relatively similar. In software, it is the same. The LOC measurement, just like square feet, serves a purpose. It is *one* of the cost drivers and normalization factors. We can use it to normalize metrics and compare different projects. We just need to be judicious in how we use it.

LOC measures the physical length of the software itself. When well specified, it is a reliable measurement. However, with visual and nonprocedural languages, such as Visual Basic, it frequently misses the mark. Moreover, it is always lacking in representing the size of the functionality of a system. Consequently, we need some other size measurements as well.

4.1.1 Measuring Lines of Code

Counting source lines of code is simple and reliable. Tools are available on the Internet that count well. The issue with counting code is determining which rules to use so that comparisons are valid.

The Software Engineering Institute (SEI) of Carnegie-Mellon University has published a framework for counting source code [1]. Included is a code counting checklist that allows you to determine explicitly how you count the code, which allows both internal and external standardization and benchmarking of code counting. Figure 4.1 is an example of the first page of a filled-in checklist.

Different organizations and studies use different rules. The most popular is NKLOC (non-commented thousand LOC) and LLOC (logical lines of code).

Your organization should be consistent in how it counts LOC. You can use the SEI checklist to decide consciously how you will count code.

4.1.2 Language Productivity Factor

Consider the problem of counting all the occurrences of "amazing" in a file. How many lines of code would this take? We would guess that in Assembler, it would

Definition name: **Physical Source Lines of Code**   Date: **8/7/92**
(basic definition)   Originator: **SEI**

| Measurement unit: | Physical source lines | ✓ |
| | Logical source statements | |

Statement type	Definition	✓	Data array			Includes	Excludes
When a line or statement contains more than one type, classify it as the type with the highest precedence.							
1 Executable	Order of precedence ->			1		✓	
2 Nonexecutable							
3 Declarations				2		✓	
4 Compiler directives				3		✓	
5 Comments							
6 On their own lines				4			✓
7 On lines with source code				5			✓
8 Banners and nonblank spacers				6			✓
9 Blank (empty) comments				7			✓
10 Blank lines				8			✓
11							
12							

How produced	Definition	✓	Data array		Includes	Excludes
1 Programmed					✓	
2 Generated with source code generators					✓	
3 Converted with automated translators					✓	
4 Copied or reused without change					✓	
5 Modified					✓	
6 Removed						✓
7						
8						

Origin	Definition	✓	Data array		Includes	Excludes
1 New work: no prior existence					✓	
2 Prior work: taken or adapted from						
3 A previous version, build, or release					✓	
4 Commercial, off-the-shelf software (COTS), other than libraries					✓	
5 Government furnished software (GFS), other than reuse libraries					✓	
6 Another product					✓	
7 A vendor-supplied language support library (unmodified)						✓
8 A vendor-supplied operating system or utility (unmodified)						✓
9 A local or modified language support library or operating system					✓	
10 Other commercial library					✓	
11 A reuse library (software designed for reuse)					✓	
12 Other software component or library					✓	
13						

Figure 4.1. Code counting checklist [1].

take about 300; in FORTRAN, around 100; in C, probably 10 to 15. In Unix Shell, it takes only one line with a "grep" in it.

Studies have shown that a proficient programmer can program approximately the same number of debugged lines of code per day regardless of the language. That is, if you are proficient at both Assembler and Java, your productivity, measured as lines of code per day, is approximately the same in both languages.

Consequently, we have the concept of a "language gearing factor," which compares the expressiveness of languages and takes into account the differences in "productivity" in languages. The more productive a language is, the fewer lines of code you should need to write, and hence, the more productive you should be.

Early gearing factors[1] were published by T. Capers Jones in 1991 [2], some of which are shown in Table 4.1.

[1]The gearing factor tables were created initially to show the relationship between LOC and function points. Function points are discussed in detail later in this book.

TABLE 4.1 1991 Gearing Factors

Language	Gearing Factor	Language	Gearing Factor
Accesss	38	Cobol (ANSI 85)	91
Ada 83	71	FORTRAN 95	71
Ada 95	49	High Level Language	64
AI Shell	49	HTML 3.0	15
APL	32	Java	53
Assembly—Basic	320	Powerbuilder	16
Assembly—Macro	213	Report Generator	80
Basic—ANSI	64	Spreadsheet	6
Basic—Visual	32	Shell Scripts	107
C	128	Visual C++	34
C++	55		

This table says that, on average, a function that took 38 LOC to program in Access would take 91 LOC to program in Cobol (assuming both languages were appropriate). If you can select the language you use, you want to pick the one with the lowest gearing factor, since you should end up writing the fewest LOC. In other words, if you can use a spreadsheet, do it, rather than writing code.

The concept of gearing factors is powerful: it allows us to normalize across languages. Recognize though that these numbers are only initial guidelines or averages and that they will vary based on a number of factors such as problem domain and programmer skill.

Other companies such as QSM, The David Consulting Group, and SPR have later gearing factors based on their clients and benchmarking research. Table 4.2 shows results from the 2005 QSM report, based on 2597 QSM function point projects [3] and The David Consulting Group's data.

4.1.3 Counting Reused and Refactored Code

You need to indicate the extent of the reuse in order to validly compare measures such as productivity and defect density. Refactored[2] code offers some special challenges due to the predominance of changed and deleted code.

For reused code, NASA uses a classification scheme that has an ordinal scale with four points: reused verbatim, slightly modified ($<25\%$), extensively modified ($\geq 25\%$ modified), and new [4]. This classification scheme can be simplified to reused ($<25\%$ changed) and new, since, typically, if you change more than 25%, the effort is the same as if all of the code were new. Informal industrial surveys show 25% count a verbatim module each time it is used, 20% only count it once, 5% never count it, and 50% never count code at all [2].

---

[2]In case you are unfamiliar with the term refactoring, it is a disciplined technique for restructuring an existing body of code by altering its internal structure without changing its external behavior. Refactoring is frequently used in object-oriented development, in which class and object evolution is a natural and preferred method of development. There are tools that refactor code for some of the more popular OO languages such as Java and C++ and automatically produce many code structure metrics.

TABLE 4.2   2005 Gearing Factors

| Language | QSM SLOC/FP Data | | | | David Consulting Group Data |
	Average	Median	Low	High	
Access	35	38	15	47	—
Ada	154	—	104	205	—
Advantage	38	38	38	38	—
APS	86	83	20	184	—
ASP	69	62	32	127	—
Assembler	172	157	86	320	575 Basic/ 400 Macro
C	148	104	9	704	225
C++	60	53	29	178	80
C#	59	59	51	66	—
Clipper	38	39	27	70	60
Cobol	73	77	8	400	175
Cool:Gen/IEF	38	31	10	180	—
Culprit	51	—	—	—	—
DBase III	—	—	—	—	60
DBase IV	52	—	—	—	55
Easytrieve +	33	34	25	41	—
Excel	47	46	31	63	—
Focus	43	42	32	56	60
FORTRAN	—	—	—	—	210
FoxPro	32	35	25	35	—
HTML	43	42	35	53	
Ideal	66	52	34	203	—
IEF/Cool:Gen	38	31	10	180	—
Informix	42	31	24	57	—
J2EE	61	50	40	60	—
Java	60	59	14	97	80
JavaScript	56	54	44	65	50
JCL	60	48	21	115	400
JSP	59	—	—	—	—
Lotus Notes	21	22	15	25	—
Mantis	71	27	22	250	—
Mapper	118	81	16	245	—
Natural	60	52	22	141	100
Oracle	38	29	4	122	60
Oracle Dev 2K/FORMS	41/42	30	21/23	100	—
Pacbase	44	48	26	60	—
PeopleSoft	33	32	30	40	—
Perl	60	—	—	—	50
PL/1	59	58	22	92	126
PL/SQL	46	31	14	110	—
Powerbuilder	30	24	7	105	—
REXX	67	—	—	—	—
RPG II/III	61	49	24	155	120
Sabretalk	80	89	54	99	—
SAS	40	41	33	49	50

(*continued*)

Table 4.2 *Continued*

Language	QSM SLOC/FP Data				David Consulting Group Data
	Average	Median	Low	High	
Siebel Tools	13	13	5	20	—
Slogan	81	82	66	100	—
Smalltalk	35	32	17	55	—
SQL	39	35	15	143	—
VBScript	45	34	27	50	50
Visual Basic	50	42	14	276	—
VPF	96	95	92	101	—
Web Scripts	44	15	9	114	—

For counting reused code, you need to decide what makes the most sense in your environment. Our personal preference is to count reused code as new if greater than 25% has changed, and only count it once. Again, it is important to be consistent and to understand what behaviors you want to encourage and discourage.

4.1.4 Counting Nonprocedural Code Length

Until the early 1990s, most code was text. With visual languages, such as Visual Basic, the size of the text is irrelevant, as "selections" and "clicks" became the "code." For these types of language and for generated languages, the typical length measurements do not work well. Functional size measurements, discussed later in this chapter, are typically used instead.

For object-oriented code, text size is still used, although it may not be as meaningful as with procedural languages.

4.1.5 Measuring the Length of Specifications and Design

It is enticing to consider that the length of the specifications and/or design of a system might predict actual code size and hence effort. Many researchers have tried to find generic correlations without great success. Fenton and Pfleeger [5] suggest that the success of the correlation depends greatly on the organization. We agree that these simple techniques can be effective in a disciplined environment with a consistent style and level of detail in the documents. They do need to be tuned and calibrated for the specific environment and tested to understand their validity.

Two length measurements for specifications and design are number of pages and number of "shalls."

The simplest technique is to use the number of pages of specifications and look for a correlation with either LOC or effort. If you use LOC, this is called the *specification-to-code expansion ratio*. Similarly, you can measure the length of the design specification and determine the *design-to-code expansion ratio*.

For example, from previous projects, you know that your design-to-code expansion ratio is 300, that is, 300 NLOC for every page of design. Your current project has 12 pages of design. You estimate that you will write 3600 NLOC.

Many organizations that are ISO-9000 certified and/or CMM Level 3 or higher use "shalls" within their requirements documents for mandatory requirements. For example, "the system shall record the time and date of every update" is a mandatory requirement. These mandatory requirements can be traced to design, to code, and to test cases, allowing an organization to certify that they have indeed developed and tested every mandatory requirement. If you have a consistent style and level of detail in your requirements, you may find a strong correlation between the number of shalls and the overall effort or LOC in your project.

EXERCISE: Within your organization, you have found that the average number of staff months per "shall" in a requirements document is 1.05 with a standard deviation of 10%. You have a new project that has 100 "shalls" in the requirements. What do you estimate the number of staff months to be? This estimate is for your boss, and you need to be as accurate as possible.

Answer: First, verify that this project and team is similar to the other projects. Next, estimate the percentage of "shall" changes that you expect to receive as the requirements "evolve" (e.g., change after they are finalized). Assume it is 10. Then you would estimate the number of staff months to be $110 * 1.05 = 115.5$ with two standard deviations of 20%. (Use 2 SD rather than 1 SD for the increase in accuracy.) Twenty percent is $\sim$23 staff months. In other words, you expect the effort to be between 92 and 138 staff months $\sim$95% of the time. If you do not assume any requirements creep, then it is $100 * 1.05 = 105$ staff months $\pm$ 21 staff months.

Although there are no benchmarks nor standards to use in predicting code length from requirements or design documents, if you have a well-disciplined organization with a consistent style, you may want to try using the length of the documents or the number of mandatory requirements. You need to gather sufficient data to create a historical trend. If your organization is not well-disciplined or does not have a consistent style, these techniques will not work.

4.2 MEASURING FUNCTIONALITY

One issue with using LOC, or any physical size measurement, as a measure of productivity is that it has little to do with the problem being solved and more to do with the software development technology itself. Customers want solutions and care little for the language or technology used to create them.

Consider what strategy you might use to size a system, based on what it needs to do rather than how it does it internally. It is a little difficult, isn't it? One possible way would be to count the inputs, outputs, interfaces, and databases in a system. That is the function point (FP) approach, once you add inquiries as well.

Function Point Analysis (FPA) [6] was invented as an indirect measure for the functional size of a system. Although many other measures have evolved from function points, it is arguably still the most widely used Functional Size Measurement (FSM).

Alan Albrecht originally developed function points at IBM in 1979, after he determined that you could estimate the size of a system from its external transactions and databases. Function Point Analysis has grown to become a standardized measure of size, with an international standards group (International Function Point Users Group, IFPUG), certification procedures, and over 1400 members. The IFPUG's website, www.ifpug.org, is a comprehensive source for FP information, including a function point counting manual. In addition, there are many excellent texts [7] and training courses if you desire a deeper understanding or to become certified in Function Point Analysis.

The IFPUG version of Function Point Analysis is the predominant function point methodology within the United States, but there are many other extensions and evolutions. Feature Points is a simple extension of function points for scientific applications. MKII Function Points was developed in the 1980s in the United Kingdom by Charles Symons with the objective of improving accuracy and being more compatible with structured analysis and design concepts. It was used extensively throughout Europe and Asia. COSMIC Full Function Points is a new international standard, which is gaining popularity in Europe and Canada. In addition, there are other FSM methodologies such as the Lorenz–Kidd Method, Object points, WebMO [8], and Use Case Points [9]. We will examine a few of the function point counting methodologies in this chapter, and a few more of the other functional sizing methodologies in the estimation chapter, since they are used for effort estimation.

FSMs are also called "proxy points." With proxy points, you count "something else," that is, a proxy, as a measure of the "functional size" of a system. You usually can count proxies early in the development process—some of them are effective during the high-level specification phase. From the proxy points, you extrapolate to estimate either LOC or effort. Most of the methodologies start with a "size" based on the "proxy" measurements and adjust it based on "difficulty" factors, such as complexity and environment.

From a user viewpoint, proxy points (including function points) are a better measure of productivity than lines of code because they measure the external rather than the internal behavior of the system. Increases in productivity as measured by function points means that the user is getting more functionality for the effort applied. Increases in productivity as measured by LOC means the user is getting more code for the effort applied, whether or not it is useful code.

4.2.1 Function Points

4.2.1.1 *Counting Function Points*   In the IFPUG Function Point Analysis,

- the system's functionality is decomposed into components of inputs, outputs, external interface files (maintained by another system), internal data files (maintained by this system), and inquiries;

- each component's difficulty is rated as simple, average, or complex;
- a complexity rating is given to each component based on its type and difficulty, as shown in Table 4.3;
- the unadjusted function points (UFPs) are counted by summing all of the complexity ratings;
- a value adjustment factor (VAF) is calculated based on the complexity of the overall system; and
- the adjusted function point (AFP) count is calculated by multiplying VAF by the UFPs.

TABLE 4.3   Function Point Complexity Ratings

Component	Simple	Average	Complex
Inputs (I)	3	4	6
Outputs (O)	4	5	7
Data Files (F)	7	10	15
Interfaces (N)	5	7	10
Inquiries (Q)	3	4	6

The complexity ratings represent the relative implementation effort. For example, from the FPA viewpoint, an average interface to an external file is harder to implement than an average inquiry; hence, the weighting for the average interface is 7 versus 4 for the average inquiry. That is, the external interface file requires 1.75 times more effort than the inquiry.

The specific IFPUG rules such as how to determine whether a component is simple, average, or complex, and how to count graphical user interfaces (GUIs) can be found on the IFPUG website. Unfortunately, the inherent number of rules and details in the Function Point Analysis process can be daunting and may deter some from using FPA. David Herron, a leading FP consultant, recommends a getting-started strategy of rating everything as average complexity. You can then evolve into a more precise FP counting method with experience.

EXERCISE: You have a small program with four simple inputs, one data file (trivial), and two outputs, both of average complexity. How many unadjusted function points would this be?

Answer:

Inputs $= 4 * 3 = 12$
Data File $= 1 * 7 = 7$
Ouputs $= 2 * 5 = 10$
Total UFPs $= 12 + 7 + 10 = 29$

An additional adjustment is made based on the expected implementation difficulty of the system. Using the IFPUG standards, you calculate the VAF based on

14 General Systems Characteristics (GSCs), each of which is rated on a scale of 0 to 5, with 0 meaning no influence (or not present) and 5 meaning that characteristic has an extensive influence throughout the project. The 14 GSCs are described in Table 4.4. These characteristics are really "implementation difficulty" factors. Tremendous transaction rates (GSC #5) are more difficult to support than low ones. Automated backup and recovery (GSC #12) requires more implementation effort than manual.

The formula for adjusted function points is AFPs $=$ UFPs $* (0.65 + 0.01 * $ VAF$)$.

TABLE 4.4 General System Characteristics [10]

General System Characteristic (GSC)	Brief Description
1. Data Communications	How many communication facilities are there to aid in the transfer or exchange of information with the application of the system?
2. Distributed Data/Processing	How are distributed data and processing functions handled?
3. Performance Objectives	Are response time and throughput performance critical?
4. Heavily Used Configuration	How heavily used is the current hardware platform where the application will be executed?
5. Transaction Rate	Is the transaction rate high?
6. Online Data Entry	What percentage of the information is entered online?
7. End-User Efficiency	Is the application designed for end-user efficiency?
8. Online Update	How many data files are updated online?
9. Complex Processing	Is the internal processing complex?
10. Reusability	Is the application designed and developed to be reusable?
11. Conversion/Installation Ease	Are automated conversion and installation included in the system?
12. Operational Ease	How automated are operations such as backup, startup, and recovery?
13. Multiple Site Use	Is the application specifically designed, developed, and supported for multiple sites with multiple organizations?
14. Facilitate Change	Is the application specifically designed, developed, and supported to facilitate change and ease of use by the user?

The VAF adjusts the function point count based on the "implementation difficulty" (i.e., the general system characteristics) of the system. Observe that for an "average" system, with all average values of 2.5 for the 14 GSCs, the VAF $= 14 * 2.5 = 35$, such that the AFP $=$ UFP $* (0.65 + 0.35) =$ UFP, that is, the AFP equals 100% of the UFP. The VAF can adjust the function point count by $\pm 35\%$ (if all of the GSCs are five or all are zero).

EXERCISE: You have a small project that has 25 UFPs. You rate the GSCs of your system as trivial in all categories except complex processing and data communications, which have a high influence. All trivial factors are scored as 1. Complex processing and data communications both get scores of 5. How many AFPs do you have?

Answer:

$$VAF = 12 * 1 + 2 * 5 = 22$$
$$AFPs = UFPs * (0.65 + 0.01 * VAF) = 25 * (0.65 + 0.22) = 21.75$$

Software Productivity Research (SPR) has an alternative calculation for the VAF, which "achieves results that are very close to the IFPUG method, but it goes about it in quite a different manner" [11]. The SPR method uses only two factors—problem complexity and code complexity—to adjust the function point count. These are each rated on a scale of 1 to 5, as shown in Table 4.5. In this method, the $VAF = 0.4 + 0.1$ (Program Complexity Score + Data Complexity Score). Notice that if both factors are average, the $VAF = 1$ and the adjustment range is $\pm 40\%$ in this method versus $\pm 35\%$ in the IFPUG method. The SPR method can be calculated manually but is automated in some of the SPR estimation tools.

TABLE 4.5   SPR Function Point Complexity Adjustment Factors [11]

Program Complexity Rating
  1. All simple algorithms and simple calculations
  2. Majority of simple algorithms and simple calculations
  3. Algorithms and calculations of average complexity
  4. Some difficult or complex algorithms or calculations
  5. Many difficult algorithms and complex calculations

Data Complexity Rating
  1. Simple data with few elements and relationships
  2. Numerous variables and constant data items, but simple relationships
  3. Average complexity with multiple files, fields, and data relationships
  4. Complex file structures and complex data relationships
  5. Very complex file structures and very complex data relationships

EXERCISE: Assume you have a program with a UFP count of 35. You determine that the program has many difficult algorithms but simple data with few elements and relationships. What is the AFP count using the SPR FP complexity adjustment method?

Answer:

$$AFPs = UFPs * (0.4 + 0.1 * (PC + DC)) = 35(0.4 + 0.1 * (5 + 1)) = 35 * 1 = 35$$

4.2.1.2 Function Point Example Assume you work for a company that currently makes home safety and security monitoring devices and controllers. Now your company wants to sell home safety *systems*.

You need to design and build the software part of the system. The available components are:

- Controller (with associated monitoring devices) for door and window alarms
- Controller (with associated monitoring devices) for motion detectors
- Controller (with associated monitoring devices) for panic buttons
- Controller (with associated monitoring devices) for fire detector
- Controller (with associated devices) for light activator and deactivator
- Controller/monitor for key device (to turn system on and off)
- Wireless dial-out device with controller

(a) Estimate the effort to build the system. Assume a productivity of 10 FPs per staff month, with a standard deviation of ± 1 staff month.

(b) Now you are told that your company can only afford 75% of the estimated staff months to build the system. What do you do now? Be specific. Answers such as work 20% unpaid overtime will not get much credit, although your boss may be impressed. *Hint*: Figure out multiple ways to reduce the AFPs, showing the FP change and the impact on the estimate.

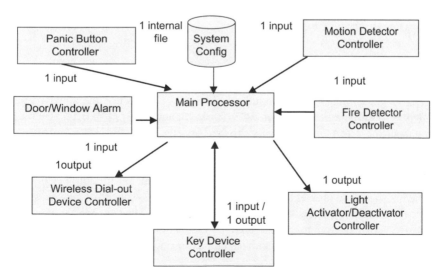

Figure 4.2. *Home security architecture.*

Solution for (*a*). You specify and design the system using block diagrams as shown in Figure 4.2.[3]

The component count is:

Simple Input $= 5$
Simple Output $= 2$
Simple Internal Database $= 1$
Medium Output (to Dial-out Controller) $= 1$

$$\text{UFPs} = 3*5 + 4*2 + 1*7 + 1*5 = 15 + 8 + 7 + 5 = 35$$

The values for the GSCs are[4]:

Data Communications	3
Distributed Functions	2
Performance	3
Heavily Used Configuration	1
Transaction Rate	0
Online Data Entry	1
End-User Efficiency	1
Online Update	1
Complex Processing	1
Resuability	3
Installation Ease	5
Operational ease	5
Multiple Sites	5
Facilitation of Change	2
VAF	33

$$\text{AFPs} = 35 * (0.65 + 0.33) = 35 * 0.98 = 34.3$$

The estimated number of staff months $= 34.3/10 = 3.4$. Since the standard deviation is ± 1 staff month, 1 SD is $34.3/9 = 3.81$ and $43.3/11 = 3.12$. Therefore, you expect the effort on this project to be between ~ 3.1 and ~ 3.8 staff months $\sim 68\%$ of the time.

Solution for (*b*). You need to reduce the expected staff months by at least 25%. There are many ways to reduce the staff months by reducing the number of AFPs.

The first step is to look at the UFPs. How can these be reduced? One answer is to reduce the functionality, but that might hurt the product. The next idea is to simplify the design. You can change the interface to the monitoring devices to be one generic monitoring input rather than 4 separate inputs. So now, instead of having 4 simple

---

[3]There are many possible designs. This is just one.
[4]The values for the GSCs are based on the assumption made about the system requirements and specifications. Other values are reasonable as well.

inputs, which total 12 AFPs, there is 1 average input for a total of 4 AFPs. The design change actually results in a better product, because it allows additional monitoring devices (such as pressure monitors) to be added easily. You can also reduce the VAF by changing some of the assumptions that you have made concerning the GSCs. For example, you could choose to use a faster processor, which would allow you to adjust the performance factor.

With only the design change, the AFPs are reduced from 34.3 to $27 * 0.98 = 26.46$, for a reduction of ~ 7.8 AFPs, which results in a reduction of $\sim 23\%$. Also, if we select a faster processor, so that the GSC for performance is 1 instead of 3, then the VAF becomes 0.31 which reduces the AFPs to $27 * 0.96 = 25.92$, which is a reduction of ~ 8.4 AFPs or nearly 25%.

This example illustrates an important point and the value of proxy point analysis. Budgets and staffing will always be inadequate. The question that must be answered is how to reduce the required effort. There are hosts of factors that generate effort. The best software engineers understand these factors and figure out how to simplify the solution, which reduces the proxy points, rather than working more overtime or cutting features.

4.2.1.3 *Converting Function Points to Physical Size* The primary purpose of the gearing factors in Tables 4.1 and 4.2 is to convert function points to lines of code, based on the implementation language.

EXERCISE: In Section 4.2.1.2, we ended up with a FP count of ~ 26. How many lines of code would you estimate if you were writing this system in Java? In Ada? Which would you prefer to use if you knew both well? Use the QSM data (Table 4.2) and the average SLOC/FP.

Answer: For Java, the average SLOC/FP is 60. For Ada, it is 154. There are 26 AFPs. Therefore, the estimated LOC is 1560 for Java and 4004 for Ada. Rounding, it is 1.6 KLOC for Java and 4.04 KLOC for Ada. We would choose to use Java and spend the extra time at the gym.

The only issue with converting FPs to LOC is which gearing factor to pick. You could choose the average, the maximum, the minimum, the median, The David Consulting Group (DSG) number, or the Jones number. We prefer the QSM or DSG data because they are newer and have more data points. After that, hopefully we would have some experience with past projects to guide us. If not, and unless we had more insight into the ease of using the language for this specific system, then we would start with the average, use a range to demonstrate the potential variance, and factor it into our risk management plan.

4.2.1.4 *Converting Function Points to Effort* Once you count function points, how do you use them to estimate effort? The primary method is to convert the function points to KLOC and use the methods and tools discussed in later chapters to estimate schedule and effort.

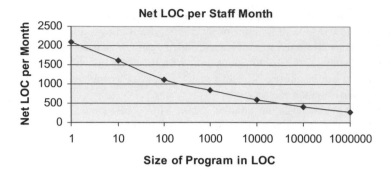

Figure 4.3. *Productivity engineering rule in LOC.*

Our second method, assuming you are using a procedural language, is to use the Jones engineering rules[5] for procedural languages [11]. He suggests using these engineering rules in situations where you are looking for only rough estimates or as a sanity check against other estimation methodologies. The essence of his data for productivity in LOC versus project size is captured in Figure 4.3. This data assumes 132 hours per month and includes all project efforts from requirements through testing.

The productivity decreases logarithmically as the size of the program increases. This decrease is due in large part to the increase in nonprogramming activity in larger projects.

EXERCISE: Estimate the effort for the system in Section 4.2.1.2.

Answer: For 1.6 KLOC, we would estimate the productivity to be ~2 KLOC per month, based on Figure 4.3. Therefore, we would estimate the total effort to be ~1 staff month. For 4 KLOC, the productivity is 1.8 KLOC per month, so we would estimate it to be 4/1.8 or ~2.2 staff months.

4.2.1.5   *Other Function Point Engineering Rules*   Jones also has other engineering rules for function points. Some of the more interesting ones are:

- Schedule = $FP^{0.4}$, where schedule is in calendar months.
- Staff = $FP/150$, where staff includes developers, testers, quality assurance personnel, technical writers, project managers, and database administrators.
- Effort = Staff * Schedule.

For the schedule equation, the power factor ranges from ~0.32 to ~0.45 with 0.32 for the smaller, simpler projects, and 0.45 for the larger, complex military projects.

---

[5]We use the terminology of "engineering rules" throughout this text. It is similar in meaning to "rules of thumb" without the potential negative connotations.

The schedule covers the period from requirements through delivery. In his text, Jones remarks that the schedule engineering rule has been one of the most useful ones to come out of the FP data. He also urges readers to collect their own historical data and tune these rules to their own environment, which we thoroughly endorse.

EXERCISE: Estimate the effort for a system with 25.93 FPs, using the Jones engineering rules for function points.

Answer: First, we would round the number of function points to 26. The precision of this methodology certainly is worse than 0.1 FP. To estimate schedule, you need to decide on the power factor: 0.4 is the average for 1000 FP projects. We know that smaller projects have greater efficiencies, so we would use the smallest power factor, which is 0.32. Therefore,

$$\text{Schedule} = 26^{0.32} = 2.84 \text{ calendar months}$$
$$\text{Staff} = 26/150 = 0.173 \text{ (!!!)}$$
$$\text{Effort} = 0.173 * 2.84 = 0.5 \text{ staff month}$$

Hmm. . . The schedule seems to be a reasonable number, but the staffing is basically 1/5 of a person. This does not seem reasonable, or at least it does not match up that well with the LOC engineering rules.

Actually, this is an excellent example of using the engineering rules and estimation methodologies. The FP engineering rules result is 50% less than the Java estimate and ~75% less than the Ada estimate.[6] Our experience is that the staffing rule does not hold up well for very small projects, although the schedule rule might. The accuracies may seem low, but the point in estimation, especially using engineering rules, is to get in the right ballpark, not in the third row of the upper deck. These rules give a starting point and a sanity check and are extremely useful when you understand both their strengths and limitations.

4.2.1.6 *Function Point Pros and Cons* Function points have been a tremendous addition to software estimation and counting methodologies. Function points are:

- technology independent,
- effective early (requirements phase) in the software life cycle,
- well-documented and specified,
- supported by standards and an international users group,
- backed by substantial data that supports the methodology,
- reasonably reliable and accurate,

---

[6]Note that the language chosen can have a huge impact on the FP productivity, which is not taken into account in the FP engineering rules. Consequently, since the range of gearing factors is large, it is reasonable to expect the FP engineering rules for effort to be even more imprecise.

- useful in negotiations with users and management, and
- insightful for understanding the sources of effort.

However, function points do have their issues, which include:

- They are semantically difficult. Many of the terms and factors are from the 1970s and 1980s and are difficult to understand in the context of today's systems. In this chapter, we have actually simplified the components for ease in understanding [12].
- They include many steps.
- Significant effort is required to become a certified function point counter.
- There are no tools that automatically count function points.
- There can be significant subjectivity in adjustment factors.

Nevertheless, function points are an important size metric and are still used successfully today. Albrecht's function point concepts are the foundation for all of the other FSMs.

4.2.2 Feature Points

Function points were originally designed for use with management information systems (MISs). The perception was that FPs were not optimal for heavily algorithmic systems, such as military, communications, and systems software. Feature points were developed by SPR [13] as an extension to function points to give additional weight to algorithmic complexity. SPR also reduced the relative weight of the average interface from 10 to 7. You can use the information in Table 4.6 to calculate the number of feature points. You use the VAF to convert UFPs to AFPs.

TABLE 4.6 Feature Point Component Weights

Component	Empirical Weight
Algorithms	3
Inputs	4
Outputs	5
Inquiries	4
Data Files	7
Interfaces	7

EXERCISE: You have a program that converts N, the number of days past A.D. 0, into the calendar date D. For example, if N = 10, then D would be January 10, 0001. How many total unadjusted feature points are there?

Answer:

Algorithms = 1
Inputs = 1
Outputs = 1
Inquiries = 0
Data files = 0
Interface Files = 0

Therefore, UFPs = 3 + 4 + 5 = 12

Feature points never reached widespread acceptance. They are interesting in that they show an evolution of FPs to better match another problem domain space.

4.3   SUMMARY

Size is one of the fundamental measures of software. We use it to normalize effort, quality, and cost. Although lines of code may have a poor reputation as a measure of size, since it does not indicate the complexity, functionality, or technology, it is a fundamental and useful metric, just as square feet is a fundamental and useful metric for buildings. It is important to have specific counting rules for lines of code—what should be included and what should not—so that you are consistent across projects and so that you understand how your counting compares with other projects.

We also need to measure the functionality, not just physical length, of software. Customers care about features and functionality, not how many lines of code it took to write it. Function Point Analysis was the first significant functional size measurement (FSM) and, although not perfect, a huge step forward for software estimation. It is the foundation for later FSM metrics.

The important concept of language gearing factors comes from function points. Gearing factors indicate the comparative number, on average, of statements required within a language to implement a function point. They allow us to both predict the number of lines of code required from a function point count and compare projects normalized by functionality rather than lines of code.

For both function points and lines of code, there are many engineering rules and algorithms to predict effort and schedule. These rules are extremely useful, especially for quick, rough estimates.

PROBLEMS

4.1   You have a system that has 3 inputs, 1 output, and 1 database file. All are of average complexity. The Technical Complexity Factors are all 2. You are writing this in Java, using The David Consulting Group's gearing factors.

   (a) How many UFPs are there?

      (b) What is the AFP count?

      (c) What is the expected LOC?

4.2 You are the development manager and your team comes up with an estimate of 6 people for 9 months (e.g., 54 staff months). You know that the job needs to be done in 36 months, and you cannot add more people. (You also think that more people may actually slow you down anyway.) You find out that your team estimated by taking FPs and converting them into LOC, and then using Jones' productivity guideline.

      (a) How many lines of code did they initially estimate?

      (b) You know they intend to write the project in Java. How many function points did they calculate?

      (c) You know you can reduce the functionality to cut the schedule, by working with the customer. How many function points do you need to reduce to have the estimate be 6 months instead of 9?

4.3 If you could program a system in Java or C equally well, which language would you expect would lead to less effort? Why?

PROJECT

The *Theater Tickets Project* is used throughout this book. The first step is to create a high-level design. In later chapters, you will continue to use it.

4.1 Theater Tickets Reservation System. This system reserves and allows you to purchase theater tickets. It has a database for tickets, a system administration interface, a user interface, and an interface to an online credit card validation system. The credit card validation system is a different system, which you do not need to build.

      (a) Create a high-level design for this system (preferably, a block diagram).

      (b) Without using any of the estimation tools you have learned so far, guess at the LOC and the number of staff months of effort it would take to build the system. Java is the programming language.

      (c) Now count the number of function points.

      (d) How many LOC do you estimate?

      (e) Using Jones' table, what is the estimated effort?

      (f) Compare your estimates. How do they differ?

      (g) Now your boss listens nicely to your estimate and tells you it is 20% too large. How do you cut the effort by 20%? *Hint*: Change your design/plan so that there really is 20% less effort rather than by working overtime or just saying a component is simpler.

REFERENCES

[1] R. Park. "Software size measurement: a framework for counting source statements," CMU/SEI-92-TR-020. Available from http://www.sei.cmu.edu/pub/documents/92.reports/pdf/tr20.92.pdf. Accessed Jan. 20, 2005.

[2] T. C. Jones. *Applied Software Measurement*, McGraw-Hill, New York, 1991.

[3] QSM website, QSM Function Point Languages Table, Version 2.0 July 2002, from http://www.qsm.com/FPGearing.html#MoreInfo. Accessed Feb. 7, 2005.

[4] Software Productivity Consortium, *Software Measurement Guidebook*, International Thomson Computer Press, London, 1995.

[5] N. Fenton and S. Pfleeger, *Software Metrics*, PWS Publishing Company, Boston, 1997.

[6] A. J. Albrecht. "Measuring application development productivity," in *Proceeding IBM Applications Development Symposium*. GUIDE Int and Share Inc., IBM Corp., Monterey, CA, Oct. 14–17, 1979, p. 83.

[7] D. Gamus and D. Herron, *Function Point Analysis: Measurement Practices for Successful Software Projects* (Addison-Wesley Information Technology Series), Addison-Wesley, 2000.

[8] D. Reifer, "Estimating web development costs: there are differences," *CrossTalk*, June 2002.

[9] G. Karncr, *Metrics for Objectory.* Diploma thesis, University of Linköping, Sweden. No. LiTH-IDA-Ex-9344:21. December 1993.

[10] D. Longstreet, "Fundamentals of function point analysis," www.softwaremetrics.com. Accessed Jan. 31, 2005.

[11] T. C. Jones, *Estimating Software Costs*, McGraw-Hill, New York, 1998.

[12] L. Fischman, "Evolving function points," www.stsc.hill.af.mil/crosstalk/2001/02/fischman.html. Accessed Feb. 14, 2005.

[13] "Feature points," http://www.spr.com/products/feature.shtm. Accessed Feb. 4, 2005.

5

Measuring Complexity

Simplicity is an acquired taste. Mankind, left free, instinctively complicates life.
—**Katharine Fullerton Gerould (1879–1944)**
Technical skill is mastery of complexity while creativity is mastery of simplicity.
—**Catastrophe Theory, 1977**
Be as simple as possible, but no simpler.
—**Albert Einstein**

Unnecessary complexity is the Typhoid Mary[1] of software development. With it come unwanted and occasionally fatal guests—additional defects and lower productivity.

The objective of complexity metrics is to identify those factors that cause these "unwanted guests" to appear. There is inherent complexity in any system or any module, based on the problem (e.g., weather prediction or interrupt handling) it needs to solve. Whatever the problem being solved, we want to minimize the complexity of the solution. That is, we want to implement the solution as simply as possible.

By measuring the complexity of the software itself, we seek to predict and understand what causes increased defects and lower productivity. The hypothesis is that the more complex the code, the more difficult it is to understand and, therefore, the more difficult to debug and maintain, which in turn implies more defects and lower productivity. Consequently, we want complexity metrics that have the capability of predicting defect proneness and productivity, which means that these metrics actually become the operational definition of complexity. We can use these metrics to identify designs and code that should be considered for simplification and, if not simplification, additional testing.

---

[1] A *Typhoid Mary* is a carrier of disease or misfortune who spreads it to those nearby.

Software Measurement and Estimation, by Linda M. Laird and M. Carol Brennan
Copyright © 2006 John Wiley & Sons, Inc.

We look at three different aspects of complexity—structural, conceptual, and computational.

5.1 STRUCTURAL COMPLEXITY

Structural complexity looks at the design and structure of the software itself. Simplicity in design brings in the concepts of modularity, loose coupling, and tight cohesion.[2] Simplicity in structure brings in the concepts of simple control flows and simple interfaces. The structural complexity metrics are operational definitions of these concepts.

There are many structural complexity metrics that have been defined, tried, and evolved. We have selected the following metrics to consider, as they contain most of the important structural complexity metric concepts.

Size: Typically measures LOC or function points.

Cyclomatic Complexity: Measures the control flow within a module.

Halstead's Complexity: Measures the number of "operators" and "operands" in the code.

Information Flow: Measures the flow of data into and out of modules.

System Complexity: Measures the complexity of the entire system in terms of maintainability and/or overall design.

Object-Oriented Structural Metrics: Measures the different structure of object-oriented programs (versus functionally designed programs).

5.1.1 Size as a Complexity Measure

5.1.1.1 *System Size and Complexity* Given that complexity is most basically defined as the quality of "interconnectedness" of parts, the simplest and most obvious metric for structural complexity is size. Size can be thought of as the sheer number of basic "parts," be it LOC or function points, that work together to accomplish a task. When function points are used as the measure of size, they are usually converted into LOC by the language gearing factors. KLOC is the primary factor in most effort estimation models.

The common wisdom is that defect density increases as a system increases in size. Empirical studies have shown that this belief is not true. The data and this relationship are examined in detail in Chapter 7. As a system increases in size, the relationship between defect and size is relatively linear. This is a key concept,

---

[2]If you are unfamiliar with the concepts of coupling and cohesion, you may wish to refer to a software engineering design text. Simply stated, coupling refers to the strength of the connections between the software modules that comprise a particular system. The more interdependent the modules are (i.e., the tighter the coupling), the more difficult the system is to understand and the more likely it is that changes to one module will impact the other modules. Good design has loose coupling. Cohesion refers to how strongly the elements within each module are related to each other. Good design has tight cohesion.

so we will repeat it. As a system increases in size, the relationship between defect and size is relatively linear. In other words, we expect the defect *density* to be relatively constant as a system increases in size.

At first glance, system size may appear overly simplistic as a complexity metric, but consider the data. LOC has remained over the years the primary factor in predicting effort. LOC is also a primary factor in predicting defects in many accepted models. Typically, other factors are modifiers and adjustments rather than the primary factor.

5.1.1.2 *Module Size and Complexity* What is the "best size" for a module? Is there a best size?

We believe the answer is yes—there is a sweet spot, although it will vary based on the skill of the individual programmer. In this sweet spot, the defect density (e.g., the number of defects per LOC) is the lowest. It is typically between 200 and 750 LOC per module. There is some controversy on this point, however. We agree with the analysis and findings of a curvilinear relationship rather than the alternative and earlier view of a random relationship (see Figure 5.1).

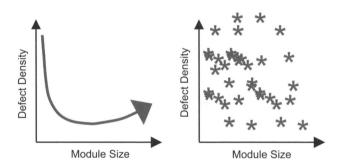

Figure 5.1. *Two views of module size versus defect density [1].*

A key issue is the difficulty in cleanly isolating the independent variables. Malaiya and Denton [2] do a fine job in analyzing the published data (including earlier data that implied a random distribution conclusion) and proposing an algorithmic model. Although the curvilinear relationship is surprising to most, we agree with the analysis and the reasoning behind it.

Hatton [3] and Malaiya and Denton [2] analyzed published defect density versus module size and concluded that for very small modules, as the module size increases, the defect density decreases linearly, until it hits a point somewhere between 200 and 400 LOC, at which point, it flattens out and then starts to increase linearly. This is quite a surprising finding. Another important conclusion is that the language is not a large factor. The fault density behavior is consistent across languages.

Malaiya and Denton constructed a composite defect density model to explain the defect density data. They postulated, in this context, that there are two types of faults—module-related faults and instruction-related faults. That is, the number of defects is based on the number of modules and the number of lines of code. For each module, there are faults caused by having a module rather than by having the code be integrated into another module, for example, interface defects, initialization defects, and handling of global data. Therefore, for module-related faults, if a module is of size s, its expected defect density D_m (in defects/LOC) is given by

$$D_m(s) = a/s$$

where s must be greater than zero and a is an empirically derived constant. In terms of defect density, this factor decreases as module size grows.

The instruction-related defects are a function of number of lines of code written, with two components. The first component, called b, is that there is a certain probability that any line of code has a bug in it. The second component is that each line of code within a module has a probability of incorrectly interacting with another line of code within that module. Therefore, for instruction-related faults, the defect density $D_i(s)$ is given by

$$D_i(s) = b + c * s$$

where c is the empirically derived interaction factor. Therefore, the total defect density, $D(s)$, is

$$D(s) = a/s + b + c * s$$

The optimum module size, S_{min}, for minimal defect density, which can be calculated by taking the derivative and setting it equal to 0, is

$$S_{min} = \sqrt{a/c}$$

S_{min} is based on the skill and expertise of the programmer and typically ranges from 200 to 400 LOC, independent of language. Hatton postulates that this number is based on the amount of code programmers can hold in their short-term memory at once. The more swapping that occurs, in and out of the human short-term memory, the more mistakes. This certainly seems intuitively reasonable.

We recommend that you issue guidelines for module size, either by starting with a recommendation such as such as 200–750 LOC for module size, or by solving for a, b, and c from your own project data.[3] We highly recommend that you gather your own data, analyze it, and draw your own conclusions. If you find a relationship, as we hope you will, use it to improve your guideline and quality. Then publish the results (in either case) to share with the rest of the software engineering community.

---

[3]The simplest way to algorithmically solve for a, b, and c is to initially ignore c and look at the smaller modules, such as less than 750 LOC. Once you have a and b, then solve for c using the larger modules.

5.1.2 Cyclomatic Complexity

The most famous complexity metric—and arguably the most popular—is McCabe's cyclomatic complexity (CC), which is a measure of the number of control flows within a module. The underlying theory is that the greater the number of paths through a module, the higher the complexity. McCabe's metric was originally designed to indicate a module's testability and understandability. It is based on classical graph theory, in which you calculate the cyclomatic number of a graph, denoted by $V(g)$, by counting the number of linearly independent paths within a program, which allows you to also determine the minimum number of unique tests that must be run to execute every executable statement. A module is defined as a set of executable code that has one entrance and one exit. The cyclomatic number can be calculated in two ways (which give the same result), either by counting the nodes and edges of the graph or by counting the number of binary decision points. That is:

$V(g) = e - n + 2$, where g is the control graph of the module, e is the number of edges, and n is the number of nodes.

$V(g) = bd + 1$, where bd is the number of binary decisions in the control graph. If there is a n-way decision, it is counted as $n - 1$ binary decisions.

We expect modules with higher CC to be more difficult to test and maintain, due to their higher complexity, and modules with lower CC to be easier.

Let us look at some examples. We will start with the three flow graphs in Figure 5.2 and then try some code. In these examples, the nodes are the vertices and the edges are the bodies of the arrows.

First, what does your intuition say about the complexity of A, B, and C? Ours says that A is the least complex, then B, then C. Now let us compute CC by counting

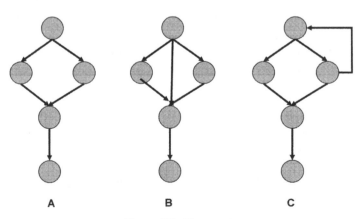

A   B   C

Figure 5.2. Flow graphs.

the nodes and edges:

$$V(A) = 5 - 5 + 2 = 2$$
$$V(B) = 6 - 5 + 2 = 3$$
$$V(C) = 6 - 5 + 2 = 3$$

So by the McCabe complexity metric, A is less complex, and B and C have the same complexity. This example demonstrates that loops are not weighed higher than any other branch, which is counter to our intuition of complexity. Now let us compute $V(g)$ using the number of binary decisions instead:

$$V(A) = 1 + 1 = 2$$
$$V(B) = 2 + 1 = 3$$
$$V(C) = 2 + 1 = 3$$

These are equivalent, which is as it should be.

EXERCISE: Recall the code strncat, which concatenates two strings together.

```
/ * The strncat() function appends up to count characters
from  string  src  to  string  dest,  and  then  appends  a
terminating  null  character.  If  copying  takes  place
between objects that overlap, the behavior is undefined.
* /
  char *strncat(char *dest, const char *src, size_t count)
  {
        char *temp=dest;
        if (count) {
              while (*dest)
                    dest++;
              while ((*dest++ = *src++)) {
                    if (--count == 0) {
                          *dest = '\0';
                          break;
                    }
              }
        } return temp;
  }
```

What is the $V(g)$ of this code?

Answer: The easiest way to calculate it is to count the number of binary decisions, which is four, one for each "if" statement and one for each "while" statement. Therefore,

$$V(\text{strncat}) = 4 + 1 = 5$$

EXERCISE: What is the CC for the flow graph in Figure 5.3?

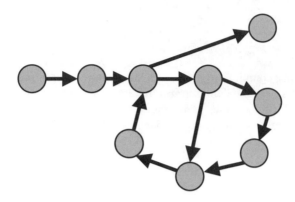

Figure 5.3. Example flow graph.

Answer: First, count the number of nodes and edges: $V(g) = 10 - 9 + 2 = 3$. Double check by counting the number of binary decisions: $V(g) = 2 + 1 = 3$.

Certain language constructs such as case statements and Boolean operators (and, or, xor, eqv, andalso, orelse) within a conditional statement can legitimately be counted in different ways. For example, case statements can be counted as one or as the number of cases minus one. Variations of CC have been defined, which count these in specific ways. Since all tend to be highly correlated with each other, we recommend using the rules that you believe are the more accurate model of complexity (and are easiest to count for you).

The objective, of course, for any metric is to give additional insight and understanding. What do we do with CC numbers? High CC numbers imply a high complexity and difficulty in maintaining and testing. NASA's in-house tests show that 20 is a threshold for error proneness [4]. Other published engineering rules [5, 6] for the cyclomatic complexity for a module are shown in Table 5.1.

TABLE 5.1 Cyclomatic Complexity Recommendations

CC	Type of Procedure	Risk
1 to 4	A simple procedure	Low
5 to 10	A well-structured and stable procedure	Low
11 to 20	A more complex procedure	Moderate
21 to 50	A complex procedure, worrisome	High
>50	An error-prone, extremely troublesome, untestable procedure	Very high

Remember that the cyclomatic complexity represents the minimum number of tests required to execute every path in the code. CC > 20 is definitely cause for concern, and CC > 50 is cause for alarm.

Cyclomatic complexity to us seems to be more of a problem when maintaining and testing code, rather than when originally writing it. As the cyclomatic complexity increases, the difficulty of fixing the code increases. One view [5] of the probability of inserting a defect while trying to fix another defect, based on the CC, is:

CC	Bad Fix Probability
1 to 10	5%
20 to 30	20%
>50	40%
Approaching 100	60%

There have been many studies that have looked at the relationship between cyclomatic complexity and defect rates. The results are mixed [7]. Many believe that using LOC is just as good and simpler than using CC. In student experiments that we ran, the correlation between LOC and CC was extremely strong.

Our view is that cyclomatic complexity is useful to:

- Identify overly complex parts of code needing detailed design inspections
- Identify noncomplex parts not in need of inspections
- Estimate maintenance effort, identify troublesome code, and estimate testing effort

One interesting extension to cyclomatic complexity is cyclomatic complexity density (CCD). CCD is the CC divided by LOC. Gill and Kemerer [8] conducted a small study that indicated that this is "shown to be a statistically significant single-value predictor of maintenance productivity." That is, a lower CCD predicts a higher maintenance productivity.

Another extension is the essential cyclomatic complexity (ECC) metric [9]. It is a measure of the "unstructuredness" of code, such as gotos in the middle of while loops. That is, it is the cyclomatic complexity of a piece of code after you remove all of the structured constructs (if, case, while, repeat, sequence). Let us now relook first at Figure 5.2. Graphs A and B only have structured constructs that can be reduced to a single node, with an ECC of 1. But what about graph C? How can you reduce it? The loop plays a role—and graph C reduces to the graph on the right in Figure 5.4, with an ECC of $2 + 1 = 3$.

EXERCISE: What is the ECC of Figure 5.3?

Answer: This graph is composed completely of structured constructs and can be reduced to a single node, which has an ECC of 1.

EXERCISE: What is the ECC if we have the control flow shown in Figure 5.5?

Answer: To calculate the ECC, we need to remove all of the structured constructs. This reduces our flow graph to Figure 5.6, which has a complexity of 4 (3 binary decisions + 1).

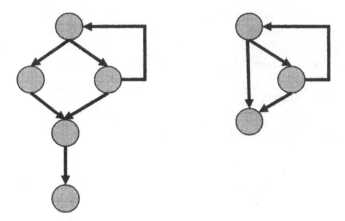

Figure 5.4. *Essential cyclomatic complexity reduction.*

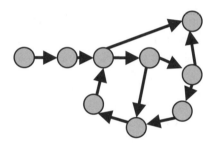

Figure 5.5. *ECC exercise flow graph.*

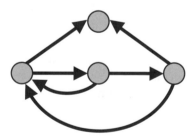

Figure 5.6. *ECC reduced flow graph.*

The ECC of programs that contain only structured programming constructs is 1. ECC is a measure of a program's unstructuredness.

There are tools available (many as freeware) that calculate the complexity metrics for a wide range of languages and are easy to use. We recommend trying them to see if they are useful in your organization. Our experience, on large projects, is that they do indeed indicate modules in need of additional testing attention and potential candidates for simplification.

5.1.3 Halstead's Metrics

In 1977, Halstead introduced complexity metrics based on the number of operators and operands in a program (think of the analogy to verbs and nouns in a document). He developed equations for difficulty, effort, and volume, which he called "software science." Halstead considered programs to be constructed of tokens, which could be either operands or operators. Operands were tokens with a value, such as variables and constants. Operators were everything else, including commas, parentheses, and arithmetic operators.

Halstead's metrics are defined as:

Length: $N = N_1 + N_2$
Vocabulary: $n = n_1 + n_2$
Volume: $V = N(\log_2 (n))$
Difficulty: $D = (n_1/2) * (N_2/n_2)$
Effort: $E = D * V$

where

n_1 = number of distinct operators
n_2 = number of distinct operands
N_1 = total number of operators
N_2 = total number of operands

The determination of the number of operators is neither completely clear nor unambiguous. One working definition is that operands are variables, constants, and strings, and operators are everything else. Operators that are paired (such as while do or { }) only count as one. Again, it is typically more important to decide how you will count and to be consistent, rather than worrying about the details of the specific rules.

EXERCISE: Calculate V, D, and E for strncat (repeated here for convenience).

```
/* The strncat() function appends up to count characters
from string src to string dest, and then appends a
terminating null. If copying takes place between objects
that overlap, the behavior is undefined. */

char *strncat(char *dest, const char *src, size_t count)
{
    char *temp=dest;
    if (count) {
```

```
        while  (*dest)
           dest++;
        while  ((*dest++= *src++))  {
           if  (--count  ==  0)  {
                  *dest= '\0';
                  break;
                  }
             }
   }       return temp;
  }
```

Answer:

n_1: {}; ++ if while break === – * return, therefore $n_1 = 11$

n_2: temp count dest src 0 '\0', therefore $n_2 = 6$

Operand	Number
{ }	4
;	5
++	3
if	2
while	2
break	1
=	3
==	1
*	3
return	1
–	1
Total	26

$N_1 = 26$

$N_2 = 10$

Length: $N = 10 + 26 = 36$

Vocabulary: $n = 11 + 16 = 17$

Volume: $V = 36 \, (\log_2 (17)) = 147$

Difficulty: $D = (11/2) * (10/6) = 9.2$

Effort: $E = D * V = 1348$

Halstead's metrics were extremely useful in opening the discussion on code structure metrics. In usage, they tend not to be practical. Since they are calculated after the code is written, they have no predictive power for development effort. They are in use as a predictor of maintenance effort. In general, though, they have not been shown to be a better predictor than lines of code, which is simpler.

5.1.4 Information Flow Metrics

Information flow metrics measure the information flow into and out of modules. The underlying theory is that a high amount of information flow indicates a lack of cohesion in the design, which causes higher complexity. They were originally proposed by Henry and Kafura in 1981 [10] and have evolved into the IEEE Standard 982.2. Information flow metrics use some combination of fanin (the number of local flows into a module), fanout (the number of local flows out of a module), and length to compute a complexity number for a procedure. Fanin, fanout, and length are defined in a number of ways by different variations of the metric.

Henry and Kafura defined the Information Flow Complexity (IFC) of a module to be IFC $= (\text{fanin} * \text{fanout})^2$ where fanin is the number of local flows into a module plus the number of data structures that are used as input. Fanout is the number of local flows out of a module plus the number of data structures that are used as output. Length is length of a procedure in LOC.

The IEEE 982.2 definitions, which are a little more specific, are:

- IFC $= (\text{fanin} * \text{fanout})^2$
- Weighted IFC $= \text{length} * (\text{fanin} * \text{fanout})^2$
- Fanin $=$ local flows into a procedure $+$ number of data structures from which the procedure retrieves data
- Fanout $=$ local flows from a procedure $+$ number of data structures that the procedure updates
- Length $=$ number of source statements in a procedure (excluding comments in a procedure)
- A local flow between procedures A and B exists if:

  A calls B

  B calls A and A returns a value to B that is used by B

  Both A and B are called by another module (procedure) that passes a value from A to B

High information complexity of a procedure may indicate:

- More than one function (lack of cohesion)
- A potential choke point for the system (too much information traffic)
- Excessive functional complexity (lack of cohesion)
- A good candidate for redesign/simplification or extensive testing

EXERCISE: What would be the IFC of the module in Figure 5.7? Assume module length is 100 LLOC.

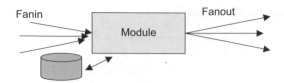

Figure 5.7. Information flow exercise.

Answer:

$$\text{Fanin} = 3 + 1 = 4$$
$$\text{Fanout} = 3 + 1 = 4$$

$$\text{IFC} = (4 * 4)^2 = 256$$
$$\text{Weighted IFC} = 100 * 256 = 25{,}600$$

EXERCISE: What would be the IFC of the strncat function, repeated here for convenience?

```
/* strncat() appends up to count characters from string
src to string dest, and then appends a terminating null
character. If copying takes place between objects that
overlap, the behavior is undefined. */

char *strncat(char *dest, const char *src, size_t count)
{
    char *temp=dest;
    if (count) {
        while (*dest)
            dest++;
        while ((*dest++ = *src++)) {
            if (--count == 0) {
                *dest = '\0';
                break;
            }
        }
    }   return temp;
}
```

Answer:

Number of flows in = ???
Number of data structures read = 3
Number of flows out = 0
Number of data structures written = 1

Ignoring the issues of counting flows in,

$$\text{IFC} = (3*1)^2 = 9$$
$$\text{Weighted IFC} = 10*25 = 90$$

This exercise points out one of the problems with flowin. For procedures such as library functions, flowin needs to be redefined.

There have been various studies (e.g., [11]) that examined the usefulness of the information flow metrics in their ability to predict fault-prone modules and modules that are considered "complex." It was discovered that fanin was not well correlated with either fault proneness or a subjective "expert opinion" of the complexity of a procedure. Fanout seems to be a much better indicator.

From a theoretical standpoint as well, fanin seems to be a poor choice for information flow complexity, since routines that are called frequently may just be evidence of good design technique and reusability. We recommend evolving the metric to have fanin equal the number of data structures read, and ignoring the number of calls. Various metrics packages calculate the information flow complexity with a variety of formulas.

EXERCISE: Using the evolved IFC definition (do not count the number of calls), what would be the IFC for the two exercises above?

Answer: For Figure 5.7, fanin = 1, fanout = 4, therefore IFC = $(1*4)^2 = 16$.
For the code, fanin = 3, fanout = 1, therefore IFC = $(3*1)^2 = 9$.

5.1.5 System Complexity

5.1.5.1 *Maintainability Index* We want complexity metrics to indicate modules and software that are difficult to maintain as well as to develop initially. In the 1990s, considerable progress was made on a maintainability index, which is a composite metric based on lines of code, Halstead's metrics, and cyclomatic complexity [6]. The work was done jointly by industry and academics (including HP and the University of Idaho) and was successfully used on both large-scale military and industrial systems for over ten years [12]. The intent was to define a metric which an individual programmer could use while maintaining code to determine if he/she was improving or diminishing the maintainability.

The maintainability index (MI) of a system is defined as [6]

$$\text{MI} = 171 - 5.2\ln(aV) - 0.23aV(g') - 16.2\ln(aLOC)$$
$$+ 50\sin[(2.4*\text{perCM})^{1/2}]$$

where

$\text{a}V =$ average Halstead volume V per module

$\text{a}V(g') =$ average extended cyclomatic complexity[4] per module

$\text{aLOC} =$ average count of lines of code (LOC) per module

$\text{perCM} =$ average percent of lines of comments per module (optional)

The coefficients were empirically derived from actual usage data.

Here are some engineering rules for the MI [13]:

Maintainability	MI Score
Highly maintainable	>85
Moderately maintainable	>65 and ≤85
Difficult to maintain	≤65

EXERCISE: MI is for a system, and we cannot reproduce one here. Consequently, we will apply it to strncat, just to see how it works. Instead of using the average, we will use the one value.

Answer:

$\text{a}V = 147$

$\text{a}V(g') = 4$

$\text{aLOC} = 17$ (depending on the rules you use)

$\text{perCM} = 3/17 = 0.18$

$$MI = 171 - 5.2\ln(147) - 0.23*4 - 16.2\ln(17) + 50\sin[(2.4*0.18)^{1/2}]$$
$$= 128$$

So based on this metric, strncat appears to be extremely maintainable.

Once you do the exercise, you can begin to see how the metric works. You start off with a score of 171. The only positive factor that you can have is from the perCM component, which has a ceiling of +50 (if and only if there are 100% comments, e.g., perCM = 100). All of the other factors impact the MI negatively; that is, the

---

[4]The extended cyclomatic complexity takes into account the added complexity resulting from compound conditional expressions. A compound conditional expression is defined as an expression composed of multiple conditions separated by a logical OR or AND condition. If an OR or AND condition is used within a control construct, the level of complexity is increased by one.

higher the volume, essential complexity, or LOC, the lower the score. For a system (rather than a module as in our exercise) MI uses the average per module; consequently, for a system (or library) made up of routines similar in style and size to strncat, you should expect a similar MI. More detail on the construction of this metric can be found in Oman and Hagemeister [14].

Studies have shown that the MI seems to be consistent with experts in assessing which modules and systems are more or less maintainable and can give potential targets for redesign. It is also useful in that tools exist (or can be written for a given environment) that automatically calculate the MI so that when programmers change code, they can readily see (based on the metric) the impact on maintainability.

5.1.5.2 The Agresti–Card–Glass System Complexity Metric The
Agresti–Card–Glass metric is a design metric based on the structured design modularity principles of coupling and cohesion. The intent is to examine high-leverage design and architectural decisions and use those as a measure of the "goodness" of a top–down design. It uses both the intramodule complexity and the intermodule complexity to arrive at a system complexity metric [16, 17].

The initial equation is

$$C_t = S_t + D_t$$

where

C_t = total system complexity
S_t = total structural (intermodule) complexity
D_t = total data model (intramodule) complexity

S_t is based on the Henry–Kafura metric, without the fanin component. That is,

$$S_t = \Sigma(f(i))^2$$

where

$f(i)$ = fanout of module i (internal data store writes are not counted).

D_t is based on the concept that the internal complexity of a module increases as the number of internal variables increases (similar to some of Halstead's concepts) and decreases as the functionality is deferred to other lower level modules, which is measured by the fanout of that module. So for each module, the internal complexity is defined to be the number of internal variables divided by the fanout of the module. D_t is the mean of all the internal complexity measures for all of the modules. That is, for each module i,

$$D(i) = \frac{V(i)}{f(i) + 1}$$

and

$$D_t = \sum \frac{D(i)}{n}$$

The relative system complexity, RSC, is a normalization of the system complexity based on the number of modules. It is the average complexity per module. That is,

$$\text{RSC} = S_t/n + D_t/n.$$

where n is the number of modules in the system and n' is the number of new modules. New modules (n') are used with the data complexity in recognition of the stability of reused modules.

RSC allows you to compare the complexity of systems, regardless of the overall size.

EXERCISE: We have a small system with a call graph as shown in Figure 5.8. Assume that each vertex is a module. All modules are new (i.e., $n = n'$) Also assume that the number of I/O variables per module is 1 for module 1, 2 for module 2, ..., and 5 for module 5. Calculate the Agresti–Card–Glass metrics.

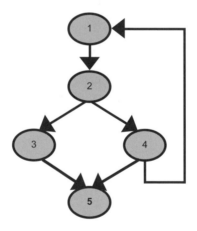

Figure 5.8. Flow graph for Agresti–Card–Glass exercise.

Answer: Since

$$V(\text{exercise}) = \langle 1, 2, 3, 4, 5 \rangle^5$$

---

[5] The notation $V(G) = \langle a, b, c \rangle$ means given program G, with modules 1, 2, and 3, then $V(1) = a$, $V(2) = b$, and $V(3) = c$.

and

$$f(\text{exercise}) = \langle 1, 2, 1, 2, 0 \rangle$$

then

$$D(\text{exercise}) = \langle 0.5, 0.67, 1.5, 1.33, 5 \rangle$$

Therefore,

$$D_t = 9$$

and since

$$f(\text{example})^2 = \langle 1, 4, 1, 4, 0 \rangle$$

then

$$S_t = 10$$

Therefore, RSC $= 10/5 + 9/5 = 3.8$.

So what do these numbers mean? What are good values versus bad values? And what do you do about them?

There are limited published results of using these metrics to predict defect densities, and the data is old. That which exists suggests that RSC is a good predictor of defect rates. The reference value RSC ≤ 26 is good, while RSC > 26 is an overly complex system [16]. If you choose to use this metric, you should establish your own engineering rules for the individual measurements, tuned to your environment.

You can also use these metrics as operational definitions of design "goodness" and work to reduce both the data and system complexity metrics (such as less fanout and fewer I/O variables) that will improve the module cohesion and reduce the coupling between modules.

The Agresti–Card–Glass metric was designed for large systems using top–down design methodologies and reinforces top–down design techniques. It was successfully used in large projects at companies such as HP and Motorola. Although cumbersome to calculate manually, it can be calculated using tools and is a good example of a design metric that encourage good design techniques.

5.1.6 Object-Oriented Design Metrics

Structural metrics for object-oriented design (OOD) need to be somewhat different from those used for functional or data-driven design because the programs are structured differently. OOD programs are structured around objects, which encapsulate the state, the characteristics, and the possible set of actions for that object. Functional designs are structured around procedures and modules, and the decomposition of those into smaller and smaller procedures and modules. Although we want to measure the structural complexity for both types of code, the *operational definition* of structural complexity differs. For example, we have found that

LOC is a measure of size for procedural code, but, intuitively, it does not make as much sense for OO code. Similarly, fanout may not make much sense either. Instead, we need metrics that indicate the complexity of the OOD and implementation. We would like them to measure classes, modularity, encapsulation, inheritance, and abstraction.

The Chidamber and Kemerer (CK) metrics suite [18] is a popular set of OOD metrics that is similar to many other proposed OOD metrics. It consists of six metrics that measure class size and complexity, use of inheritance, coupling between classes, cohesion of a class, and collaboration between classes. These metrics are:

- *WMC—Weighted Methods per Class*: This metric focuses on the number and complexity of methods within a class. The complexity typically defaults to one, in which case this is the number of methods per class. Alternatively, the complexity may be computed by a variety of methods, such as McCabe's CC or LOC. Operationally, it equals the sum of the complexity for all methods within a class. This metric has been shown to be an indicator of the amount of effort required to implement and test a class. High values suggest that the class is too large and should be split [19].

- *DIT—Depth of Inheritance Tree*: This metric measures how many inheritance layers make up a given class hierarchy. Large values imply more design complexity, but also more reuse.

- *NOC—Number of Children*: This is a measure of the number of immediate successors of the class. Again, large values imply that the abstraction of the parent class has been diluted, the increased need for testing and, more reuse. Redesign should be considered.

- *CBO—Coupling Between Object Classes*: This is a measure of how many other classes rely on the class and vice versa. It is a count of the classes to which this class is coupled. Two classes are consided coupled when methods declared in one class use methods or instance variables of the other class. Large values imply more complexity, reduced maintainability and reduced reusability.

- *RFC—Response for Class*: This metric is the size of the set of methods that can potentially be executed in response to a message received by an object. It is calculated as the sum of the number of methods plus the number of methods called by local methods (count only one level down). Complexity increases as the RFC increases, as well as the need for increased testing.

- *LCOM—Lack of Cohesion on Methods*: This metric counts the number of different methods within a class that reference a given instance variable. Complexity and design difficulty increase as LCOM increases.

OOD metrics are still evolving. Some are operationally not well defined, some may not count exactly what they intended to count, and some are extremely difficult to count manually. Fortunately, tools do exist. Although refinement is required, studies on the CK metrics have shown that the OOD metrics appear to give added insight beyond the traditional size metrics and that high values of the CK OOD metrics correlate with:

- Lower productivity
- High effort to reuse classes
- High effort to design classes
- Difficulties in implementing classes
- Number of maintenance changes
- Number of faulty classes
- Faults
- User reported problems [19]

In 1999, Rosenberg et al. [20] of NASA published guidelines specifying that any class that meets *at least two* of the following criteria needs to be flagged and investigated for possible refactoring:

- Response for class > 100
- Coupling between objects > 5
- Response for class > 5 times the number of methods in the class
- Weighted methods per class > 100
- Number of methods > 40

Others have published similar guidelines.

The CK metrics are useful when they are well defined locally. When used in concert with some of the other traditional metrics, they will identify outliers in need of further investigation and potentially more testing, as well as giving you additional insight into the structure and maintainability of your OOD system. You may also be able to come up with additional local practices and guidelines for "good OOD," which you can codify into your own metrics.

5.1.7 Structural Complexity Summary

We described the most popular and well-known structural metrics that are useful in judging and/or predicting defect proneness, productivity, and maintainability. LOC, amazingly, is really the top metric. The value of many of the others as individual indicators is, in many cases, still not clear. Nevertheless, when used in combination, they can be extremely useful.

5.2 CONCEPTUAL COMPLEXITY

Conceptual complexity refers to difficulty in understanding. You want to be able to measure how hard it is to understand the system/requirements and/or code itself. It tends to be more psychological, based on mental capacity and thought processes of programmers. As an analogy, consider calculus versus algebra. Calculus is much more conceptually complex and difficult than algebra. There are leaps of understanding and insight that need to be mastered. In software, consider interrupt handling versus payroll systems. Payroll systems are relatively straightforward, with typically clear requirements. Interrupt handling systems need to handle the unexpected, such as timing issues, and race conditions. The typical interrupt handling system is conceptually more complex than the typical payroll system.

Consider two different implementations of a factorial routine, written below in pseudocode. Which routine do you consider more difficult to understand?

```
Factorial Routine 1
        Int fact(int n){
            If (n= =0)
                    { return 1}
            Else
                    {return n* fact (n-1)}
            }
Factorial Routine 2
            Int fact(int n) {
            total=1
            For i=1 to n
                    {total=i*total }
            Return total
            }
```

For most people, Routine 1 is conceptually more difficult due to the recursion. Note that the CC of the two routines are equivalent.

Conceptual complexity is difficult to quantify. In some cases, such as the interrupt handling, it could be based on how difficult it is to specify a solution. In other cases, it may be the amount of effort required to understand the code itself. There are metrics that measure recursion, if recursion is the source of complexity, but there are no specific metrics of which we know that measure conceptual complexity. Nevertheless, it can be an important consideration when comparing designs and implementations.

Now consider this question: "Since maintaining someone else's code is harder than writing new code . . . and if we are as clever as possible when we write it . . . then who will maintain it?" [21]

5.3 COMPUTATIONAL COMPLEXITY

Computational complexity refers to the complexity of the computation being performed. An example is weather forecasting. This kind of complexity can be measured by determining the amount of time (number of instructions) and space (disk and/or memory) required for the calculations. Algorithms that we as humans consider "complex," because they are difficult for us to evaluate, may or may not be computationally complex.

Consider the previous Factorial Routines 1 and 2. Which is more computationally complex? Routine 1 requires a call stack on the order of size $n + 1$, one for each call. This can become infinitely large as n becomes infinitely large. Routine 2 requires a call stack of size 1, and a limited amount of storage for variables. Hence, from a space viewpoint, Routine 1 is far more computationally complex than Routine 2. From a time viewpoint, both increase linearly as n increases and, hence, have a similar order of magnitude of computational complexity, although again we expect Routine 2's complexity to be less because the computation required for each iteration is less.

Computational complexity is used to evaluate and compare implementations and designs for efficiency and to ensure that the complexity of the solution does not exceed the inherent complexity of the problem being solved.

5.4 SUMMARY

We have examined structural, conceptual, and computational complexity and ways to measure them. Structural complexity looks at the structure of the software itself. There are many metrics: source lines of code is one of the best, although the others can give additional insight into error proneness and maintainability. Many structural complexity metrics are embodied in easy-to-use tools. Conceptual complexity looks at how hard the software is to understand. This concept is important and needs to be considered in design, but it is difficult to measure. Computational complexity looks at the difficulty of computing the algorithms used, in terms of amounts of storage and CPU required. It is used to compare designs for efficiency.

The complexity metrics are operational definitions of good design and good programming and are indicators for productivity and defect proneness, which, in turn, are factors in the cost effectiveness of our work. Use these metrics to identify simpler designs and to identify high-risk areas that may need special attention.

As a final thought, we offer Bob Colwell's view, who wrote: "I believe design complexity is a function of the number of ideas you must hold in your head simultaneously, the duration of each of those ideas, and the cross product of those two things, times the severity of interactions between them." [22]

PROBLEMS

5.1 The following pseudocode implements the Sieve of Eratosthenes, which finds all prime numbers less than n.

```
Eratosthenes (n) {
   e[1]:=0
   for i: = 2 to n do e[i]:=1
   p:=2
```

```
while p*2<n do {
  j:=p*2
  while (j<n) do {
    e[j]:=0
    j:=j+p
  }
  repeat p:=p+1 until e[p]=1
  }
  return(a)
}
```

Calculate the following complexity metrics for this program: LOC, CC, ECC, Halstead, Agresti–Card–Glass, information flow, and maintainability index.

5.2 The pseudocode below is of an object-oriented implementation of the same program, using a different algorithm. Calculate the following metrics for this program: CK, LOC, CC, ECC, Halstead, Agresti–Card–Glass, information flow, and the maintainability index.

```
//Initiate an instance IEEval of class ESieveEval
public class ESieveEval implements IEEval{
    private EFilterEval EFilterEval;
    private integer newVal=new Integer(2);

//initiate the class ESieveEval
public ESieveEval() {
  LRStruct src=(new EIncEval(2,1)).makeELRS (); // src=2,3,4,5,...
  EFilterEval=new EFilterEval(newVal, src); //filter out numbers
}

//inherit predefined class LRStruct,
public LRStruct nextLRS() {
  newVal=(Integer)EFilterEval.nextLRS().getFirst();
  EFilterEval= new EFilterEval (newVal, EFilterEval.makeELRS ());
  return makeELRS();
}

//use the design pattern Singleton to define method makeELRS()
public LRStruct makeELRS() {
  return LRSFactory.Singleton().makeLRS (newVal, this);
}}
```

Calculate the CK metrics for this program as well as all of the others from Problem 5.1 that you can. Compare the results from Problems 5.1 and 5.2. What conclusions and observations can you make?

5.3 What can you say about the computational complexity of the program in Problem 5.1?

5.4 What is the difference between computational complexity and structural complexity? What is an example of a program that is computationally complex but structurally simple? What is an example of a program that is structurally complex and computationally simple?

5.5 True or False: If you decrease the complexity of a system, the function points will always decrease as well.

5.6 True or False: The Agresti–Card–Glass metric attempts to measure both coupling and cohesion.

5.7 True or False: If you have a module with a CC >50, you should seriously consider refactoring/rewriting it.

5.8 True or False: If you have a high information flow count for a module, there is a high degree of cohesion in the module.

5.9 True or False: Your module size should always be under 150 LOC.

5.10 True or False: A DIT of 10 indicates a good candidate for redesign.

5.11 According to the Maintainability Index, decreases in which of the following improve code maintainability? LOC, number of unique variables, fanout, and number of children.

PROJECTS

5.1 Determine the optimal size for your modules. (a) Gather your defect density versus module size for your own data. (b) Graph it. (c) Determine a, b, and c.

5.2 Calculate complexities using tools.

    (a) Find a free complexity counting tool on the Web. There are demo downloads and other freeware. Some possible tools are listed below (these were good links as of July 2005).

        http://user.cs.tu-berlin.de/~fetcke/measurement/products.html
        http://www.chris-lott.org/resources/cmetrics
        http://www.scitools.com/
        http://www.semdesigns.com/Products/Metrics/JavaMetrics.html

    (b) Next, select two programs (not just modules). These could be your own code or even Linux code if you want.

    (c) Include the Sieve of Eratosthenes as a program. Browse through the three programs and rank order them by your intuitive view of complexity.

    (d) Calculate the complexity metrics (LOC, CC, HK, DIT—whichever you can do) using the tool you've selected.

    (e) Document any assumptions in using the metrics and graph the results.

    (f) How do the results compare to your intuition?

    (g) What did you think of the tool—good or needs improvement?

REFERENCES

[1]   N. E. Fenton, "A critique of software defect prediction models," *IEEE Transactions on Software Engineering* **25**(5): 675–689 (1999).

[2]   Y. Malayia and J. Denton, "Module size distribution and defect density," in *11th International Symposium on Software Reliability Engineering (ISSRE'00)*, October 2000. Available from www.cs.ttu.edu/~denton/papers/modsize.pdf. Accessed Apr. 15, 2005.

[3]   L. Hatton, "Software failures: follies and fallacies," *IEE Review*, Mar. 1997.

[4]   http://mdp.ivv.nasa.gov/complexity_metrics.html. Accessed June 15, 2005.

[5]   Avisto web site, http://www.aivosto.com/project/help/pm-complexity.html. Accessed Feb. 1, 2005.

[6]   SEI website, http://www.sei.cmu.edu/activities/str/descriptions/mitmpm.html. Accessed June 15, 2005.

[7]   Available from www.cs.ttu.edu/~denton/papers/modsize.pdf. Accessed Apr. 15, 2005.

[8]   G. K. Gill and C. F. Kemerer, "Cyclomatic complexity density and software maintenance productivity," *IEEE Transactions on Software Engineering* **17**(12): 1284–1288 (1991).

[9]   Available from http://hissa.ncsl.nist.gov/HHRFdata/Artifacts/ITLdoc/235/chaptera.htm. Accessed June 15, 2005.

[10]   S. Henry and D. Kafura, "Software structure metrics based on information flow," *IEEE Transactions on Software Engineering* **7**(5): 510–518 (1981).

[11]   B. Kitchenham, L. Pickard, and S. Linkman, "An evaluation of some design metrics," *Software Engineering Journal*, January 1990.

[12]   K. D. Welker, and P. W. Oman, "Software maintainability metrics models in practice," *Crosstalk, Journal of Defense Software Engineering* **8**(11): 19–23 (1995).

[13]   D. Coleman, D. Ash, B. Lowther, and P. Oman, "Using metrics to evaluate software system maintainability," *IEEE Computer* **27**(8): 44–49 (1994).

[14]   P. Oman and J. Hagemeister, "Constructing and testing of polynomials predicting software maintainability," *Journal of Systems and Software* **24**(3): 251–266 (1994).

[15]   W. Agresti, private correspondence, July 2005.

[16]   D. N. Card and W. W. Agresti, "Measuring software design complexity," *Journal of Systems and Software* **8**(3): 185–197 (1988).

[17]   D. Card and R. Glass, *Measuring Software Design Quality*, Prentice Hall, Englewood Cliffs, NJ, 1990.

[18]   S. R. Chidamber and C. F. Kemerer, "A metrics suite for object-oriented design," *IEEE Transactions on Software Engineering* **20**(6): 476–493 (1994).

[19]   C. Kemerer, "Metrics for object oriented software: a retrospective," from http://www.software.org/metrics99/kemerer.ppt. Accessed June 25, 2005.

[20]   L. Rosenberg, E. Stapko, and A. Gallo, "Applying object oriented metrics," ISSRE Nov. 1991, NASA–Goddard Space Flight Center, http://www.software.org/metrics99/rosenberg.ppt. Accessed July 10, 2005.

[21]   Source unknown, Bell Labs, circa 1978.

[22]   B. Colwell, "Complexity in Design," *IEEE Computer*, **38**(10): 10–12 (2005).

6

Estimating Effort

Good estimation is based on the understanding and use of a range of tools and techniques and the expert judgment as to which combinations are most appropriate in each situation.
—*F. Wellman, 1992*

Anyone who expects a quick and easy solution to the multi-faceted problem of resource estimation is going to be disappointed.
—*Alfred M. Pietrasanta at IBM System Research Institute, 1968*

We are sure you are going to be disappointed. Effort estimation still has a long way to go.

Effort is probably the most popular metric we have in software. It is the question that everyone always wants answered. How much effort is it going to take?

Effort is easily defined as the number of staff days/weeks/months or even years associated with a project. The only possible issue in measuring effort is determining *which* effort is counted for a project. Do you include the upfront specification effort? The bid and the proposal effort? Or only the development and testing effort? Do you include the "overheads" of other organizations, such as a metrics or a quality organization? This is a simple issue easily resolved by clear rules and clear definitions.[1]

The complication with effort is that it is typically more useful to be able to *predict*[2] the effort rather than count it. In order to predict effort, we usually need

---

[1]When others quote effort numbers and when you use estimation tools, make sure you understand what is included in effort. It is easy to swing effort by over 250% by definitions alone.

[2]Some make a distinction between prediction and estimation, especially when discussing quality and reliability within the context of effort and schedule; however, the distinction is confusing and frequently not terribly useful. Therefore, within this chapter, you should consider the terms interchangeable.

---

to have taken the first steps of predicting the size and understanding the inherent difficulties and complexities of the project.

In this chapter, we give you a bevy of estimation tools and techniques, with examples, since different ones work better in different situations, and you should always estimate using at least three different methodologies. We give you a number of methods of combining them into one estimate. But let us set some expectations first. These tools and methodologies will, without a doubt, significantly improve your estimations and your ability to bring in projects on-time and on-budget. But they are not silver bullets. Estimates are just probabilistic views. Consequently, we also discuss and provide methods for dealing with the issues, uncertainties, and inherent risks with estimation. Remember that the unknown and uncertain will always be with us and will continue to cause havoc to our schedules and plans as long as we solve problems that have not been solved before, and implement systems that have not been implemented before.

6.1   EFFORT ESTIMATION: WHERE ARE WE?

How well do you estimate? How do you know? Do you actually track the estimates throughout the life cycle of a project, and understand where you under- or overestimated so that you can do better the next time? Do you actually have a documented estimation process you follow?

How well do most people estimate? The 1995 Standish Group's Chaos Report found overruns on 89% of projects. The most common value reported in other surveys is that 30–40% of the programs overrun [1]. Molokken and Jorgensen, who studied software estimation results, point out that the root causes of the overruns are complex, the data is not always reliable, and those responding to the surveys "may have a tendency to over-report causes that lie outside of their responsibility..., e.g., customer-related causes." We resonate with their observations and comments. What goes awry on a project is usually not one factor. One factor can usually be compensated for or fixed. It is the combination and interplay between factors, such as schedules, changing requirements, new technologies, resource unavailability, unforeseen problems, and personnel (management and staff), that lead to overruns.

Popular common causes for overruns listed in the literature are:

- Specifying incomplete or unclear requirements
- Failing to adjust schedules when scope changes
- Setting development schedules that are too aggressive
- Insufficient resources

It is interesting to note what the last three really say:

- Too much work
- Too little time
- Not enough people/equipment

Our view is a little different. In our experiences, we see the primary causes as:

- Confusion of the desired schedule/effort target with the estimate. Development teams are frequently pushed into dates because of the "needs of the business" rather than because they have a rational plan to deliver on those dates.
- Hope-based planning. Developers know what the "right answer" is—it is on-time and on-budget based on the target that marketing or higher management tells them is needed. This is extremely related to confusion between the estimate and the target. Hope is not a plan.
- Inability of software personnel to credibly communicate and support their estimates. The lack of a good estimation process and knowledge frequently leads to the tightest schedule you cannot prove you won't make rather than a rational one based on probable outcomes.
- Incomplete, changing, and creeping requirements. Nothing reeks havoc on project estimates more than changing and growing requirements.
- Quality "surprises." Projects can easily spend half of their time in test-and-fix, especially when the need for speed causes the development team to take additional risks and to turn over inadequately tested code.

6.2 SOFTWARE ESTIMATION METHODOLOGIES AND MODELS

There are hundreds of documented software estimation methodologies, tools, and models. The first ones that we recall are those that actually estimated the software cost as a percentage of the hardware cost. (Hardware cost a lot more in those days.) The output of most of them is an estimation of staff effort from a wide variety of inputs. Many use an analytical formula that takes as input parameters descriptions of project characteristics, system size, complexity,[3] and development methodology, which are typically called "cost drivers." You need to be sure you understand what phases of the life cycle are included, since many models may cover only software design, development, and testing. All of the methodologies and models have significant limitations.

We categorize estimation methodologies as:

- Expert opinion
- Using benchmark data
- Analogy
- Proxy points
- Custom models
- Algorithmic models

---

[3]Complexity in this context typically means project complexity, such as the need for high security or reliability, rather than the complexity of the design or the code.

Expert opinion usually will give you the best estimates, but it requires you to have true experts available. If you have an estimated size (FP or LOC), you can use benchmark data as a great place to get an effort estimate very easily. Unfortunately, estimating LOC is typically as difficult as estimating effort directly. Analogy can either be a very simple method, where you extrapolate from a very similar system, or an extremely complex method, requiring significant processing capability and historical databases. Proxy points determine the size of a project based on external characteristics of the system, such as screens, inputs, or use cases. Algorithmic models typically take as input size (LOC or FP) and the project and process characteristics and determine effort, schedule, and cost. There are both manual and tool-based algorithmic models. In research studies, use case points (one of the proxy point methods) generated results as good as or better than expert opinion.

You can also classify estimation methodologies as either top–down or bottom–up. The top–down methodologies generate an estimate based on the global properties of the software. The advantage is that the estimation process follows the structure and natural evolution of the top–down software design process. The disadvantage is the same as for top–down design: that is, difficult technical issues may be masked and cause later problems. The bottom–up models involve the costing of components in the form they will be developed. Bottom–up models have the disadvantage of being highly reliant on a well-defined design (which occurs later in the development process) and the skill and expertise of the estimators.

So how do you select which methodology to use? The current thinking, with which we strongly concur, is that you should *use at least three different methods*. Each gives you some insight and understanding, and three allow you to triangulate on an answer.

Note: You will find that few of the methods work well all of the time, and many work poorly frequently. Results may vary significantly. Models and methodologies are not a replacement for common sense and sound engineering judgment. You need to be careful.

6.2.1 Expert Estimation

There are two approaches to expert estimation methodologies—*activity decomposition* and *system decomposition*. One looks at the tasks to be performed, while the other looks at the components and modules of the system.

With experts, you need to be able to converge the expert opinion when they disagree and to handle the uncertainties of their estimates. The Delphi and wideband Delphi methods are both designed to gain convergence.

6.2.1.1 Work and Activity Decomposition
This method is a tried and true method and probably the most widely used (other than the popular, but highly dangerous, method of pulling numbers out of the air). The estimator, typically the person who will be responsible for ensuring the work is accomplished, thinks about the work to be done and the skill of the people who will do it, and creates

| | Months | | | | | | | | | | | | | | | Total |
	1	2	3	4	5	6	7	8	9	10	11	12	13	14	15	
Requirements	4	4	6	8	6	4	1	0	0	0	0	0	0	0	0	33
Scenario Development	3	3	3	2	1											
Data Model Development	1	1	1	1												
Sequence Diagrams			2	2	2	2										
Detailed Requirements				3	3	2	1									
Design	0	1	3	4	5	4	3	1	0	0	0	0	0	0	0	21
High Level Architecture		1	1	1	1											
Performance Model				1	1	1										
Data Base Design			1	1	1	1										
Detailed Architecture			1	2	2	2	2	1								
Coding & Unit Testing	0	0	0	3	8	14	14	14	13	12	9	8	7	2	2	106
Module Design & Coding				3	6	9	9	9	7	5	3	3	3	1	1	
Data Base Implementation				2	2	2	2	2	1							
OA&M Implementation					3	3	3	2	1	1						
Unit Testing									2	5	5	5	4	1	1	
System Testing	0	0	4	4	4	4	3	3	6	6	6	5	5	5	3	58
Test Case Development			3	3	3	2										
Test Environment			1	1	1	2	3	3								
Test Case Execution									5	5	5	5	5	5	3	
Project Mgmt & Administration	1	1	1	1	2	2	2	2	2	2	2	2	2	2	2	26
Training & Documentation				2	2	2	4	4	2	2	1	1	1	1	1	23
Total Project Staffing	5	6	14	22	27	30	27	24	23	22	18	16	15	10	8	267
Total Project Cost (staff years)																22.3

Figure 6.1. Work and activity decomposition example.

an outline of the required activities, durations, and number of people required to do those activities per time period (see Figure 6.1).

This example subdivides the work into six areas of responsibilities, Requirements, Design, Coding & Unit Testing, System Testing, Project Management & Administration, and Training & Documentation. In this case, the estimation effort may have been done by one person for the whole project, or by a set of people, each responsible for one of the areas. In this case, it assumes a waterfall development process. Obviously, for different processes and different projects, you would use a different activity breakdown structure.

This estimation process is really a gestalt-type process, based on the wonderfulness of the human brain to think about the system that must be built, weigh potential risks and uncertainties, and arrive at an answer. Its success comes from the estimator's skill and experience. It requires no intermediate sizing, such as KLOC or FPs, and no explicit handling of complexity factors or productivity factors. It can be difficult to defend ("Why do you need six people in the third month? Aren't four enough?") because it is usually based on subjective personal opinion rather than quantitative data and history. Feedback from past project's estimations usually improves the results.

6.2.1.2 *System Decomposition* In the system decomposition method, you decompose the system into lower level modules, estimate the effort associated with each module, and total the estimates. Again, this is a tried and true estimation methodology, especially for development effort. Issues include needing a detailed

design, needing experts both to do the design and to estimate the effort for the subsequent lower level modules, and extrapolating from the effort to build the modules to the total project effort.

A variation on this approach is the *function block* estimation method. It is based on the concept of having an average size for function blocks (or components) and having an average size for subfunction blocks (or modules). In this method, you decompose your system into function blocks, which tend to be about the same size. You count the number of function blocks, multiply it by the average size of a function block (or the average effort, if you have that data), and voilá, you have an estimate for the size of the system. You then decompose each of the function blocks into your standard sized subfunctions, count the numbers of subfunctions, multiply by the standard size, and now you have a second estimate. You then compare and adjust the estimates.

This function block approach can work well if you have a design process that creates similarly sized modules and components. Again, you need to be in the design process or to have a very good idea of the expected design to use this method.

6.2.1.3 The Delphi Methods

The Delphi methods are named after the Oracle at Delphi, in Ancient Greece. The Oracle was a priestess who would answer (supposedly correctly, although cryptically) any question that was asked, assuming that the supplicant had sufficient gold. With the Delphi method, you go to the experts (potentially with a bag of gold) and ask their opinion for schedule and effort estimates. The methods facilitate the convergence of answers among the experts and, hopefully, result in better answers than just one expert's opinion.

In the Delphi method (developed at the Rand Corporation in 1948), a small team of experts is given the system specifications, system goals, assumptions, and estimation issues. They anonymously generate individual estimates and reach consensus on a final set of estimates through iteration. Frequently, after two or three rounds, if consensus has not been reached, the group's estimate is determined by discarding both the highest and lowest estimates and taking the average of the remainder.

The wideband Delphi method (developed by Rand Corporation in the early 1970s) is an extension to the Delphi method that includes more estimation team interaction. Typically, it starts with the distribution of the system specifications and goals. Before the estimation meeting, each expert anonymously generates a list of tasks that must be performed and his/her overall estimate. At the meeting, the estimates are given to a moderator, who lists them on a linear scale but does not identify who created them. Each participant then reads through their list of tasks and assumptions, raising any questions or issues he/she might have but not identifying his/her own estimate. Anonymity is an important aspect of the Delphi technique: it prevents reputation from ruling or an outspoken colleague from intimidating the other participants. Discussion ensues, and as a result, a common list of tasks, issues, and assumptions typically emerges. The process is then repeated within the meeting. It continues for four rounds or until the estimates have converged into an acceptable range (defined in advance).

The wideband Delphi method is becoming increasing popular, especially when there is no historical cost data available to aid in other estimation techniques.

6.2.2 Using Benchmark Size Data

An extremely simple method of estimation, which we call the *EZ estimation model*, is based on the concept that productivity is a function of size and application domain. If you believe this to be true for your project, and you are able to determine the size in lines of code or function points, then you only need a simple division to calculate your initial estimate. As illustrated in Figure 6.2, take the project size and divide it by the delivery rate to get effort.

Figure 6.2. *EZ estimation model.*

In 2004, Donald Reifer published [2] LOC productivity data based on the most recent 600 projects in his database of 1800 projects, which is reproduced in Table 6.1. All projects were completed since 1997. The David Consulting Group has function point productivity data from over 8740 projects that were completed between 2000 and 2004. These benchmarks can be used, *with care*, to project a delivery rate and predict effort.

With care is an important caveat. This data tells you the productivity on a certain set of projects. It may or may not hold true for your project. The data set is large, which is good. But never use these numbers blindly. They are useful, and a good part of the picture, but not the whole picture.

If you have a function point count rather than LOC, you have two choices: either use the function point benchmarks or convert the FPs to LOC by selecting the target programming language(s), and then converting to LOC by using the gearing factors presented previously (see Chapter 4).

6.2.2.1 *Lines of Code Benchmark Data* Reifer presents his data subdivided by application domain, reproduced in Table 6.1.

EXERCISE: You are in a military project that aims mobile howitzers. You have estimated the size of your program to be 150 KLOC. What do you estimate the effort to be?

Answer: This is a military ground project, where the average productivity is 195 LOC per staff month. We would estimate $150K/195 = 0.77K$ staff months $= 770$ staff months. Since the productivity range is from 80 to 300, the staff month range could be from 500 to 1870. Since this is a large range, we'd try to get more

TABLE 6.1 Software Productivity (ESLOC/SM) by Application Domain

Application Domain	Number of Projects	Size Range (KLOC)	Average Productivity (LOC/SM)	Range (LOC/SM)	Example Application
Automation	55	25 to 650	245	120 to 445	Factory automation
Banking	30	55 to 1000	270	155 to 550	Loan processing, ATM
Command and control	45	35 to 4500	225	95 to 350	Command centers
Data processing	35	20 to 780	330	165 to 500	DB-intensive systems
Environment/tools	75	15 to 1200	260	143 to 630	CASE, compilers, etc.
Military—all	125	15 to 2125	145	45 to 300	See subcategories
Airborne	40	20 to 1350	105	65 to 250	Embedded sensors
Ground	52	25 to 2125	195	80 to 300	Combat center
Missile	15	22 to 125	85	52 to 175	GNC system
Space	18	15 to 465	90	45 to 175	Attitude control system
Scientific	35	28 to 790	195	130 to 360	Seismic processing
Telecommunications	50	15 to 1800	250	175 to 440	Digital switches
Test	35	20 to 800	210	100 to 440	Test equipment, devices
Trainers/simulations	25	200 to 900	225	143 to 780	Virtual reality simulator
Web business	65	10 to 270	275	190 to 985	Client/server sites
Other	25	5 to 1000	182	65 to 481	All others
Totals	**600**	**10 to 4500**		**45 to 985**	

information to determine if the expected productivity was going to be higher or lower than average for this type of application, and we would use that to narrow down the range for the initial estimate.

The EZ estimation methodology is a good method when you have an estimate for LOC or FP. Unfortunately, especially for LOC, that may be difficult.

6.2.2.2 Function Point Benchmark Data
Figure 6.3 is an example of the benchmark data for function point productivity by size of a project within a particular organization from The David Consulting Group.

Figure 6.4 contains The David Consulting Group's function point productivity data by platform type for projects completed between 2000 and 2004 [3].

In addition, the International Software Benchmarking Standards Group (ISBSG) compiles submitted data and will provide it for a small fee.

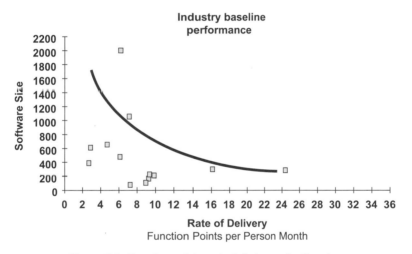

Figure 6.3. *Function point productivity by application size.*

EXERCISE: You need to build a system having an estimated 500 FPs. You need to generate an effort estimate in the next hour for a meeting. All you have are the benchmark data in Table 6.1, Figure 6.3, and Figure 6.4. What do you estimate? It will be written in Java (25%), Powerbuilder (50%), and SQL (25%), and is an E-business application. *Note:* the percentages are based on the size in FPs, not LOC.

Answer: You want to see first what answers all of these benchmarks give you.

1. Using the industry baseline performance (Figure 6.3), you get a productivity of ~14 FPs per staff month. Therefore, you have an effort of $500/14 = 36$ staff months.
2. Using the FPs by platform type (Figure 6.4), you get productivity of ~15 FPs per month. Therefore, you have an effort of $500/15 = 33$ staff months.

Average Function Points per Month Across Different Platforms	
Client Server	17
Main Frame	13
Web	25
E-business Web	15
Vendor Packages	18
Data Warehouse	9

Figure 6.4. *Function point productivity by platform type.*

3. Using the gearing factors from Chapter 4, you decide to use 60 LOC per FP for Java, 30 for Powerbuilder, and 40 for SQL.

Since 500 FPs $=>$
125 FPs in Java $=>60*125 = 7.5$ KLOC
125 FPs in SQL $=>125*40 = 5.0$ KLOC
250 FPs in Powerbuilder $\rightarrow 250*30 = 7.5$ KLOC
You have a total of 20.0 KLOC.

Using the LOC productivity chart (Table 6.1), you decide to use 275 LOC per staff month. Therefore, you estimate that the system will take $20/0.275 = 73$ staff months.

This says it looks to be between 33 and 75 staff months. Our choice would be to estimate roughly between 3 and 6 staff years. If we needed one number, we'd use the weighted average of $(1*L + 4*M + 1*H)/6$ and round up, which would be 4.33 staff years ... or round up to 4.5 staff years, with an equal probability of being over or under.

6.2.3 Estimation by Analogy

Estimation by analogy is the preferred approach when you have decent analogs. It will probably give you the most accurate estimation possible. The idea is to find completed projects (the analogs) that are similar and use the experience and data from those to estimate your new project. The typical breakeven point is $\pm 25\%$: if it is more than 25% different, get a closer analog or use a different method.

Rewrites and ports of systems are wonderful examples of simple estimates by analogy. Assume your organization was responsible for porting all of your company's old FORTRAN systems into Java and making them web based. How would you estimate the effort? The easiest way would be to do an experiment to determine the cost factors. Then use your new knowledge to predict the remainder. You might even learn that simple measures like LOC were adequate for prediction (e.g., 10 staff weeks per KLOC). But what if you needed to estimate before you ported the first one? Obviously, many other companies and organizations have done similar ports. Email them and see what you can find out. Alternatively, you could run a few smaller experiments (prototypes of the port) and extrapolate from those.

6.2.3.1 Traditional Analogy Approach The traditional analogy approach is a structured approach that characterizes a project by multiple attributes (variables) and uses that characterization to identify other, similar project(s). The effort for the new project is based on the effort for the identified, completed projects. This approach is being pursued in research, with good results using tools that calculate the similarities algorithmically and using large databases of projects. It differs from the estimation model approach in that it looks for similar projects and uses those as the primary data points to predict, rather than using parameters based on a regression of data sets. This method can be tool based or manual, although the manual is usually tedious and time consuming. Shepperd and Schofield [4] have validated this method on nine different industrial data sets (a total of 275 projects) using a PC-based tool, *and in all cases their analogy method outperformed the algorithmic models such as COCOMO*. They calculated the similarities of the analogies by measuring the Euclidean distance in *n*-dimensional space, where each dimension corresponded to an attribute.[4]

You can also use a similar, simplified approach manually. The concept is shown in Figure 6.5.

For the analogy method:

- Choose a similar system, typically similar in structure, users and environment, system construction and schedule, and implementation and operational environment
- Analyze the differences
- Express the differences as modifiers
- Break out costs for the full project (e.g., requirements, project management, hardware)
- Modify base system costs to arrive at a new estimate

The validity of the estimate is highly dependent on the degree of similarity of the systems.

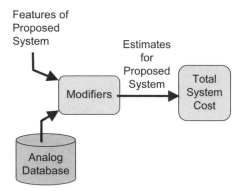

Figure 6.5. *Analogy estimation model.*

[4]The tool used in the studies is called ANGEL. As of March 2005, it was available on-line for free. You may wish to try it.

As an example, consider that you have a system to estimate. You have five other systems you think may be similar. You research them and decide that one of them is the most similar. Then you look at what you consider the key differences between the systems—these are the modifying factors. For each one, you estimate the extent ỏf the impact of key differences, by estimating the percentage of the difference in effort that this factor would cause. Table 6.2 shows that, in this example, we consider that there are eight modifying factors. For each, we specify the impact it is expected to have on the base estimate. For example, we expect that the interfaces will cause a 20% increase in effort. The product of all the modifiers is the compound modifier, which leads to the first-order estimate for our new system, which would be 1.31 ∗ effort for the old system.

TABLE 6.2   Modifying Factors Worksheet

Modifying Factor	Effect on Base	Estimated (%)	Modifier
System feature complexity	+	15%	1.15
Menus and screens	+	10%	1.10
Database structure	−	5%	0.95
Interfaces	+	20%	1.20
Staff familiarity with development environment	+	20%	1.20
Development environment	−	10%	0.90
Development team experience	−	20%	0.80
Customer environment	+	5%	1.05
	Compound modifier		**1.31**

The next refinement is to look at the different cost elements of the project and make a determination of the extent of applicability for the compound modifier. Table 6.3 shows the expected applicability for a large project using a waterfall development methodology. The effort in requirements through system test are all expected to scale linearly with the compound modifier. For cost elements, such as integration test, if there are differences in process, such as a need to integrate with the customer's system, the modifier may or may not be applicable. For cost elements such as hardware, which are purely project dependent, the modifier is not applicable.

TABLE 6.3   Applicability of Modifiers

Cost Element	Applicability of Modifier
Requirements specification	Applicable
Product design	Applicable
Detailed design	Applicable
Code and unit testing	Applicable
System testing	Applicable
Integration test	Depends on project methodology and business arrangement
Documentation and training	Depends on business arrangement
Project management and administration	Depends on project methodology
Third party software	Depends on product and project definition
Capital equipment	Depends on project definition

Cost Element	Base System (staff months)	Compound Modifier	Macro Estimate
Requirements Specification	15	1.31	20
Product Design	10	1.31	13
Detailed Design	35	1.31	46
Code and Unit Test	35	1.31	46
System Test	50	1.31	66
Integration Test	25		10
Training	3		2
Project Mgmt & Administration	6		9
3rd Party Software	$20,000		$25,000
Capital Equipment	$225,000		$135,000
Total Staff	179		212
Staff Cost/mo (fully loaded)	$9,200		$10,000
Project Costs	$1,891,800		$2,280,000

Figure 6.6. Effort and cost estimate spreadsheet.

Continuing our example, we would put the cost elements (as shown in Figure 6.6) in a spreadsheet and for those items for which the modifier doesn't work, we would create a macro estimate manually.

6.2.3.2 *Analogy Summary* If you can find a system that is similar to the one you need to build, use it as the basis for your estimation. It will probably give you the most accurate estimation possible.

6.2.4 Proxy Point Estimation Methods

Proxy point estimation methods determine the size of a project based on external characteristics of the system—that is, characteristics that can be used as a *proxy* for size. The underlying concept is that the proxy point is directly related to the size and effort to build the system.

There are a large number of proxy point methods. In our judgment, the primary ones at this time are:

- *Function Points*: The initial and most widely known proxy point method.
- *Object Points*: Used with COCOMO II—object points are screens, reports, and 3GL objects
- *Use Case Points*: Second generation proxy point based on use cases. Use case points has had excellent results and is used in industry today.

6.2.4.1 *Meta-Model for Effort Estimation* The proxy point models all have a three-step process for estimating effort, as shown in Figure 6.7.

1. First you estimate size, typically in either KLOC, FP, or some other "proxy point" metric.

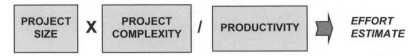

Figure 6.7. *Effort estimation meta-model.*

2. Next, you adjust your estimate for "complexity" or "difficulty" factors, such as security, algorithmic complexity, reliability requirements communication requirements, and warranty requirements.

3. Finally, you adjust by a productivity factor, such as FP per staff month. In manual methods, this tends to be a simple division. With tools, more complex functions (rather than just division) and factors (such as size, environment, development process) are taken into account. The result is an effort estimate. It may be one number, a range, or a number with confidence percentages.

The boundaries between adjustments for complexity and productivity are blurry and change with different methodologies. Where do we account for factors such as an embedded system environment? We can argue that it should be a "complexity factor" or just as easily a "productivity factor" (albeit a negative factor). Different methodologies classify these factors differently.

6.2.4.2 Function Points

Counting IFPUG function points was addressed in Chapter 4. To estimate using function points, you need a method of converting the function points to effort, duration, and schedule. The possibilities include:

1. Using the FP count directly with the benchmark data or algorithmic tools (such as COCOMO).

2. Converting to LOC and using the LOC methods such as benchmark data and algorithmic tools

3. Using engineering rules

Function Point Engineering Rules The benchmark data and tools methods are described in their own sections within this chapter. Several engineering rules are shown below. They can be useful when doing quick, rough estimations.

Project Duration: The length of a project in calendar months equals
the number of FP raised to the Dth power, where D ranges from 0.32 to 0.5. The recommended values of D are as follows [5, 6]:

Project Type	Recommended D
Military	0.45
Average	0.4
Simple	0.32
Large Web	0.32
Small Web	0.5

Staffing: The number of staff on a new development project equals the number of function points divided by 150. The number of staff on a maintenance project equals the number of function points divided by 750 [6].

Effort: The number of staff months on a project equals the number of people multiplied by the duration [6].

Creeping Features: The number of user requirements will increase at a rate of 1% to 5% per month from the design through coding phades, based on the development methodology. The average is 2% [6].

EXERCISE: Assume that you have a new, 1000 FP military project. What is the estimate for effort, staffing, and duration? Assume design through coding is 50% of the schedule.

Answer:

Duration $= 1000^{0.45} = 22.4$ calendar months $= \sim 2$ years

Staffing $= 1000/150 = 6.7$ staff $= 7$ staff

Effort $= 7*2 = \sim 14$ staff years

Creeping FP $= 12.2\%. 1000 = 240$ FP, which means that your project just added another ~ 6 months and ~ 3.5 staff years if you consider creeping features.

COSMIC Function Points   Function points have their strengths, but they also have their shortcomings, such as the difficulty of counting consistently without extensive training, the awkwardness and/or difficulty of counting embedded, highly algorithmic, and web systems, and the difficulty of using automated tools to count.

The COSMIC full-featured function points method [7] is an evolution of function points, designed to address some of the shortcomings of function points. It has been defined primarily outside the United States and has an international standard, ISO/IEC 19761:2300. It is a "second-generation" method designed to measure a functional size of real-time, multilayered software such as used in telecommunications companies, process control systems, and operating systems, as well as traditional business application software.

The COSMIC method introduces the concept of multiple measurement viewpoints. You can decide to measure from the end-user viewpoint, which is the same as IFPUG, or you can select the "developer" viewpoint, which considers the intended architecture of the system and allows inclusion of nonbusiness functionality such as security and navigation. For example, consider a project developed on a single platform versus the same project on multiple platforms of differing technologies. We naturally expect the development effort to be different in the different environments. With IFPUG, since it primarily looks at the external behavior of a system, this difference is hidden or extremely deemphasized.

The primary counting activity for COSMIC function points is to determine the number of "data movements" and to use it as the primary size driver. There are four types of data movements: entry, exit, read, and write. Entries move data from the user across the boundary to the inside of the functional process. Exits move data from inside the functional process across the boundary to the user. Reads and writes move data from and to persistent storage.

It appears to us that the COSMIC function point method is an up-and-coming methodology that deserves notice and trial. The latest manual, news, tools, and case studies can be found through www.cosmicon.com (as of Jan. 2006).

6.2.4.3   Object Points

The object points method [8] is an alternative method to function points when 4GLs[5] or similar technologies are used for development. The original method was developed in 1991 for use with CASE tools and extended [9] as an alternative to LOC for early input to the COCOMO model. In the early work, it was shown to closely approximate function point estimates with less than half the effort. Although object points is no longer of interest in research, it is simple to use (and tune) manually and is recommended as one of the methods (remember, you need three) for a 4GL development.

Object points are not related to object-oriented development and are not object classes. The objects in object points are screens, reports, and the 3GL modules that are needed to support the 4GL development.

The scheme for counting object points is extremely similar to the other proxy point methods, with the exception of the explicit consideration of reuse.

1. The complexity of each object is determined and assigned a numerical weighting factor, which is the object point. For screens and reports, the complexity and object point count is determined by the number of views and data tables (see Figures 6.8, 6.9, and 6.10). For each 3GL module, the object point count is 10.
2. The system's object point total (OP) is the sum of the individual object points.
3. The new object point total (NOP) is calculated by removing the percentage of reuse. That is, $NOP = OP * (1 - \% \text{ Reuse})$.
4. Environment productivity and programmer productivity are factored in to determine staff months. The nominal value for the environmental productivity

Number of Views Contained	Total Number and Source of Data Tables		
	<4	4 to 7	>7
<3	Simple	Simple	Medium
3 to 7	Simple	Medium	Difficult
>7	Medium	Difficult	Difficult

Figure 6.8. Object points—screen complexity.

[5]4GL means "fourth-generation programming language." 1GLs are low-level machine languages. 2GLs are low-level languages as well, but assembly languages such as NASM, S1F, and gas. 3GLs are high-level machine languages such as C and FORTRAN. 4GLs consist of statements similar to human language, such as SQL. 4GLs are typically used in database scripts. 5GLs, such as Visual Basic, contain visual tools that are used in software development.

Number of Sections Contained	Total Number and Source of Data Tables		
	<4	4 to 7	>7
<2	Simple	Simple	Medium
2 or 3	Simple	Medium	Difficult
>3	Medium	Difficult	Difficult

Figure 6.9. Object points—report complexity.

Object Type	Simple	Medium	Difficult
Screen	1	2	3
Report	2	5	8
3GL component	10	10	10

Figure 6.10. Object point weights.

is 1. It can be adjusted based on a view of the percentage difference from nominal. The nominal programmer productivity is 13 NOPs per staff month, with a range of 4 to 50.

EXERCISE: We have a new 4GL application that will consist of the following:

1. Three input screens, each of which has two views and references six different data sources
2. One output report that has four sections and references eight data sources
3. Three existing 3GL components and requires an additional three to be programmed. In addition, the programmers' productivity on past projects was 15 OPs per staff month, and the environment is average.

What would be a reasonable estimate for this new application?

Answer:
1. The three input screens are all simple. ➜ $3 * 1 = 3$ object points.
2. The one output report is difficult ➜ $1 * 8 = 8$ object points.
3. There are six 3GL components ➜ $6 * 10 = 60$ object points.
4. Total OPs = 71.
5. It appears that ∼40% of the application is reused ➜ $71 * 0.6 = 43$ NOPs.
6. Effort = NOP * Environment Factor/Productivity Factor = $43 * 1/15 = 2.87$ ≈ 3 staff months.

6.2.4.4 Use Case Sizing Methodologies

The use case method[6] is a popular method for capturing and specifying functional requirements of a system.

---

[6]Use cases became part of UML in the early 2000s. There are many references and texts that explain both. You can start at www.uml.org to look for more information.

As of early 2005, there were a few closely related methodologies and/or approaches to using use cases for estimation. Some of the most noteworthy ones are:

- *Using Use Cases with Function Points Analysis*: Use cases are a method of specifying requirements. Function Point Analysis (FPA) is an estimation methodology based on requirements. FPA can easily use a use case specification as input. An example of using use cases for FPA can be found on the IFPUG website [10].
- *Using Use Cases with LOC Estimates*: One method [11] uses system decomposition and predicts LOC from use cases. This method is relatively complex, time consuming, and not, to our knowledge, in widespread use. It relies on the other traditional methods to estimate effort and schedule from LOC.
- *Use Case Points*: Use case points (UCPs) were introduced by G. Karner [12] in 1993 and have been gaining in popularity, with significant trials and research by Anda and others at Simula Research Laboratories. UCPs are quite similar in approach to function points and achieved [13] results better than experts in both industrial trials and student projects.

Use Case Points Methodology   The use case points methodology [13] is a series of steps similar to function point counting, except you start with use cases and actors[7] rather than inputs, outputs, queries, external interfaces, and internal interfaces. The steps are:

1. Classify each actor as simple, average, or complex (Figure 6.11), count the number of each kind, and then calculate the unadjusted actor weight (UAW) by multiplying each total by weight and summing the products.
2. Classify each use case as simple, average, or complex (Figure 6.12), count the number of each kind, and then calculate the unadjusted use case weight (UUCW) by multiplying each total by weight and summing the products. The criteria in Figure 6.12 are traditional UUCP criteria. Others [14] have adjusted it to include additional factors of complexity, such as information flow, with good results for their companies.
3. Determine the total unadjusted use case points (UUCs). Total UUCPs = Total UAWs + Total UUCWs.

Classification	Unadjusted Actor Weight Description of Actor	Weight
Simple	Well-defined API	1
Average	Protocol such as TCP/IP, HTTP, FTP or the actor is a data store	2
Complex	GUI interface or any human interface	3

Figure 6.11. Unadjusted actor weight (UAW).

---

[7]In the use case methodology, actors are types of users or other external systems. At a minimum, you will probably have a typical user and a system administration interface for the human interfaces, and unless the system is standalone, another actor for each external interface.

Classification	Unadjusted Use Case Weight Description	Weight
Simple	<4 Transactions	5
Average	≥4 and ≤7 Transactions	10
Complex	>7 Transactions	15

Figure 6.12. Unadjusted use case weight (UUCW).

4. Compute the weighted technical and environmental factors. Each factor needs to be assigned a value from 0 to 5 depending on the complexity within the project, and then multiplied by the weights in Figures 6.13 and 6.14 to give a weighted factor. A 0 value means it is irrelevant to the project. A 5 value means it is crucial.

5. Calculate the Tfactor by taking the sum of all the individual weighted technical factors.

6. Calculate the TCF (technical complexity factor) $= 0.6 + 0.01 *$ Tfactor.

7. Calculate the Efactor by taking the sum of all the individual weighted environmental factors.

8. Calculate the EF (environmental factor) $= 1.4 - (0.03 *$ Efactor).

9. Calculate the AUCPs (adjusted use case points) $=$ UUCP $*$ TCF $*$ EF.

10. Effort $=$ AUCPs $*$ Use Case Productivity Factor.

11. Karner [12] proposed 20 staff hours per UCP. Schneider and Winters [15] recommended using the environmental factors to modify the productivity factor: count the number for factors in F1 through F8 that are below 3 and add them to the number of factors in F7 and F8 that are greater than 3. Call the result X. If X is ≤2, then use 20 hours per UCP. If X − 3 or 4, then use 28 hours per UCP. If X > 4, adjust the project to reduce the risk, or use 38 hours per UCP.

Factor	Technical Complexity Factors Description	Weight
T1	Distributed System	2
T2	Response or Performance Objectives	2
T3	End-User Efficiency	1
T4	Complex Internal Processing	1
T5	Reusable Code	1
T6	Easy to Install	0.5
T7	Easy to Use	0.5
T8	Portable	2
T9	Easy to Change	1
T10	Concurrent	1
T11	Security Objectives	1
T12	Provides Access for 3rd Parties	1
T13	Special User Training Facilities Required	1

Figure 6.13. Technical complexity factors (TCFs).

	Environmental Factors	
Factor	Description	Weight
F1	Familiarity with Project	1.5
F2	Application Experience	0.5
F3	OO Experience	1
F4	Lead Analyst Capability	0.5
F5	Motivation	1
F6	Stable Requirements	2
F7	Part-Time Workers	−1
F8	Difficult Programming Language	−1

Figure 6.14. Environmental factors (EFs).

Use Case Point Methodology Example: Home Security System There are some good examples of the use case methodology in the literature, such as [13, 15, 17], which start with defining the use cases and actors. Our focus is on the counting, once the cases and actors are defined, so the use cases and actors in this example will be simplified.

As our example, we will estimate the Home Security System, as shown in the block diagram in Figure 6.15. The Controllers are components that are being reused, and their development effort is not considered as part of the project.

Step 1: Determine the unadjusted actor weight (UAW). See Figure 6.16 (System Config file is not an external data store and is not counted as an actor).

Step 2: Determine the unadjusted use cases weight (UUCW). See Figure 6.17. The use cases are:

- Initialize/Reconfigure System and System Configurations
- Alarm: Receive Alarm, Recognize It, Callout, and Flash Lights
- Arm/Disarm System

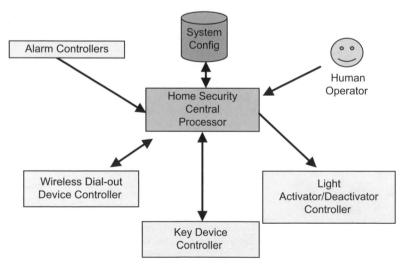

Figure 6.15. Home security architecture.

Unadjusted Actor Weight		
Actor	Complexity	Score
Human	Complex	3
Alarm Controller	Simple	1
Callout Controller	Simple	1
Key Device Controller	Simple	1
Light Controller	Simple	1
Total		7

Figure 6.16. UAW example.

Step 3: Calculate the total unadjusted use case points.

$$\text{Total Unadjusted Use Case Points} = 20 + 7 = 27.$$

Step 4: Determine Tfactor (Figure 6.18). Note that the project complexity values are really assumptions we have made about how the system will work and the requirements.

$$\text{Total Tfactor} = 33$$

Step 5: Calculate TCF $= 0.6 + 0.01 * 33 = 0.93$.

Step 6: Determine Efactor (Figure 6.19).

Step 7: Calculate the EF (environmental factor) $= 1.4 - (0.03 * 18) = 1.4 - 0.54 = 0.86$.

Step 8: Calculate the AUCPs (adjusted use case points) $= \text{UUCPs} * \text{TCF} * \text{EF} = 27 * 0.93 * 0.86 - 22$.

Step 9: Determine effort; use 20 hours per UCP.

$$\text{Effort} = 20 * 22 = 440 \text{ hours}$$

Assuming 35 real work hours per week (overheads, meetings, vacations, etc.), Effort $= 12.6$ staff weeks.

Unadjusted Use Case Weight		
Actor	Complexity	Score
System Config	Simple	5
Alarm Callout	Medium	10
Arm/Disarm System	Simple	5
Total		20

Figure 6.17. UUCW example.

Factor	Description	Weight	Project Complexity	Weighted Value
T1	Distributed System	2	4	8
T2	Response or Performance Objectives	2	2	4
T3	End-User Efficiency	1	2	2
T4	Complex Internal Processing	1	2	2
T5	Reusable Code	1	1	1
T6	Easy to Install	0.5	5	2.5
T7	Easy to Use	0.5	5	2.5
T8	Portable	2	2	4
T9	Easy to Change	1	3	3
T10	Concurrent	1	1	1
T11	Security Objectives	1	3	3
T12	Provides Access for 3rd Parties	1	0	0
T13	Special User Training Facilities Required	1	0	0
Total Tfactor				33

Figure 6.18. *Tfactor example.*

Our estimate for effort required to build the Home Security System, assuming all the other controllers exist, is ~13 staff weeks.

	Environmental Factors			
Factor	Description	Weight	Value	Weighted Value
F1	Familiarity with Project	1.5	5	7.5
F2	Application Experience	0.5	3	1.5
F3	OO Experience	1	4	4
F4	Lead Analyst Capability	0.5	4	2
F5	Motivation	1	5	5
F6	Stable Requirements	2	1	2
F7	Part-Time Workers	−1	1	−1
F8	Difficult Programming Language	−1	3	−3
Total				18

Figure 6.19. *Efactor example.*

Use Case Point Methodology Effectiveness   There are a few issues with UCPs, the most signficant of which are:

- *Variance in Use Case Level of Detail*: The use cases produced for a 5 KLOC system versus a 500 KLOC system will differ dramatically in level of detail.
- *Large Variance in Use Case Complexity*: Use cases can be exceedingly simple or exceedingly complex.

One company, Brilasoft Limited, initially found that its effort per UCP varied from 15 to 30 hours [14]. After use case standardization, guidelines, and training, effort reached an average of 12 hours per UCP with an acceptable variance.

In another study [18], the method was evaluated on a large (100+ staff year) project that used incremental development. In this study, researchers found they needed to standardize the size and adjust the complexity definition of use cases as well.

Our view, based on these commercial projects (in multiple companies and on both small and large projects) and our own student projects, is as follows:

- The UCP method is simple, quick, and transparent to use.
- A tuned, calibrated UCP method works well. The calibration appears to be relatively easy and quick.
- The size and level of detail of use cases must be standardized within an organization.
- The complexity classification rules for use cases may need to be adjusted based on the complexity of the transactions.
- For large projects, which are expected to have diseconomies of scale (e.g, lower productivity because the project is so large), an additional overhead factor may be needed. Alternatively, this factor can be incorporated into the productivity variable (e.g., increase the number of hours per UCP by 50% or 100%). This tuning is simple.

We highly recommend use case points as an estimation methodology. It has been shown to give results as good as or better than expert estimation. In addition, there are commercially available tools, such as Duvessa, which support these estimation methods and give additional flexibility in using local sizing parameters.

6.2.5 Custom Models

You probably know your environment and cost drivers better than anyone else. Your cost drivers may be relatively simple. Perhaps you try some of the standard estimation methods and feel that if you just tweaked them a bit here or there, they would better match your environment. So . . . tweak them!

Here is a simple, four-step process for custom models [19]:

Step 1: Decompose costs.
Step 2: Formulate a cost theory.
Step 3: Collect data.
Step 4: Correlate the data.

Let us illustrate this by way of an example. Suppose that you have a large custom system for which you need to estimate ∼400 features each year, ∼100 of which you will actually build. Your current methodology for estimating each feature is to pull two of your experts in to estimate each one. Unfortunately, this means that these two experts seem to spend almost all of their time doing cost estimation and little else. This is a problem, so you decide that you will build your own estimation model.

The first step is to decompose the costs. When you estimate, you look at the impact on each of your five modules—A, B, C, D, and E. For each feature that is implemented, you see that it may impact the database, logical interface, screen, reports, and/or algorithms of each module.

The second step is to formulate a cost theory. Your theory is that the cost is primarily based on two variables: the number of database schema changes and the number of interface changes. You estimate the typical impact (in weeks) on each module for a database change and an interface change, as shown in Table 6.4.

For example, Table 6.4 says that if there is a database change, then there is no expected effort in Module A, but the overall impact on the system is 14 weeks.

You now need a cost function. From Table 6.4, you derive your first theory:

$$\text{Effort (in weeks) of a Feature} = 14 * \text{Number of DB Changes}$$
$$+ 8 * \text{Number of Interface Changes}$$

You also believe that the complexity of each feature may be important. So you consider a complexity adjustment factor (CAF) from 0.5 to 1.5 for each feature. Your second theory is

$$\text{Effort (in weeks) of a Feature} = \text{CAF} * (14 * \text{Number of DB Changes}$$
$$+ 8 * \text{Number of Interface Changes})$$

The third step is to gather data. You would gather historical data from past feature estimates made by the experts and the actual costs if possible.

The fourth and final step would be to do a statistical correlation to see how well your models performed, adjust as required, and then select the better one, assuming the predictions were satisfactory.

In this example, if one of your models is satisfactory, you have reduced the cost of your estimation process dramatically. Instead of having two experts spending most of their time estimating, you have created a straightforward process that takes a few hours per feature.

TABLE 6.4   Custom Model Example

Module	Impact (in Weeks) of a Database Change	Impact (in Weeks) of an Interface Change
A	0	4
B	3	1
C	5	1
D	2	0
E	4	2
Total	14	8

6.2.6 Algorithmic Models

The algorithmic models are empirically derived, using regression analysis. The initial ones are simple and can be used manually. More complex ones are embodied in tools.

These parametric models are all empirically based on certain data sets from a certain environment. Because the environmental factors are significant cost drivers, it is best to use multiple methods and not rely on tremendous accuracy. Ferens and Christensen [20] report that "in general, model validation showed that the accuracy of the models was no better than within 25 percent of actual development cost or schedule, about one half of the time, even after calibration."

In most projects, we are primarily interested in first estimating effort and then estimating schedule. Most algorithmic models take the intermediate step of estimating size, usually KLOC or FP first, and then using the size to drive the effort (e.g., staff days/months/years), which in turn, is the fundamental driver for cost, schedule, and staffing.

6.2.6.1 Manual Models   The typical manual, algorithmic model is of the form

$Effort = A + B*(Size)^C$, where A, B, and C are empirically determined constants, and Size is the length in either LOC or FPs.

There are many different KLOC equations for effort, calibrated to different project data sets. For example [21]:

$$\text{Walston–Felix:} \quad Effort = 5.2*(KLOC)^{0.91}$$

$$\text{Bailey–Basili:} \quad Effort = 5.5 + 0.73*(KLOC)^{1.16}$$

$$\text{Boehm Simple:} \quad Effort = 3.2*(KLOC)^{1.05}$$

$$\text{Doty:} \quad Effort = 5.288*(KLOC)^{1.047}$$

As Figure 6.20 shows, they all give different predictions. This is a surprising result to most first-time students of estimation. We all expect more consistency.

The reason for the variance is that they are based on different data sets, and they are extremely simple models, using only LOC to predict effort.

The most important factor is C—the scaling factor—which accounts for the economies (or diseconomies) of size. Three out of the four equations show decreases in productivity as the projects increase in size. One, the Walston–Felix equation, shows increases in productivity as the projects increase in size. B is the productivity factor—the smaller B, the higher the productivity on the project.

Similarly, three equations that predict effort from function points are:

$$\text{Albrect–Gaffney:} \quad Effort = 13.39 + 0.0545*FP$$

$$\text{Kemerer:} \quad Effort = 60.62 + 7.728*(10^{-8})*FP^3$$

$$\text{Matson–Barret–Meltichamp:} \quad Effort = 585.7 + 15.12*FP$$

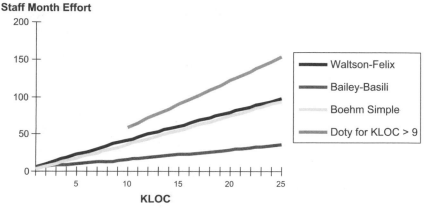

Figure 6.20. *Comparison of KLOC models.*

These again all give different results, although two of them predict the productivity to be constant, independent of size.

These models were all derived from specific environments, some with small data sets. Use with extreme caution! If you have a stable environment, and past data, you may be able to determine these constants $(A, B,$ and $C)$ for yourself and use them as your own model. Note, however, that when you improve productivity, B will decrease. When you improve how you manage large projects, C will decrease.

COCOMO is probably the most famous, popular, and influential algorithmic model. It originally was developed in the late 1970s by Barry Boehm and has continued to grow and evolve through COCOMO II in 1996 and COCOMO 2000. It continues to become more complex, more flexible, and able to handle more software development methodologies. In COCOMO I, there are three classes of projects, with different parameters for each. Organic projects are typically small projects, with a known environment and a small experienced team. Semidetached projects are a mixture with medium size projects of medium complexity. Embedded systems work in tight, inflexible environments. COCOMO I uses the same basic effort equation, $B*\text{LOC}^C$, where B and C vary by the class of the project. (See Figure 6.21.)

You can use the COCOMO I equations manually. The later equations in COCOMO II become more complex and are only practical in tools.

Class of Project	Effort	Duration
Organic	$E = 2.4 * \text{KLOC}^{1.05}$	$D = 2.5 * E^{0.38}$
Semidetached	$E = 3.0 * \text{KLOC}^{1.12}$	$D = 2.5 * E^{0.35}$
Embedded	$E = 3.6 * \text{KLOC}^{1.2}$	$D = 2.5 * E^{0.32}$

Figure 6.21. *COCOMO I equations.*

6.2.6.2 *Estimating Project Duration* COCOMO I also has duration equations based on effort, of the form Duration $= 2.5 * \text{Effort}^C$, where C varies by type of project as shown in Figure 6.21, and Duration is in staff months. Other empirical studies are consistent with the COCOMO I rules and have the same form, that is,

$$\text{Duration} = B * \text{Effort}^C$$

where C tends to be between 0.3 and 0.4 [22], with military projects occasionally at 0.42. Reifer researched web development projects and found the same type of relationship between effort and duration, with $C = 0.5$ for smaller projects and $C = 0.33$ for larger ones. B ranged from 1.5 for business-to-business applications to 2.2 for financial applications, (Reifer's algorithms are for web development only.)

EXERCISE: You need to build an embedded controller for a state-of-the-art weapons system. You have estimated 5 staff years of effort. What is a reasonable estimate for the project duration? How many people should you assign to the project?

Answer: You would prefer to use estimation tools to look at different schedule scenarios, but assuming you cannot, you can use the COCOMO I equations:

$$\text{Duration} = 2.5 * 60^{0.32} = 9.27 \text{ months}$$

This is the nominal solution. So you might assign $60/9.27 \approx 6.5$ people to the project with a schedule of 9.25 months. Or you might decide to assign fewer people and extend the schedule. Or, for the most effective solution, you may choose to have just a few people on it initially, ramp up to 12 or so, and then ramp back down, such that the total staff effort is 5 staff years.

You also may want to know how much you can shorten the schedule and how that impacts the effort. The engineering rule is that the limit to schedule compression (how much you can compress the normal software development schedule) is about 75%. That is, if the normal schedule would take about 8 months, it is highly unlikely that the project can be completed in less than 6 months. As you approach the 75% mark, the amount of extra effort to achieve the compressed schedule increases rapidly. At 75% schedule compression, the amount of extra effort is about a factor of 1.43 [9]. So, if the nominal effort for an 8 month project was 24 staff/months, then an accelerated project at 6 months would take 34 persons/ months or about 43% more effort.

6.2.6.3 *Tool-Based Models*[8] In the 1970s and 1980s, function points were developed, and the first estimation tools, SLIM and Price-S, were released. In

[8]T. Capers Jones published an overview [23] of software estimation tools in 2002, which is the source for much of the overview material in this section.

1981, the COCOMO I models and equations were developed. From 1985 to 2004, the estimation tool market expanded rapidly, such that today, there are over 100 commercial estimation tools available. These tools take a preliminary size estimate (typically LOC or FP) and some project attributes and create a schedule, a staffing plan, a total effort estimate, and cost estimates. Today, COCOMO, SPR, and Checkpoint are the primary tools, although our students are always finding new ones to try.

Many of these tools are highly sophisticated, and utilize various techniques such as Monte Carlo modeling for risk analysis. A brief description of the generic functionality of the tools follows [23]. After you read it, we urge you to search for "software estimation tools" online and try a few. Most are available either as a demo version or freeware. If you have not used them before, we expect that you will have some fun and be impressed.

In addition to a size estimate, these tools take many items as input to their models, including:

- Software taxonomy

  Nature of software (new, old, port, enhancement)

  Scope (system or module)

  Class (internal vs. external, civilian vs. military vs. e-business)

  Type (system, application, embedded, management information)
- Project goals—allowing trade-offs between schedule, total effort, and staffing
- Work patterns, staff salaries, and overhead rates

Most have the following features:

- Sizing logic for specifications, source code (if FPs are input), and test cases
- Phase-level, activity-level, and task-level estimation
- Support for object-oriented technology
- Conversion between LOC and FP
- Reusability support
- Support for variety of languages (C, Cobol, Visual Basic)
- Quality and reliability estimation

Many have the following features as well:

- Risk and value analysis
- Estimation templates from historical data
- Links to project management tools
- Cost and time-to-complete estimates mixing historical data with project data
- Inflation calculations for long-term projects
- Estimates keyed to the SEI model

Our view is that the real difficulty with software estimation is determining the effort, not the schedules and staffing. Many of the tools also have extremely nice capabilities, which allow you to trade off effort and schedule. *Whatever the method you use in determining size and effort, we highly recommend using the tools to work through the schedule, the staff, and the risks and tie it into the project plan.*

Now go try some of these tools and see what you think.

6.3 COMBINING ESTIMATES

We frequently have said to estimate using three or more different methods and combine them together. When selecting the methods to use, do not select the same methods with the same biases. Methods that would be considered complementary are [24].

- Top–down with bottom–up
- Expert opinion with analogy
- Expert opinion with proxy points
- Expert opinions by experts with different project experiences and responsibilities
- Proxy points and analogy

Methods that would be considered to have the same biases are [24]:

- Algorithmic models based on the same underlying algorithms (such as all of the COCOMO derivatives)
- Experts who have had similar responsibilities on similar projects

When combining estimates, do not ignore your engineering judgment. If you feel that, under the given circumstances, an estimation method is highly flawed, discard the estimate. You ultimately are responsible for the estimate rather than the algorithms or the methodology.

There are many ways to take your three (or more) estimates and arrive at your final estimate.

1. Just take the one you think is the best (very simple, but not recommended!).
2. Use the mean, with standard deviations to show the variance.
3. Use a weighted mean based on standard distribution, which would be $(1 * \text{Largest} + 1 * \text{Smallest} + 4 * \text{Mean})/6$.
4. If you have a range of confidence levels in the estimate, you can create your own weighted mean by:
   (a) assigning a weight between 0 and 1 to each estimate, where the weight represents your relative confidence in the estimate, and the sum of all of the weights equals 1.0;

    (b) multiplying each estimate by its weight; and

    (c) summing up all the weighted estimates for the combined estimate.

Here's a custom weighted mean example. You have the following estimates:

FP using gearing factors: 150 staff months
Expert opinion—activity decomposition: 100 staff months
Use case points: 125 staff months
Expert opinion—module decomposition: 250 staff months

You have been using these methodologies for the past year, and you have been getting very good results with use case points. This is the first time you've tried module decomposition. Hence, you decide to use the following confidence weights:

FPs: 0.2
Expert opinion—activity decomposition: 0.2
Use case points: 0.5
Expert opinion—module decomposition: 0.1

$$\text{Weighted Mean} = 0.2 * 150 + 0.2 * 100 + 0.5 * 125 + 0.1 * 250$$
$$= 30 + 20 + 62.5 + 25 = 137.5$$

6.4   ESTIMATING ISSUES

6.4.1   Targets Versus Estimates

In the introduction to this chapter, we stated that a primary reason for projects coming in over-budget was the confusion between the target for a project—that is, what the senior management or marketing wants the cost to be—and the actual estimates.

    When requested to provide an estimate, one of the first questions you should ask is: "Are you asking me for an answer or telling me what the answer needs to be?" Frequently, because of the realities of business, you are being told what the answer must be; that is, you are given the "effort budget" for the job. In this case, all of the same tools and methodologies still apply. But instead of using them to create an estimate, you use them interactively to create a rational plan that can match the budget. For example, think of all the ways you could reduce the number of adjusted use case points. You could reduce actors. You could reduce scenarios. You could decrease the technical factors. You could improve the environmental factors. You could even reuse large chunks of code and classes rather than reprogramming them. There are infinite potential solutions, some of which are feasible, most of which are not. But the point is to use the same methodologies to consider the changes to your plan to reduce the effort on the project so that you can come in on-budget.

Some people, when faced with an inadequate budget, try adjusting the parameters of the estimation model without changing the work involved. This will only create more overtime, unless you actually made mistakes in the initial estimate. Another favorite technique is to plan on overtime. Our view is that overtime is for contingency and risk management. Have a plan you believe you can meet without overtime. Use overtime to get out of trouble when the unforeseen occurs, as it always will. The third favorite technique is to cut features. We see this option as a last resort, unless you can justify to yourself and to your customer that the feature is either truly unneeded or optional. Instead, use your creativity and your problem solving skills to simplify the project or increase productivity. Features are what people pay money for!

Managers who recognize the inherent uncertainties in estimates, and the tendency for work to expand to fill the available time, may purposefully understaff and aggressively schedule a project in order to reap the highest efficiencies possible. This strategy is a reasonable strategy but needs to be understood and managed appropriately.

6.4.2 The Limitations of Estimation: Why?

It is easy to agree that the state of the practice is ragged. Although we have some excellent results in estimation, we also have a lot of disappointing ones. We are sure you were disappointed at the expected accuracy of estimations. In practical terms, it really comes down to the question of the extent of invention and problem solving required.

Consider the situation of building six new apartment buildings, one after the other, all of which have the same design, all of which are being built on the same type of vacant land. The estimate for the first one may have been $\pm 25\%$ of what actually happened. By the third, the estimate is probably $\pm 5\%$. But consider the impact of new technology. Instead of using brick and mortar, you change to precast concrete, because of the expected savings in cost. And instead of building on flat vacant lots, you need to build on a rocky hillside. And you decide to add a penthouse on top because you have a customer who really wants one. Now what happens to your estimate? That $\pm 25\%$ looks awfully good now.

The same is true of software projects. If you are building similar systems to those you have previously built, with similar teams and technologies, and can manage the requirements processes, you will become quite accurate with your estimates. If you are building fundamentally new systems, where invention is required, $\pm 25\%$ will be quite an achievement.

6.4.3 Estimate Uncertainties

We need to remember what an estimate really is and frame our estimates appropriately. Estimates have inherent probabilities. Remember the normal distribution—what we typically give are estimates that are our most accurate view, which is also known as the 50% view, which means that we have the same probability for being under as well as over-budget.[9]

In order to estimate more accurately, we need to:

- Understand, accept, and manage the inherent uncertainties in estimation
- Change our terminology in estimation to include the uncertainties

The size of the uncertainty in the estimate differs based on how close you are to the end of the project. Barry Boehm published the classic chart shown in Figure 6.22 in 1981 [25], which became known as the "cone of uncertainty." It represents the estimated accuracy of estimates at different phases in the software life cycle. It says that during the initial feasibility phase of a project, the accuracy of an estimate is a factor of ± 4. For example, if you estimate a project to be 200 staff months, it could take anywhere between 50 and 800 staff months (?!). As you progress through the life cycle of the project, the estimate accuracy increases, such that in detailed design, it is a factor of approximately ± 1.3 rather than the initial ± 4.

Most practitioners agree that the scale has changed due to improved estimation practices and processes. Also, there is a much greater tendency to underestimate (due to market/organizational pressures, optimism, and overconfidence) rather than to overestimate. Our experience leads us to believe that it is now typically

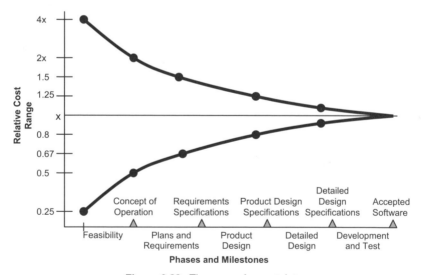

Figure 6.22. The cone of uncertainty.

[9]Unfortunately, Parkinson's Law, which states that work expands to meet the time available, holds extremely well for software projects. So really this 50% view is the one that says we'll be on-budget 50% of the time, and over-budget the other 50% of the time.

closer to $+100\%/-50\%$ at the feasibility stage, but still not much better than $+20\%/-10\%$ at the detailed design stage.

Uncertainties can be categorized as statistical variance, known risks, and unknown events. You will always have statistical variance. The only question is the size of it. The known risks need to be addressed explicitly in the risk management plan. (See Chapter 12 for a more detailed discussion of how to plan for and quantify risks.) The unknown events are obviously the toughest to handle. The typical strategy is to use experts to minimize the number of unknown events and, in the absence of any other information, have a 10% management contingency buffer, as recommended by the Project Management Institute (PMI).

We also need to improve the way we talk about estimates to include the probabilistic nature of the estimates. Instead of giving "the number," we need to give ranges and views based on probabilistic distributions. The "pX view" means that there is an X% probability of not exceeding the estimate; for example, the p10 view means that we believe we will exceed the estimate 90% of the time.

Consider the difference in information between the statements below.

- My estimate is 12 staff months.
- My estimate is between 10 and 14 staff months.
- My p50 estimate is 12 months.
- I estimate that 95% of the time it will be between 10 and 14 months.
- I estimate that 98% of the time it will be less than 14 months.

The first statement is the easiest for others to deal with. You take on all of the risk and uncertainties for making the date. With the other statements, you now are sharing the risks, allowing others to help manage the risks, and providing significantly more information.

The ranges can be specified by the experts as part of the estimation process. Unfortunately, *experiments have shown that experts tend to be consistently overconfident in their estimations of ranges* [24]. The reasons for the overconfidence are very human, such as the need to appear confident and professional, belief in one's own abilities, and lack of immediate feedback, but they still result in overly optimistic ranges of estimates. Experiments show that you will get more accurate ranges by using either predetermined organizational guidelines or probability distributions based on previous projects. We recommend the engineering rules in Figure 6.23 as a starting place until you have your own organizational baseline. For example, if your current p50 estimate is 50 staff months, and you are in the design phase, then using our engineering rules, you would say that the expected range is between 45 and 60 staff months.

Project Phase	Feasibility	Requirements	Design	Coding	Testing
% Uncertainty	+100/−50	+50/−25	+20/−10	+10/−5	+5

Figure 6.23. *Estimation uncertainty engineering rules.*

To use the distribution from previous projects to derive the X% effort, start with your best estimate (determined by other methods) [24]. For example, assume your estimate is 10 staff years and, on previous similar projects,

- 30% came in on-budget,
- 10% came in under-budget by 10%
- 40% came in over-budget by 50%
- 20% came in over-budget by >50%

Then your % estimates are:

- p10 estimate—9 staff years
- p40 estimate—10 staff years
- p80 estimate—15 staff years

Little [26] published data for 120 delivered systems from Landmark Graphics, all based on the agile methodology. His study revealed the following for these 120 systems:

(1) estimation accuracy follows a log-normal distribution,[10] *(2) our initial estimates are targets with only a small chance of being met, (3) the range between the target and an estimate with 90% confidence is about four times greater, and (4) this behavior and uncertainty range is nearly identical at all stages in the project lifecycle, in conflict with the "cone of uncertainty" presented by Boehm.*

These results are not that surprising, especially considering the agile methodology, and its embracement of change.

In summary, to deal with the uncertainties of estimates:

- Change your terminology from one number to a pX number.
- Use probability intervals to specify the range on your estimates.
- Use methods other than "gut feelings" for determining the range, since over-confidence is typical and becomes more pronounced as the staff becomes more and more experienced.
- If you are using agile methods, especially if you are following the principle of "responding to change over following a plan," expect to have a low probability of meeting your initial estimates (10%?), and expect a large estimate uncertainty throughout your projects.

6.5   ESTIMATING EARLY AND OFTEN

When should you estimate? And how much effort should you spend on it?

It depends on the project and the methodology. Effort estimation is usually overhead—you are not producing a deliverable product. So you need to ensure that the

---

[10]Very simplistically, the log-normal distribution means that it was underestimated far more frequently than overestimated.

benefit exceeds the cost. If it really does not matter how much you spend on development or how long it takes, do not bother. If you are dealing with frequently changing requirements and specifications, you need to understand how to give ballpark estimates quickly and efficiently, and expect to update them (quickly and efficiently) when the situation changes.

In some projects, estimates are crucial and important to do well. They can greatly impact the quality of the decision making. When we bid for jobs, if our estimate is greatly under, we may lose money and damage our company. If we overestimate, we may unnecessarily lose a job to a competitor. When we estimate well, it gives us a chance to win the jobs we should win and lose those we shouldn't win, as well as provides us with a foundation to manage the schedule and budget risks. Typically, our customers and management demand it.

For traditional developments, you should estimate the job at least three times:

- *Feasibility Phase*: Macro estimation
- *Requirements Phase*: Detailed estimation
- *Design Phase*: Refined estimation

The need for accuracy of an estimate is related to its purpose at that point in time. A cost estimation at the feasibility stage of a project need only be accurate enough to support a decision to prepare a more detailed definition of the project. Detailed product and project definitions are not available, so the estimate will be high level. The estimate at the requirements specification stage is a critical project decision point and must be reasonably accurate. You are potentially committing significant resources based on the business case, which is based on the cost estimate. The required accuracy depends on the business model. If it is for an in-house project or consulting services, they may be "pay as you go," in which case the estimate is really about establishing credibility. For external product sales or for a fixed-cost project, the required accuracy depends on when a final price will be set. Once the detailed design has been completed, and hopefully most of the unknowns have become known, a reasonably accurate estimate and plan can be created.

Because of the inherent uncertainties throughout all projects, you may need to reestimate as you learn more. Whenever you have major unplanned events, you will need to understand how they impact the schedule and the effort. Do not ignore them and just hope it will all work out. Typically, it does not. At least, roughly estimate the impacts to make sure your plan is still viable. By estimating early and often, you can take appropriate action to adjust the program and project plan when you find that the work is not aligned with either the budget or the schedule.

6.6 SUMMARY

Well, were you disappointed? There certainly is no silver bullet (although we personally believe use case points have great potential). We presented you with a bevy of methods and, hopefully, a tremendous amount of insight into their practical use, including the need to present estimations as probabilities and some of the human frailties of over-optimism. Remember also to set your expectations based on the amount of uncertainty in a project. If there is very little, then your estimations should be pretty good. If there are unknowns, and significant invention is required, the variation will be high.

The good news here is that if you do follow the methodologies, you will have better results than you had before. Even with projects that have many unknowns, these techniques and tools can help you to quantitatively understand where you are at any point, and you can use them to intelligently adjust the program, be it the schedule, the design, or just the expectations.

Remember that the cone of uncertainty dictates that the farther you are from the finish point, the greater the uncertainty, so try to keep your project or release on the smaller side. Then start managing with all of your effort to keep it on track, and revisit the estimates, so that you can adjust your plan before it is history.

PROBLEMS

6.1 You have a relatively simple project for which the specifications have been agreed and signed off on. There are 1200 function points. Now you are told that you will have 6 months to develop it. Is this reasonable or not? You are in a customer meeting and need to respond with something intelligent right now.

6.2 You need to build a web application that automatically orders materials for your manufacturing company. You have estimated 5 staff years of effort. What is a reasonable estimate for the project duration? How many people should you assign to the project?

6.3 You have the following estimates:

FP using gearing factors: 150 staff months

Custom model: 100 staff months

Use case points: 125 staff months

Combine them into one estimate. You believe the custom model is twice as good an estimate as the other two estimates.

6.4 You are building a new system with 4 simple screens, 2 reports which each reference over 10 different data tables, and call 5 new C programs to do certain calculations. Historically, you have a productivity rate of 10 NOPs per staff month, with a SD of ± 1 staff month. What is the estimated number of staff months for the project? What would be the 95th percentile estimate? Assume an overall reuse rate of 40%.

6.5 Your company has been upgrading its old systems. Your system is next in line and you are responsible for estimating the cost/schedule for the upgrade. It will be an interactive, object-oriented, web-based system. How would you go about estimating the effort and schedule? Assume you have all the data from the initial implementation. This will be a complete rewrite.

6.6 You've estimated the size of a project to be 500 FPs. Using the Jones engineering rules, what is the expected duration? It is a military project. You expect to be in design through development for 60% of the duration of the entire project. You expect this customer to add in 3% new FPs for each month during design through development. How many extra function points should you expect the customer to add in?

6.7 True or False: Purchasing a good estimation tool is the best way to improve your estimations.

6.8 What are two other estimation methodologies that would be complementary with function points?

6.9 Your team tells you that the most likely view is 6 staff months for a project. Using the 6 months as the p50 view and employing our engineering rules, what would you calculate the p95 view to be? You are in the requirements phase of the project.

6.10 You've estimated a project to require 20 staff months of effort (using use case points) using a team that was good, but you did not know the RUP or OOD at all. You have the option of sending them to training in both RUP and OOD, such that they will now be considered very experienced and familiar (e.g., from 0 to 5 on the appropriate factors). What would be the breakeven point for sending them to training: that is, time spent in training = time saved by being more efficient. Assume that your previous Efactor was 10, so your previous EF was $1.4 - 0.03 * 10 = 1.1$. Use Karner's factors for productivity.

6.11 Which method(s) produced results as good as or better than experts?

6.12 True or False: You should expect to be able to estimate within 10%.

6.13 True or False: If you are told the budget for the work, there is no need to ever estimate how much effort it will take, because it doesn't matter.

6.14 True or False: Experts, as a rule, underestimate more frequently than they overestimate.

6.15 True or False: An advantage of using estimation tools is that they frequently integrate well with project management tools.

6.16 You have a system with 25 use cases, 3 different user interfaces, and 5 different external system interfaces. The development team estimates it at 10 staff years $\pm 10\%$. Is this a reasonable estimate?

6.17 Your company starts to use use case points on two different projects. They find that the productivity is 8 use case points per month on one project and 18 on the other. What do you think is going on?

PROJECTS

6.1   Select one automated software estimation tool to use. You can find many on the Web that have demo versions or short time period licenses. Determine the types of algorithms it uses.

6.2   Estimate the theater tickets project (from Chapter 4) using three different estimation methodologies, including your automated tool (from 6.1), use case points, and another method of your own choosing.

6.3   Review the automated tool you selected in 6.1. What did you like, what did you not like, and would you recommend it for use on your own projects?

6.4   Combine your estimates into one estimate.

6.5   Create a presentation of your estimate that you might use to present to your management.

REFERENCES

[1]   K. Molokken and M. Jorgensen, "A review of surveys on software effort estimation," Simula Research Laboratory, 2003.

[2]   D. Reifer, "Software cost, quality, & productivity benchmarks," *The DOD Software Tech News*, July 2004.

[3]   David Consulting Group web site, www.davidconsultinggroup.com. Accessed Mar. 15, 2005.

[4]   M. Shepperd and C. Schofield, "Estimating software project effort using analogies," *IEEE Transactions on Software Engineering* **23**(12): 736–743 (1997).

[5]   D. Reifer, "Estimating web development COSTS: there are differences," *Crosstalk*, June 2002.

[6]   T. C. Jones, *Estimating Software Costs*, McGraw-Hill, New York, 1998.

[7]   *Measurement Manual COSMIC Full Function Points 2.2, The COSMIC Implementaion Guide for ISO/IEC 19761*, COSMIC, 2003.

[8]   K. Banker, R. Kauffman, C. Wright, and D. De Zweig, "Automating output size and reuse metrics in a repository-based computer aided software engineering (CASE) environment," *IEEE Transactions on Software Engineering* **20**(3): 169–186 (1994).

[9]   B. Boehm, et al. *Software Cost Estimation with COCOMOII*, Prentice Hall, Englewood Cliffs, NJ, 2000.

[10] D. Longstreet, www.ifpug.com/Articles/usecases.htm. Accessed Mar. 15, 2005.

[11] J. Smith, "The estimation of effort based on use cases," Rational Software, 1999.

[12] G. Karner, *Metrics for Objectory*. Diploma thesis, University of Linköping, Sweden. No. LiTH-IDA-Ex-9344:21. December 1993.

[13] B. Anda, "Comparing effort estimates based on use case points with expert estimate," Department of Informatics, University of Oslo, Norway. In *Proceedings of Empirical Assessment in Software Engineering (EASE 2002)*, Keele, UK, April 8–10, 2002.

[14] G. Banerjee, "Use case estimation framework," Annual IPML Conference, 2004.

[15] G. Schneider and J. Winters, *Applying Use Cases—A Practical Guide*, Addison-Wesley, Boston, 1998.

[16] S. Koirala, "How to prepare quotation using use case points," December 2004. Available from http://codeproject.com/gen/design/usecasepoints.asp. Accessed Feb. 22, 2005.

[17] K. Ribu, *Estimating Object-Oriented Software Projects with Use Cases*. Masters thesis, University of Oslo. November 2001.

[18] P. Mohagheghi, B. Anda, and R. Conradi, "Effort estimation on uses cases for incremental large-scale software development," 2005 ACM.

[19] T. DeMarco, *Controlling Software Projects: Management, Measurement, and Estimation*, Yourdon Press, New York, 1982.

[20] D. V. Ferens, and D. S. Christensen, "Does calibration improve the predictive accuracy of software cost models?" *CrossTalk*, April 2000.

[21] T. McGibbon, *Modern Cost Estimation Tools* and *Modern Empirical Cost and Schedule Estimation Tools*. Contract Number F30602-89-C-0082 (Data & Analysis Center for Software) August 20, 1997. Available from www.dacs.dtic.mil/techs/estimation/title.shtml.

[22] S. Oligny, P. Bourque, and A. Abran, "Exploring the relation between effort and duration in software engineering projects," www.lrgl.uqam.ca/publications/pdf/558.pdf. Accessed July 15, 2005.

[23] T. C. Jones, "Software cost estimation in 2002," *Crosstalk*, June, 2002.

[24] M. Jorgensen, "Practical guidelines for expert-judgement based software effort estimation," *IEEE Software*, **22**(3): 57–63 (May/June, 2005).

[25] B. Boehm, *Software Engineering Economics*, Prentice-Hall, Englewood Cliffs, New Jersey, 1991.

[26] T. Little, "Agility, uncertainty, and software project estimation," www.macs.ece.mcgill.ca/~radu/304428W03/AgilityUncertaintyAndEstimation.pdf. Accessed July 15, 2005.

7

In Praise of Defects:
Defects and Defect Metrics

If debugging is the process of removing bugs, then programming must be the process of putting them in.
—Unknown

No software system of any realistic size is ever completely debugged—that is, error free.
—Edward Yourdon and Larry Constantine [1]

Defects do follow a Rayleigh pattern, the same as effort, cost, and code constructed. This curve can be projected before the main build begins; it can be finely tuned. It is the key ingredient for the statistical control of software reliability.
—Lawrence H. Putnam and Ware Myers [2]

Huns learn less from success than they do from failure.
—Wess Roberts [3]

7.1 WHY STUDY AND MEASURE DEFECTS?

Let us start thinking about defects by trying to answer two defect-related questions:

1. Your system has no reported field defects. It was released six months ago. Is it time to break out the champagne?
2. You are building a commercial application. Your CEO, who is very dedicated to quality, directs you to find and fix 99% of the bugs before you ship. What is your response?

Think about these two scenarios as we study defects in this chapter. We will then return to them in Section 7.9 and provide reasonable answers based on what we have learned.

This chapter is about defects—their patterns, their rhythms, their predictability, and the stories they can tell, to any and all who will listen.

Most people view software defects as undesirable and just want to get rid of all of them as soon as possible. The quantitative software engineer sees them a little differently (although still wanting to be rid of them quickly). Defects are real, observable manifestations and indications of the software development progress, process, and quality. From schedule, quality, and process engineering viewpoints, they are invaluable. From a schedule viewpoint, they give a clear indication of progress (or lack thereof). From a quality viewpoint, they give an early indication of the expected defect density of the product. From a process engineering viewpoint, they give clear indications of the effectiveness of the software development processes and indicate targets for improvement. You can see them, count them, predict them, and trend them. Defects are actually one of the best and most useful pieces of data available in software development.[1]

Defects have their own behavioral patterns and dynamics that need to be understood to manage and control software development projects and processes. To those who pay attention to them, defects give a wealth of understanding and insight into both the software product and the software development processes.

7.2 FAULTS VERSUS FAILURES

Software engineers use the terms defects, faults, and bugs interchangeably and occasionally interject the term failures when speaking about undesirable system behavior. Faults are defects that are in the system at some point in time. Failures are faults that occur in operation. Defects metrics measure faults. Reliability metrics measure failures. Bugs are synonymous with defects and faults.

If code contains faults but the faults are never executed in operation, then the system never fails. The mean-time-between-failures (MTBF) for the system will approach infinity and software availability will be 100%.

If there is only one fault in an entire system, and it is executed in the boot sequence of the system, then the system will fail every time, and the MTBF approaches 0 and the software availability will be 0%.

Faults are defects in the system that may or may never be seen in operation.

Faults can range in severity from crucial—they must be fixed immediately— to inconsequential—they may never be worth fixing. As part of any project, you need a defect severity scheme that is relevant for that project. For defect metrics and

---

[1]Think of defects as the pain of software development. Pain is a huge feedback mechanism. If we did not have it, we would damage ourselves on a daily basis. Pain and defects, by themselves, are undesirable—something you want to eliminate. When understood by trained professionals, they can lead to discovery and treatment of underlying problems, which eventually lead to better health or systems in the long term.

management, focus on the defects that will actually impact your project and product performance.

The standard measure of defects today is defect density: the number of defects per KLOC or per function point.

7.3 DEFECT DYNAMICS AND BEHAVIORS

7.3.1 Defect Arrival Rates

Defects are not detected at random intervals. Defects have certain dynamics, behaviors, and patterns. Starting with the beginning of the software life cycle, they tend to follow a Rayleigh curve, as shown in the Figure 7.1 [4]. You can predict these curves, along with the upper and lower control limits, based on the project size, process maturity, and past history.

7.3.2 Defects Versus Effort

There tends to be a linear relationship between defects and effort [4], assuming that the other factors (such as process, team skill level, and technology) stay constant (Figure 7.2). In other words, people tend to make errors, which lead to defects, at a relatively constant rate. All you can do is adjust the slope of the line, through improvements in processes, training, technology, and skill levels or through changes in schedule and staffing levels.

7.3.3 Defects Versus Staffing

Defects detected over time tend [4] to be similar to staff effort, with an additional time lag for error detection (Figure 7.3).

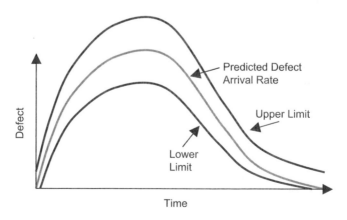

Figure 7.1. *Defect arrival rates.*

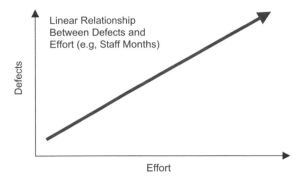

Figure 7.2. *Defects versus effort.*

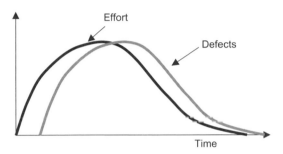

Figure 7.3. *Defects versus staffing.*

7.3.4 Defect Arrival Rates Versus Code Production Rate

Detected defects are related to the code production rate [4], which in turn is related to the staff effort curves. All of them tend to follow Rayleigh curves. Note that if you start tracking the defect data once formal testing begins, the defect discovery curve will look exponential (Figure 7.4).

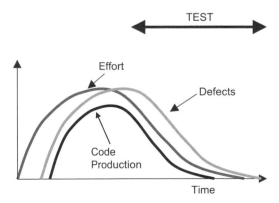

Figure 7.4. *Defects versus code production rate.*

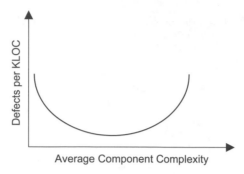

Figure 7.5. *The bathtub chart.*

7.3.5 Defect Density Versus Module Complexity

Figure 7.5 shows the relationship between the complexity of a software module and defect density, which we explored in detail in Chapter 5 [5]. It is occasionally called the "bathtub chart." It is important to remember that defect density for small software modules is high, falls exponentially as the size increases, bottoms out for a while, and then rises again. Intuitively, this seems reasonable. For any module, there is an initial set of "startup defects," which, if you have a very small module, will create a high defect density. On the other end, as the software becomes increasingly complex, the complexity engenders a higher rate of defects. The implications are clear—you want to design and build your systems such that your modules are at the bottom of the "bathtub," where the defect density is the lowest.

7.3.6 Defect Density Versus System Size

The "cloud" shown in Figure 7.6 is an approximation of Putnam–Myers QSM data for defects versus effective source lines of code from 1997 [4]. Although the number of defects varies widely based on the size of project, the trend is linear.

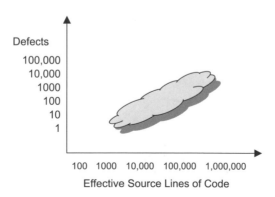

Figure 7.6. *Defects found from Integration to Delivery—QSM Data Base.*

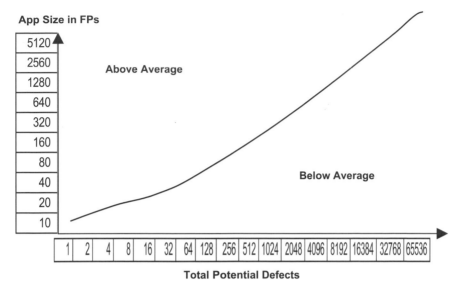

Figure 7.7. *Defects versus function points.*

The chart in Figure 7.7 is from Jones in 1991 [6]. The details are different, but the trend and pattern are the same as the Putnam–Myers data.

7.4 DEFECT PROJECTION TECHNIQUES AND MODELS

The objective of defect prediction and estimation techniques and models is to project the total number of defects and their distribution over time. The techniques vary considerably. There are both dynamic and static defect models. The dynamic models are based on the statistical distribution of faults found. The static models use attributes of the project and the process to predict the number of faults.

Static models can be used extremely early in the development process, even before the tracking of defects begins. Dynamic models require defect data and are used once the tracking of defects starts.

7.4.1 Dynamic Defect Models

Dynamic models are based on predicting—via calculations or tools—the distributions of faults, given some fault data. The primary concept is that the defects do follow distribution patterns as discussed above, and given some data points, you can generate the arrival distribution equations.

There are many different defect distribution equations, but the primary ones are Rayleigh, exponential, and S-curves. Rayleigh distributions model the entire development life cycle. Exponential and S-curves are applicable for the testing/deployment processes.

There are two distribution functions: the probability distribution function (PDF) for defect arrivals, which is called $f(t)$, and the cumulative distribution function (CDF) for total number of defects to arrive by time t, which is called $F(t)$. Note that $f(t)$ is the derivative of $F(t)$.

The Rayleigh and exponential curves are both in the family of the Weibull curves and have the forms

$$f(t) = m(t/c)^m * e^{(-t/c)^m}/t$$
$$F(t) = 1 - e^{(-t/c)^m}$$

When $m = 1$, these are equations for an exponential distribution. When $m = 2$, these are equations for a Rayleigh distribution.

7.4.1.1 Rayleigh Models

The equations for the basic Rayleigh curves, where t is time, c is a constant, and K is the total number of defects (e.g., area under the curve), are

$$f(t) = K * 2(t/c^2)e^{-(t/c)^2} \quad \text{and} \quad F(t) = K(1 - e^{-(t/c)^2})$$

Interestingly, $c = \sqrt{2}\, t_m$, where t_m is the time t at which $f(t)$ is maximum. Therefore,

$$F(t) = K\left[1 - e^{-(1/2t_m^2)t^2}\right]$$
$$f(t) = K\left[(1/t_m)^2 t e^{-(1/2t_m^2)t^2}\right]$$

The ratio of defects that should appear by time t_m is defined as $F(t_m)/K$, which is $[1 - \exp(-0.5)]$ or $\sim.4$. Therefore, $\sim 40\%$ of the defects should appear by time t_m.

There are multiple ways to use these equations to predict arrival rates and total number of defects. There are many commercially available tools that will do these calculations in a statistically valid manner. A few simple methods which you can calculate yourself and that can get you started are demonstrated next.

Method 1: Predicting the Distributions—An Extremely Easy Method   Given that you have defect arrival data, and the curve has achieved its maximum at time t_m (e.g., the inflection point), you can calculate $f(t)$, assuming the Rayleigh distribution. The simplest method is to use the pattern that $\sim 40\%$ of the total defects have appeared by t_m. This is a crude calculation but it is a place to start.

For example, assume you have the following data for arrival rates for defects:

Week	1	2	3	4	5	6	7	8	9
Defects found	20	41	48	52	62	59	52	44	33

t_m is week 5. Since ~40% of the defects appear by t_m, and the sum from week 1 through week 5 of defects is 223, then the simple calculation for the total number of defects is $223 * (100/40) = {\sim}557$.

You can determine $f(t)$ once you have K and t_m.

Continuing the example and substituting in $K = 557$ and $t_m = 5$,

$$f(t) = 557(t/25) e^{-t^2/50} = 22.3te^{-t^2/50}$$

$$F(t) = 557(1 - e^{-t^2/50})$$

Method 2: Predicting the Distributions—A Little More Complex Method You can solve for $f(t)$ by using t_m and one or more data points to solve for K and $f(t)$. The simplest way is to take just one data point; the easiest point to use is $f(1) = 20$. Substituting in $t_m = 5$, we have

$$20 = K(1/25) e^{-1/50}$$

$$K = 20 * 25 * e^{1/50}$$

$$K = 510$$

So

$$f(t) = 510(t/25) e^{-t^2/50} = 20.4 \, te^{-t^2/50}$$

$$F(t) = 510(1 - e^{-t^2/50})$$

We know that at least three points are needed to estimate these parameters using nonlinear regression analysis, and that further statistical tests (such as standard error of estimate and proportion of variance) are necessary for these parameters to be considered statistically valid. In the case where high precision is important, use a statistical package or one of the reliability tools to calculate the curve of best fit.

As an interim and easier step, we can calculate K for all values of $f(t)$, assuming $t_m = 5$ and then calculate the mean and standard deviation. That is, $K = [25f(t)e^{-t^2/50}]/t$. These calculations are easily performed with a spreadsheet. The mean for K is 491 with a standard deviation of 22.3.

Week	1	2	3	4	5	6	7	8	9
Defects found	20	33	48	60	62	59	52	44	33
K	510.1	446.9	478.9	516.4	511.1	505.0	494.8	494.5	463.2
Mean	491.2								
SD	22.37972								

Note that these calculations are sensitive to t_m and although they are not completely valid in a statistical sense, they give the statistically challenged practitioner a

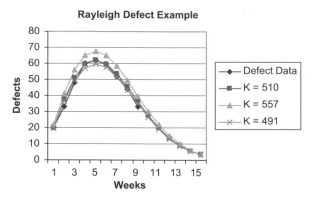

Figure 7.8. Rayleigh defect example: defect projection for different K values.

relatively easy method for calculating the defect detection distribution functions, with some initial control limits. Considering the precision of the typical data, they are reasonable. Figure 7.8 is a graph that shows $f(t)$ for $K = 510, 491, 557$. All three curves are close to the actual data and very similar to each other. From an "eyeball" perspective, $K = 491$ looks the best, as we would expect.

Method 3: Predicting the Arrival Rates Given Total Number of Defects and Schedule   Once you predict the total number of defects expected over the life of a project, you can use the Rayleigh curves to predict the number of defects expected during any time period by using the equations below. You can also compare projected defects with actual defects found to determine project performance.

T_d is the total duration of the project, at which time 95% of all defects have been found.[2] K is the total number of faults expected for the lifetime of the delivery.

Then the number of defects for each time period t is

$$f(t) = (6K/(T_d^2))te^{-3(t/T_d)^2}[2]$$

For example, you know that past, similar projects have had a defect density of 10.53 defects per KLOC and you have predicted that this project will be 100 KLOC. You also have a reasonable expectation, based on process improvements, that you expect to have 5% fewer defects. Therefore, you project that the total number of defects for this project will be $10.53 * 100 * 0.95 = 1000$.

Given a total duration of the project of 26 weeks, and a total expected number of faults of 1000, then the expected distribution of faults would be as depicted in Figure 7.9.

Based on the distributions in your data from prior projects, you can add in control limits. You may want to use 2 SD, which will give you a 95% confidence range of performance.

---

[2]The 95% number here is used as a reasonable target for delivery. The equations are derived from $F(T_d)/K = 0.95$ Another percentage would result in slightly different constants in the equations.

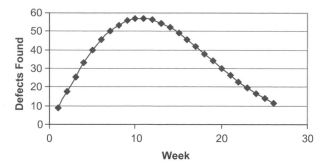

Figure 7.9. *Defects projection for 26 week project.*

If you do not have data from prior projects, you can still project overall defect densities in a number of ways, as discussed later in this chapter, and use the same technique to project arrival rates.

The Rayleigh model is used in a number of tools, which you can find on the Internet. Some of the more notable ones are:

- SPSS (SPSS Corporation)
- SAS (SAS Corporation)
- SLIM (Quantitative Software Management Corporation)
- STEER (IBM Corporation).

7.4.1.2 Exponential and S-Curves Arrival Distribution Models   Once testing begins, exponential and S-curve functions are the primary modeling functions for defect arrivals. Figure 7.10 contains both $F(T)$—the cumulative distribution function—and $f(t)$— the arrival function—for both curves.

S-curves resemble an S, with a slow start, then a much quicker discovery rate, then a slow tail-off at the end. They are based on the concept that initial defects may be more difficult to find because of either the length of time for error isolation or crucial defects that need to be fixed before others can be found. There are multiple S-curve models; all are based on the nonhomogeneous Poisson process for the

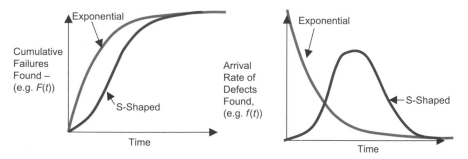

Figure 7.10. *Exponential and S-curves.*

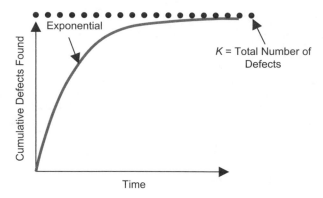

Figure 7.11. *Exponential distribution and K, the total number of defects.*

arrival distribution. One equation [7] for S-curves is

$$F(t) = K\left[1 - (1 + \lambda t)^{-\lambda t}\right]$$

Now let us look at the exponential distribution (Figure 7.11):

$$F(t) = K\left(1 - e^{-\lambda t}\right)$$

$$f(t) = K\left(\lambda t e^{-\lambda t}\right)$$

Given a set of data points, you want to know K. The techniques are similar to those for Rayleigh curves. You can (1) use reliability/statistical analysis tools, (2) solve for it using a few points, or (3) eyeball in your own K (... but don't tell anyone we said that).

7.4.1.3 Empirical Data and Recommendations for Dynamic Models
You may be extremely skeptical of these models and their ability to predict the number of total defects. So let us look at some of the empirical results of using these models:

- Putnam and Myers [8] found that total defects projected using Rayleigh curves were within 5–10%.
- Using their STEER software tool, IBM Federal Systems in Gaithersburg, Maryland, estimated latent defects for eight projects and compared the estimate with actual data collected for the first year in the field. The results were "very close." [9]
- Thangarajan and Biswas [10] from Tata Elxsi Ltd reported on using a Rayleigh model successfully on over 20 projects.

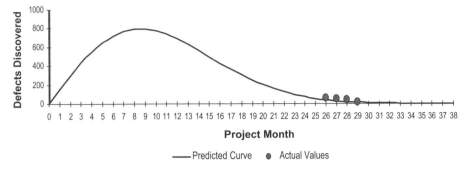

Figure 7.12. *Northrop Grumman defect discovery Rayleigh curve: discovered defects.*

- Figure 7.12 is a chart from Northrop Grumman [11] in 2001, which shows their successful use of the Rayleigh model to predict defects in the test cycle based on defects discovered earlier in the life cycle.
- Some data suggests that $m = 1.8$ for Weibull curves (see Section 7.4.1) may be best, although the calculations become more difficult.

Recommendations Over the past 15 years, and with the move to higher SEI levels, much more defect data has been recorded than ever before. Even so, organizations will vary from the standard patterns. Defect arrival rates tend to follow the Rayleigh curves, and the equations can be finely tuned to match an individual environment.

Our first and primary recommendation is to start tracking and using your defect data if you are not doing it. Our second recommendation is to try the simplest models first, especially the Rayleigh curves, and evolve if needed.

7.4.2 Static Defect Models

Static defect models are based on the software development process and past history rather than the defect data for the current project. They can be used throughout a project's life cycle, including before it begins. They are extremely useful for evaluating and predicting the impact of process changes to the overall quality of a project.

7.4.2.1 *Defect Insertion and Removal Model* The basic model, which has been credited to Barry Boehm and Capers Jones, is that defects are inserted into a product and then removed. You can improve a product by inserting fewer defects and/or by removing more of them. It is a good, high-level model to use to guide our thinking and reasoning about defect processes (Figure 7.13).

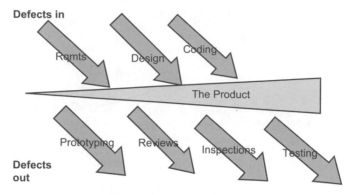

Figure 7.13. *Defect insertion/removal model.*

7.4.2.2 Defect Removal Efficiency: A Key Metric Defect removal efficiency, DRE, is a key metric that is used for measuring and benchmarking the effectiveness of the process, as well as measuring the quality of a project.

For an overall project, $DRE = E/(E + D)$, where E is the number of defects found before delivery to the end user, and D is the number of defects found after delivery. The goal is to have DRE approach 1, which would mean that no defects were found postdelivery.

For example, you found 10 defects after you delivered your product. There were 990 defects found and removed before delivery. Your $DRE = 990/1000 = 99\%$.

For each software engineering activity i, $DRE_i = E_i/(E_i + E_{i+1})$, where E_i is the number of defects found in activity i, and E_{i+1} is the number of errors found after activity i that are traceable to defects that were present during activity i. The goal is to have DRE_i approach 1 as well, so that errors are found and removed before they reach the next activity.

Projects that use the same team and the same development processes can reasonably expect that the DRE values from one project to the next are similar. For example, if on the previous project, you removed 80% of the possible requirements defects using inspections, then you can expect to remove ~80% on the next project. Or if you know that your historical data shows that you typically remove 90% before shipment, and, for this project, you have used the same process, met the same kind of release criteria, and found 400 defects so far, then there probably are ~50 defects still in the product.

The defect removal matrix is a useful matrix that identifies both the phase in which a defect was inserted and when it was removed. It is useful as an analysis tool for the defect removal process; it allows you to calculate the efficiencies of the defect removal for each step in a process.

For example, you are working on a project on which you are tracking your defects and the phases in which the defects were found and removed. You have four defect removal steps: (1) requirements review, (2) design review, (3) testing, and

(4) customer detected. You have three phases of defect insertion that you track: (1) requirements, (2) design, and (3) coding. You can represent your defect data in a DRE matrix as shown below:

	Defect Injection Phase			
Defect Removal Step	Requirements	Design	Coding	Total
Requirements Review	13			13
Design Review	2	12		14
Testing	3	5	32	40
Customer Detected	1	3	4	8
Total	19	20	36	75

This matrix indicates that 19 requirements defects have been found, 13 of which were found in the requirements review, 3 in testing, and 1 by the customer.

DRE for System = Total Detected Before Release/Total Detected = 67/75

= 89%

which, especially for a significant system, is not bad. The DRE of a phase measures the percentage of possible faults that were removed in a phase. For example, in design, there were 26 possible faults that could have been detected (6 requirements and 20 design faults); 14 of them were discovered in the design review phase, resulting in a DRE of 14/26.

The DRE for each phase[3] is shown below:

Phase	DRE by Phase
Requirements	0.68
Design	0.54
Testing	0.83
Customer Detected	1.00

In terms of analysis, this chart tells us our design defect removal process is the least effective, and the testing is the most effective at removing defects. If this were one of our projects, we would launch two quality improvement initiatives:

1. Based on the total number of requirements defects, we would look for process improvements to avoid defects being inserted in the first place: for example,

---

[3]This calculation assumes that there are no "latent bugs"—bugs that have not been found by the customer. This assumption is highly unlikely, as discussed in later sections. Alternatives would be to use an estimated total number of defects, or to explain that you expect that there are additional latent defects. In either case, the analysis of the data remains valid.

using JAD sessions or prototyping to reduce the number of requirements defects.

2. Based on the DRE of the phases, we would focus on improving the design review process. Typical engineering rules for design reviews are 60–70% removal versus the 54% we have here.

7.4.2.3   *Static Defect Model Tools*

There are tools that support the static defect model and allow you to tune it for your environment. One tool is COQUALMO [12], an extension to COCOMO II.

COQUALMO is a defect prediction model for the requirements, design, and coding phases based on the defect insertion/defect removal model. It is actually two separate models, one for defect introduction and one for defect removal. For defect introduction, COQUALMO use the COCOMO II project descriptors (size, personnel capability and experience, platform characteristics, project practices, and product characteristics such as complexity and required reliability). For defect removal, it uses ratings of a project's level of use of tools, reviews, and execution testing to determine what percentage of the introduced defects will be removed. The result is a prediction of defect density, either in KLOC or FPs. In short, COQUALMO is a mathematical model that takes as input your view of your defect injection drivers and defect removal drivers and gives you a projection of the defect density of your system at different points in the development life cycle (Figure 7.14). It can be used to estimate the impact of "driver changes" on defect density, so that you can do "what if" and "improvement investment" analysis.

COQUALMO is currently populated with data from the COCOMO clients and "expert opinion."

We strongly recommend you use a tool such as COQUALMO and tune it to your environment. It will allow you to quantitatively understand and then engineer your defect injection, prevention, and removal processes to optimize your quality and effort.

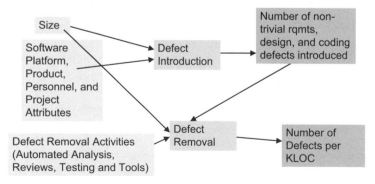

Figure 7.14. *COQUALMO.*

7.5 ADDITIONAL DEFECT BENCHMARK DATA

Defect benchmark data is surprisingly sparse. Many companies consider it proprietary. It is also easy to misuse the data, either by punishing projects that do not meet certain benchmarks or by calculating misleading results caused by differences in counting techniques, such as in size, usage, and severity. Don Reifer [13] has taken a lead in publishing software productivity, cost, and quality data, in hopes of encouraging others to do so. We fully support his position and encourage you to publish your defect data as well.

7.5.1 Defect Data by Application Domain

Reifer's delivered defect data (for 600 U.S. projects from 1997 through 2004) by domain is shown in Figure 7.15.

Reifer's additional comments include:

- Defect rates in military systems are much smaller due to the safety requirements.
- Defect rates after delivery tend to be cyclical with each version released. They initially are high and then stabilize around 1 to 2 defects per KLOC in systems with longer life cycles (>5 years). Web Business systems tend to have shorter life cycles (≤2 years) and may never hit the stabilization point.

Application Domain	Number of Projects	Error Range (Errors/ KESLOC)	Normative Error Rate (Errors/ KESLOC)	Notes
Automation	55	2 to 8	5	Factory automation
Banking	30	3 to 10	6	Loan processing, ATM
Command & Control	45	0.5 to 5	1	Command centers
Data Processing	35	2 to 14	8	DB-intensive systems
Environment/ Tools	75	5 to 12	8	CASE, compilers, etc.
Military—All	125	0.2 to 3	< 1.0	See subcategories
Airborne	40	0.2 to 1.3	0.5	Embedded sensors
Ground	52	0.5 to 4	0.8	Combat center
Missile	15	0.3 to 1.5	0.5	GNC system
Space	18	0.2 to 0.8	0.4	Attitude control system
Scientific	35	0.9 to 5	2	Seismic processing
Telecom	50	3 to 12	6	Digital switches
Test	35	3 to 15	7	Test equipment, devices
Trainers/ Simulations	25	2 to 11	6	Virtual reality simulator
Web Business	65	4 to 18	11	Client/server sites
Other	25	2 to 15	7	All others

Figure 7.15. Defect density by application domain.

7.5.2   Cumulative Defect Removal Efficiency (DRE) Benchmark

The percentage of defects removed before software is delivered to a customer tends to be significantly lower than one might expect. Jones' data from 1991 is shown in Figure 7.16 [14]. This table says, for example, that for software larger than 320 function points, typically only 75% of the faults were removed before shipment. Remember that this is data from 1991.

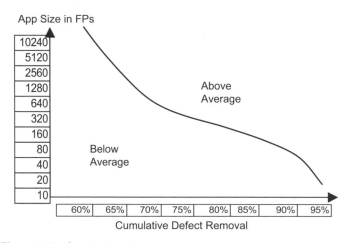

Figure 7.16. *Cumulative defect removal percentage versus function points.*

7.5.3   SEI Levels and Defect Relationships

Diaz and King [15] measured software development at General Dynamics and analyzed the relationship between SEI levels, quality, cost, and rework. They used data from ~20 projects in various stages of the life cycle, with ~360 software development engineers as shown in Table 7.1.

Jones' data from 2000 [16], which looks at DRE per FP, based on SEI levels shown in Figure 7.17. This chart tells us, for example, that the typical U.S. software project ships with only 80% of the defects removed.

TABLE 7.1   General Dynamics Decision Systems Project Performance Versus CMM Level

SEI Level	Customer Reported Unique Defects per KLOC
2	3.2
3	0.9
4	0.22
5	0.19

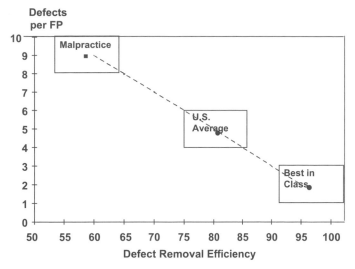

Figure 7.17. *Defect removal efficiency.*

7.5.4 Latent Defects

Two different studies by Hatton and Roberts [17] using only static code analyzers on millions of lines of debugged and released C and FORTRAN code found approximately six defects per KLOC. These were faults such as uninitialized variables. Obviously, there are more latent defects in the code than the static analyzers found.

7.5.5 A Few Recommendations

We are sure that you have noted that these benchmarks are inconsistent in the specifics. What should your goal be—less than 2 defects per KLOC or 0.25 defects per KLOC?

The differences and inconsistencies are at least partially due to differences in data sets and counting methodologies, which make it impossible to have one number. Nevertheless, there is a host of information here and some conclusions can be drawn.

- Zero defects is probably impossible. You will always have latent defects, even if you do not know they are there.
- Good software should be less than 2 defects per KLOC.
- Safe software should be at least less than 1, if not 0.5 defects per KLOC.
- Increasing SEI level conformance tremendously improves the DRE and number of delivered defects.

7.6 COST EFFECTIVENESS OF DEFECT REMOVAL BY PHASE

The later defects are removed, the more expensive they are to remove. Requirements defects that become failures in operation can be tremendously costly, easily costing orders of magnitude more to remedy.[4] Engineering rules for the cost of fixing defects range from a factor of 5 to 10 for each development phase. That is, it costs 5 to 10 times more to fix a coding defect once in formal testing and another 5 to 10 times more to fix it once it is in the field. IBM found in a 1983 study that it cost 20 times more to remove a defect in testing than in design/code inspection and approximately another 4 times more to fix it after the customer began using the system [18].

Your cost effectiveness will be based on your situation. Do you have one field site or 200? Can patches be downloaded easily, or is a site visit required along with database upgrades? Do you have extensive integration and regression testing? We recommend that you gather your own data and understand the costs for your own environment. Short of using your own data, we recommend using the following multiplicative factors as engineering rules:

Cost for fixing in requirements/design—1×
Cost of fixing in coding phase—5×
Cost of fixing in formal testing phase—25×
Cost of fixing in field—250×

7.7 DEFINING AND USING SIMPLE DEFECT METRICS: AN EXAMPLE

This section presents a sample defect construct and a few defect presentation charts. It demonstrates the wealth of information you can get from simple defect data. Notice how each one of the charts has a story to tell to those who pay attention.

The defect-related information that a program manager needs might be:

- Quality of component
- Readiness for release
- Productivity of bug fixing
- Identification of high-risk components

The defect base measures, for each module, might be:

- Defect open date

---

[4]Just think about all the costs involved in releasing a software fix to an end customer: requirements, development, and testing staff are impacted; development and test environments must be updated and maintained; new software must be packaged and shipped; documentation may need to be updated and reissued. Of course, there is also the additional possibility when making changes that other breakages may occur introducing more costs.

- Defect close date
- Lines of code

A sample defect construct is shown in Figure 7.18.

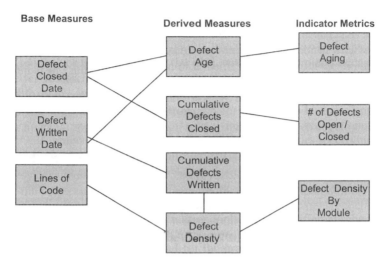

Figure 7.18. *Sample defect construct.*

From this sample construct, we can generate many different indicator metrics, a few of which could be:

- Open/closed/backlog distribution
- Open/closed/backlog cumulative distribution
- Defect density by module
- Defect aging

The objective of the open defect status (Figure 7.19) is to show, per week, the number of new defects, the number of closed defects, and the number of defects that are currently open (in backlog).

What does this chart tell you? How would you improve the chart?

- At a macro level, it looks like the quality of the release is improving, since both the arrival rate of new defects is decreasing as well as the backlog. Also, it appears that the team can fix about 10 defects per week. We need to drill down to understand new versus closed to see if we really are converging. It is not clear yet when we will be ready to release.
- This chart could be improved significantly by clearly having the goals for both ready to release and expected performance with upper and lower bounds. (In Chapter 14 will talk in more detail about how to ensure that any charts you create will be highly effective communication tools.)

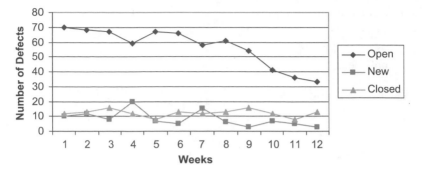

Figure 7.19. Defect status.

The module defect density chart (Figure 7.20) is designed to show the defect density of modules compared to a target rate. What does this chart tell you? How would you improve the chart?

- It looks like module 4's defect density is outside the control limits. We need to drill down/investigate to determine the reasons. If, for example, it happens to be a highly complex module, more inspections and testing may be warranted. For modules 3 and 5, we might check just to make sure that adequate testing has been done, and that we do not have a good result just because no one is really finding defects.
- We think this chart looks pretty good as it is. It might be improved if we had trend data over time to add in or some additional detail on what "defects" here really mean—Defects found after release? Defects total? Defects in formal testing?

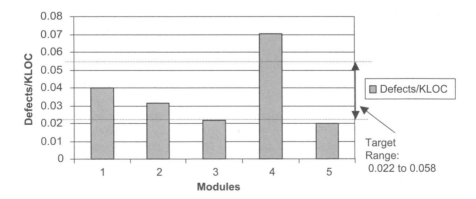

Figure 7.20. Module defect density (defects/KLOC).

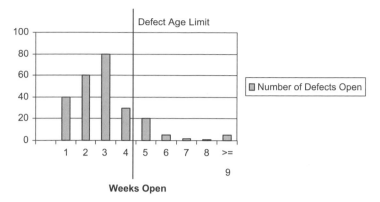

Figure 7.21. *Defect aging chart.*

The defect aging chart (Figure 7.21) is another simple chart that tells a story. What does this chart tell you? How would you improve the chart?

- First, we would be very concerned about the number of defects open past the target date, especially those at or after week 9. What is the cause? Do they really need to be fixed? Or does no one know how to fix them? It looks like, on average, it takes about three weeks to close a defect. This is just a good number to know.
- We have been assuming all the defects are critical. This chart could be improved (along with all of the others) by clearly indicating the severity of the defects.

These three charts are simple examples of the type of information you can easily get from sample defect data. They are invaluable to the project manager and to anyone wanting to understand the true progress of the project. They frequently do not tell the whole story; instead, they give clues and hints that tell you to investigate further to understand what really is going on.

7.8 SOME PARADOXICAL PATTERNS FOR CUSTOMER REPORTED DEFECTS

Jones pointed out in 1991 [6] that there are two general rules for customer reported defects:

1. The number of customer reported defects found correlates directly with the number of users.
2. The number of customer reported defects found correlates inversely with the number of defects found prior to shipment.

These general rules seem, at first, to be at odds with each other, but actually they are interrelated. They are both based on the concept that the more the software is used, the more defects that will be discovered. If the software has many users, it will have more execution time, and hence, more defects will be uncovered. Conversely, if the software is buggy, people will use it less, and fewer defects will be uncovered.

7.9   ANSWERS TO THE INITIAL QUESTIONS

1. Your system has no reported field defects. It was released six months ago. Is it time to break out the champagne?

HP had a system with no reported field defects. Initially, it was thought to be an example of "zero defects." They later discovered that was because no one was using it [17]. Be very careful to understand the usage of your system if the number of reported field defects is significantly lower than expected. It may be due to low usage.

2. You are building a commercial application. Your CEO, who is very dedicated to quality, directs you to find and fix 99% of the bugs before you ship. What is your response?

As studies repeatedly show, finding and fixing 99% of bugs is near impossible and very costly. Our suggestion is to discuss the defect benchmark data with your CEO and to suggest that a reliability or availability target may be more appropriate.

7.10   SUMMARY

Defects have their own behavioral patterns and dynamics, which need to be understood in order to properly predict, plan, and then monitor individual projects.

Defects are inserted into a project throughout its life cycle and are removed through activities such as inspection and testing. The quality of the processes, the skill of the people, and the size of the project highly impact the number of defects inserted. The number and type of defect removal activities highly impact the number of defects removed.

In this chapter we presented multiple methods of predicting and understanding both the number of defects in a project and their arrival rate during testing, development, and deployment. Some of the methods are static, based on characteristics of the project and the processes, such as SEI levels. Other methods are dynamic, based on the early test data for a project.

The two primary defect metrics are:

- *Defect Removal Efficiency* (*DRE*): The percentage of defects removed, either before shipment or for each phase of development
- *Defect Density*: The number of defects remaining in the product per KLOC.

There are benchmarks and engineering rules for both of these metrics, a few of which are:

- A DRE of 100% for a project is probably impossible. You will always have latent defects, even if you do not know they are there.
- Good software should be less than 2 defects per KLOC.
- Safe software should be 0.5–1.5 defects per KLOC.

We love defect data. It gives you real, observable events that allow you to understand how well the project is progressing, in terms of quality and schedule.

PROBLEMS

7.1 What does it mean if you have a higher arrival rate of defects for your project in the first month of system test than for other similar projects? List at least three options.

7.2 Given the defect removal matrix below, what is the defect removal efficiency for testing?

Defect Removal Step	Defect Injection Phase			
	Requirements	Design	Coding	Total
Requirements Review	10			10
Design Review	2	12		14
Testing	3	5	22	30
Customer Detected	1	3	4	8
Total	16	20	26	62

7.3 What is a reasonable number of defects in *good* quality released code?

7.4 Describe two ways in which you can predict the number of defects remaining after system test.

7.5 You have a system that is very similar to one that you built last year, except it is twice as large. In that system, you had 50 faults found in the field in year 1. You intend to roll out out this system twice as fast. How many faults do you predict to be found in year 1? Tests so far show that you have improved the defect density, as found in system test, by 50%. Discuss your reasoning.

7.6 True or False: Architecting to have small modules (<100 LOC) is a good way to reduce the number of defects in a system.

7.7 True or False: Defect density increases as system size increases.

7.8 True or False: A cost-effective way to find defects is to have a short testing cycle and then turn it over to real customers to use.

7.9   You have a one year development schedule, at which point your system is expected to be tested and 95% of the defects removed. You predict that you will have 200 defects in your system. How many defects, roughly, do you expect to find in month 8 if you are on schedule?

7.10   There are two different sets of data in Section 7.5.3. One is based on KLOC, the other on FPs. Do you think they are consistent? Why or why not?

PROJECTS

7.1   Project 1: You are now in system test. For theater tickets, you have the defect arrival data points below. Assume a Raleigh curve.

Month	1	2	3	4	5	6
Found Defects	13	22	25	22	17	5

    (a)   What do you predict as the total number of bugs in the system? Use two methods.

    (b)   How many bugs do you predict as being left in the system?

    (c)   What is the equation that predicts the defects?

    (d)   If you shipped at the end of week 6 (and assuming you removed all the defects found at that time), what would you predict as the defect removal efficiency?

    (e)   If this is a 10,000 LOC program, what would you predict as the remaining defect density after 6 months?

    (f)   Should you ship after 6 months? Why or why not?

7.2   Project 2: Download COQUALMO or another static defect prediction tool from the Internet. Use this tool to predict the number of defects inserted and removed by phase assuming a 10 KLOC program. Use your own judgment as to the adjustment factors to be used.

REFERENCES

[1]   E. Yourdon and L. Constantine, *Structured Design: Fundamentals of a Discipline of Computer Program and Systems Design*, Prentice-Hall, Englewood Cliffs, NJ, 1979.

[2]   L. H. Putnam and W. Myers, "Familiar metric management—reliability," www.qsm.com, 1995. Accessed Sept. 1, 2005.

[3]   W. Roberts, *Leadership Secrets of Atilla the Hun*, Warner Books, New York, 1995.

[4]   L. H. Putnam and W. Myers, *Industrial Strength Software—Effective Management Using Measurement*, IEEE Computer Society Press, New York, 1997.

[5]   L. Hatton, "Software failures: follies and fallacies," *IEE Review*, Mar. 1997.

[6]   T. C. Jones, *Applied Software Measurements*, McGraw-Hill, New York, 1991.

[7]   A. Wood, "Predicting software reliability," *IEEE Computer* **X**(II): (1996).

[8]   C. Putnam and W. Myers, *Measures for Excellence: Reliability Software on Time, Within Budget*, Yourdan Press, Englewood Cliffs, New Jersey, 1992.

[9]   S. Kah, *Metrics and Models in Software Quality Engineering, Second Edition*, Addison-Wesley, New York, 2003.

[10] M. Thangarajan and B. Biswas, "Mathematical model for defect prediction across software development lifecycle," www.qaiindia.com/Conferences/SEPG2000/sepg2000/sepg2_selectedPP.htm. Accessed Mar. 4, 2005.

[11] C. Hollenbach, "Quantitatively measured process improvements at Northrop Grumman IT," 2001.

[12] S. Chulani, "Modeling software defect introduction and removal: COQUALMO," University of Southern California Center for Software Engineering Technical Report USC-CSE-99-510, 1999.

[13] D. Reifer, "Software cost, quality, & productivity benchmarks," *The DoD Software Tech News*, July 2004.

[14] T. C. Jones, *Applied Software Measurements*, McGraw-Hill, New York, 1991.

[15] M. Diaz and J. King, "How CMM impacts quality, productivity, rework, and the bottom line," *Crosstalk*, 2002.

[16] T. C. Jones, "Software benchmarking: what works and what doesn't," *Software Productivity Research*, November 27, 2000. Available from www.cs.uml.edu/Boston-SPIN. Accessed Jan. 5, 2005.

[17] L. Hatton and A. Roberts, "How accurate is scientific software?," *IEEE Transactions on Software Engineering*, 1994.

[18] H. Remus, "Integrated software validation in view of inspections/review," *Proceedings of the Symposium on Software Validation*, North Holland, 1983.

8

Software Reliability Measurement and Prediction

> *Some models sometimes give good results, some are almost universally awful,*
> *and none can be trusted to be accurate at all times.*
> —*Stephan Kan* [1]

8.1 WHY STUDY AND MEASURE SOFTWARE RELIABILITY?

To start, consider the following question:

> You've educated your boss that removing 99% of all the defects is probably an
> unreasonable goal, and he agrees. But (happily) he remains extremely com-
> mitted to quality. Next, he says to you: "I want 99.99% reliability for the
> first 6 months in operation." You are still in the architecture phase of your
> project. What do you say and do?

Compare your answer with ours in Section 8.12.

8.2 WHAT IS RELIABILITY?

Software reliability is the probability that a software system will function without
failure under a given environment and during a specified period of time.

Software Measurement and Estimation, by Linda M. Laird and M. Carol Brennan
Copyright © 2006 John Wiley & Sons, Inc.

This definition may seem obvious, or even trivial, but let us look deeper.

The first interesting word is *probability*. We are not speaking about absolutes. We are speaking about probabilistic events and predictions. The system may actually have higher or lower reliability in operation, and the reliability prediction can still be correct.

The next important phrase is *without failure*. This phrase indicates that you need a good definition of what a failure is and what it is not. For the telephone network, dropping a call is not considered a failure, crashing the network is.

Under a given environment is extremely important. A system designed and tested on Windows XP may have significantly different behavior on Windows NT. Or a system built and proved to be extremely effective and safe for controlling one type of anti-ballistic missile (ABM) may not be effective or safe for the next generation of ABMs.

Finally, consider the phrase *during a specified period of time*. The requirement for a highly critical piece of software to have a reliability of 99.999% for two seconds versus two years is entirely different.

8.3 FAULTS AND FAILURES

As we learned in Chapter 7:

Faults are defects that are in a system.

Failures are faults that occur in operation.

Defects metrics measure faults.

Reliability metrics measure failures.

If the faulty code is never executed in operation, then the system never fails. The mean-time-between-failures (MTBF) will approach infinity. The software availability will be 100%.

And if there is only one fault in an entire system, and it is executed in the boot sequence of a system, then the system will fail every time, and the MTBF approaches 0. The software availability will be 0%.

8.4 FAILURE SEVERITY CLASSES

Not all failures are the same. Some are minor headaches, others are major catastrophes. We need to differentiate the different types of failures by defining the appropriate failure severity classes [2]. Failures should be categorized in the same severity class if they have the same impact. The classes may be based on cost impact, system capability impact, user impact, or whatever else makes sense for that system. You should have four or five classes at most: more classes become meaningless.

For example, consider a telephone network, an online retailer, and an ATM banking machine network. All of these systems should have significantly different failure severity classes. For a telephone network, it might be based on the ability of the network to continue to handle calls. For an online retailer, it might be revenue based. For an ATM banking machine network, it might be the number of machines impacted. Examples of failure classes are shown below.

TELEPHONE NETWORK (CAPABILITY BASED)

Severity	Definition
1	Cannot process any calls; entire network is down
2	Cannot process any calls within a region
3	Cannot process any calls within a switch
4	Inconvenient operations

ONLINE RETAILER (REVENUE BASED)

Severity	Definition—Revenue Impact in $
1	>100 K
2	10 K – 100 K
3	1 K – 10 K
4	<1 K

ATM BANKING (USER BASED)

Severity	Definition—Number of Machines Impacted
1	>1000
2	100 – 1000
3	10 – 100
4	<10

8.5 FAILURE INTENSITY

Failure intensity is the number of failures per unit. Initially, we always measured it per unit of time, where time was clock time. As software reliability evolved, we realized that failure intensity typically makes the most sense to the users when "unit" is whatever the natural unit for that system is. For airplanes, it could be either crashes per number of flights or per millions of miles flown. For telephone networks, it could be number of call failures per million of calls handled correctly. For price scanning systems, it could be number of incorrect prices per 100 items scanned. And for some other systems, it could be failures per year.

8.6 THE COST OF RELIABILITY

Reliability is not free. In fact, each percentage of improvement is costly. The exact relationship between cost and reliability is not completely understood, other than to say that the cost increases as the reliability requirement increases. This is due in part to the difficulty of isolating the variables of cost and reliability in a repeatable study. Nevertheless, when considering the relationship, we know that given a software project, if you need to improve the reliability, the methods for achieving it, such as additional testing and reviews, all cost development dollars.

There are a few models that deal with the cost of reliability. One is COCOMO II, which has required software reliability (RELY) as a cost factor. The values of RELY range from very low at 0.82 to very high at 1.26, with 1 being "nominal," which gives a factor of 1.54 to the cost equation. Nominal means "moderate, easily recoverable losses." That is, if a project were to cost \$1M, where the impact of a failure was "moderate, easily recoverable" and instead, you realized that the impact of a failure was really "risk to human life," then the same project would be projected to cost \$1.26M, in order to improve the reliability to an acceptable level.

For systems, Marcus and Stern [3] created an availability index, which shows a logarithmic relationship between system availability and cost. Assuming $R = e^{-t/\text{MTTF}}$ and $A = \text{MTTF}/(\text{MTTF} + \text{MTTR})$, then $R = e^{(A-1)/(A*\text{MTTR})*t}$, where A is availability and MTTR is mean time to repair. We can then transform the data points into a reliability versus investment chart, which has a logarithmic relationship as well, as shown in Figure 8.1. This transformation is for systems and includes hardware as well as software. The question is whether it holds for software alone.

Sha's reliability model also relates effort and reliability [4]:

$$R = e^{-kCt/E}$$

where k is a scaling concept, C is complexity, and E is the additional effort spent to improve reliability. This equation gives the same logarithmic relationship between investment and reliability, that is,

$$E = -kCt/(\ln R)$$

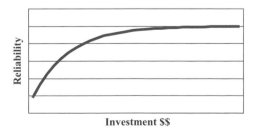

Figure 8.1. Reliability index.

We concur that there is a logarithmic relationship between cost and software reliability, as shown in Figure 8.1. We recommend that you use this relationship and/or the COCOMO factors and tune them for your environment. We also suggest that as a simple, getting started engineering rule, you use 25% more effort for a highly reliable system (NOT ultrareliable) and 20% less for "don't care" reliability software.

8.7   SOFTWARE RELIABILITY THEORY

The basic objective in reliability engineering is to predict when a system will fail, be it a probe to Mars, your website, a banking transaction, or the space shuttle.

Software reliability is similar to hardware reliability. For hardware, components wear out, due to factors such as corrosion, shock, overheating, and aging. It is usually physical in nature and probabilistic. For software, we can use the same basic approach although we do not have the same physical issues. It is probabilistic: the probabilities vary over time, we can graph them and model them, and, for each model, there is a probability distribution function (PDF).

There are many different reliability models. We will examine a few.

Software reliability theory is described well in many texts, such as Fenton and Pfleeger [5] or Shooman [6]. We recommend them to you for more in-depth treatment.

8.7.1   Uniform and Random Distributions

Let us look at a simple software reliability model. Suppose we have a software component that we know will fail sometime within 5 days, and it may fail any time up to that point with equal probability. Then, where t is an integer, $f(t) = 1/5$ for $t = 1$ to 5, and $f(t) = 0$ for $t > 5$. Graphically, this is shown in Figure 8.2.

In this case, $f(t)$ has a *uniform distribution*; that is, the probability is the same, 20%, that it will fail any day until day 6.

A uniform distribution describes some situations well, but it has a major limitation, in that you may not know the endpoint.

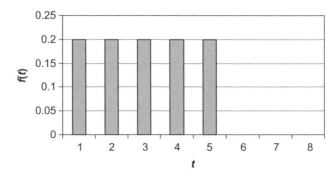

Figure 8.2. *Uniform distribution example.*

The most common model uses a *random distribution*. Failures are apt to occur randomly over time; that is, they are independent of the past events. That is, the probability of failure is equivalent for each time period t, given that the system has not failed before time t. This is also called an *exponential distribution*. The equation is

$$f(t) = \lambda e^{-\lambda t}$$

λ is also called the instantaneous failure rate, or hazard rate, and is the reciprocal of the mean-time-to-failure (MTTF). That is,

$$\lambda = 1/\text{MTTF}$$

Graphically, this function is depicted in Figure 8.3. Note that $f(t)$ never reaches 0.

MTTF is the mean time to failure. If you have failure data, with n different failure points of t_1 through t_n, then

$$\text{MTTF} = \sum_{i=1}^{n} t_i/n$$

If you have a probability distribution $f(t)$, then MTTF = expected value of $f(t)$, which is just

$$\text{MTTF} = \int_0^\infty t f(t) dt$$

For the exponential distribution [6],

$$\text{MTTF} = \int_0^\infty \lambda t e^{-\lambda t} dt = 1/\lambda$$

Here are three examples of calculating MTTF.

1. The system periodically fails. You track it for one month. It fails on days 2, 7, 8, 16, 22, and 31. To calculate the MTTF, you need to look at the intervals between

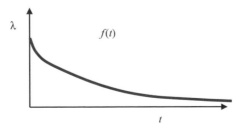

Figure 8.3. *Random distribution.*

failures. Assuming you started on day 1, the intervals are 1, 5, 1, 8, 6, and 9 days. Therefore,

$$\text{MTTF} = (1 + 5 + 1 + 8 + 6 + 9)/6 = 30/6 = 5 \text{ days}$$

2. The system periodically fails. You track the length of time it takes to fail and find that[1] $f(1) = 10\%; f(2) = 15\%; f(3) = 20\%; f(4) = 25\%; f(5) = 30\%$; all other $f(x) = 0$.

$$\text{MTTF} = 0.1 * 1 + 0.15 * 2 + 0.2 * 3 + 0.25 * 4 + 0.30 * 5$$

$$= 0.1 + 0.3 + 0.6 + 1 + 1.5 = 3.5$$

3. You have an exponential distribution. The MTTF is 2 days. Therefore, $\lambda = 1/\text{MTTF} = \frac{1}{2} = 0.5$. Therefore $f(t) = 0.5 \, e^{-0.5t}$.

Continuing with the previous example, the probability of failure on the 10th day is $f(10) = 0.5 \, e^{-5} = 0.0033 = 3.3\%$. Note that if you have completed day 9 with no failure, then $f(10) \equiv f(1) = 0.5 * e^{-0.5} = 0.30 = 30\%$.

8.7.2 The Probability of Failure During a Time Interval

The probability of failure between any two points of time is the area under the curve of $f(t)$, which is the integral of $f(t)$: that is, $\int_{t_1}^{t_2} f(t)dt$.

For our example of uniform distribution, the probability of failure between t_1 and t_2 is

$$\int_{t_1}^{t_2} 0.2 \, dt = 0.2(t_2 - t_1)$$

For the exponential distribution, the probability of failure between t_1 and t_2 is

$$\int_{t_1}^{t_2} \lambda e^{-\lambda t} dt = -e^{-\lambda t} \Big|_{t_1}^{t_2} = e^{-\lambda t_1} - e^{-\lambda t_2}$$

Here are two examples.
1. The probability of failure between time 3 and time 4 for our uniform distribution is $0.2(4 - 3) = 0.2$ or 20%.
2. The probability of failure between time 5 and time 6 for our exponential distribution is $e^{-\lambda * 5} - e^{-\lambda * 6}$, which is dependent on λ. For $\lambda = 1$, the probability of failure is 0.004. For $\lambda = 0.1$, it is 0.057. That is, the probability of failure between time 5 and 6 is 5.7% when $\lambda = 0.1$. For this example, $\text{MTTF} = 1/0.1 = 10$.

Note that for a continuous function, the probability of failure *at* any time t is really 0, because a point in time has no duration (i.e., is infinitely small). It is only during an interval, such as between $t = 2$ and $t = 3$, that it make sense.[2]

---

[1]Remember that $f(t)$ is the probability distribution function for failure.
[2]When we speak of the probability of failing on "day 5" it really means during day 5, and we are, in fact, changing the continuous function into a discrete function.

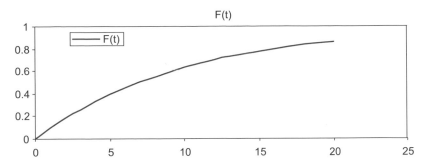

Figure 8.4. Cumulative exponential distribution: $\lambda = 0.1$.

8.7.3 $F(t)$: The Probability of Failure by Time T

The probability of failure *by* time t is written $F(t)$. This is the failure function in reliability. Notice that it is equivalent to the probability of failure during the interval 0 to t. $F(t)$ is a cumulative distribution function (CDF), where as $f(t)$ is a probability distribution function (PDF).

For our uniform distribution, $F(t) = 0.2t$, where t is an integer ≤ 5, and it is 0 for $t > 5$.

For our exponential distribution,

$$F(t) = \int_0^{t_2} \lambda e^{-\lambda t}\, dt = -e^{-\lambda t}\Big|_0^{t_2} = 1 - e^{-\lambda t_2}$$

Figure 8.4 is a graph of $F(t)$, where $\lambda = 0.1$. From looking at the graph, we see that $F(t)$ at time $t = 10$ is ~ 0.6, which means that the probability the system will fail by $t = 10$ is $\sim 60\%$.

Here are some examples.

For our uniform distribution, the probability of failure through day 4 is $0.2 * 4 = 0.8 = 80\%$.

For our exponential distribution, assuming $\lambda = 0.1$, $F(t) = 1 - e^{-0.1t}$. Then the probability of failure through day 7 would be $1 - e^{-0.7}$.

8.7.4 $R(t)$: The Reliability Function

The reliability function is the probability the system has NOT failed by time t. Therefore, it equals one minus the probability it HAS failed by time t. That is,

$$R(t) = 1 - F(t)$$

For our uniform distribution,

$$R(t) = 1 - 0.2t$$

For the exponential distribution,

$$R(t) = 1 - (1 - e^{-\lambda t}) = e^{-\lambda t}$$

For our exponential distribution, assuming $\lambda = 0.1$, the probability that the system has not failed through day 7 is $R(t) = e^{-0.7}$.

8.7.5 Reliability Theory Summarized

There are three primary functions in reliability theory:

$f(t)$ = Probability distribution function of failures
$F(t)$ = Probability of failure by time t
$R(t)$ = Probability of no failure by time t

They are related by

$$F(t) = \int_0^t f(t)dt \quad \text{for continuous } f(t)$$

$$F(t) = \sum_{i=1}^{0} f(i) \quad \text{for discrete } f(t)$$

$$R(t) = 1 - F(t)$$

$f(t)$ describes the distribution of the failure arrivals—it can be a uniform distribution, an exponential distribution, or another distribution.

8.8 RELIABILITY MODELS

Reliability models are used to estimate a product's reliability or the number of latent defects once the product is released. They give you an objective understanding of the quality of the product, so that you can make fact-based decisions such as when to ship, and so you can understand whether or not the product is expected to meet the reliability requirement. They can also allow you to plan resources for maintenance, since you can estimate the number of expected faults you will need to fix.[3]

8.8.1 Types of Models

Reliability models are extremely similar to defect models and, in many cases, are the same. With reliability models, we are trying to predict the number of defects remaining after shipment and the arrival rates of failures in operation.

---

[3]We have been faced with the discussion of the number of people required to maintain the system after release. Being able to have a quantitative, fact-based discussion based on the number of defects you project to be left in the system, when you expect them to be found, and the number of defects people can fix per month is entirely different than "Uh—I think we need 50% of the staff for the next 6 months."

There are both static and dynamic models.

Static models use attributes of the program to estimate the number of defects. They typically are of form $y = f(a, b, c, d, e, \ldots, z)$, where y is the defect rate or number of defects, and a through z are the attributes of the product, process, and/or project. A good example of this is COQUALMO [7], which is based on COCOMO and which we examined in Chapter 7. Static models usually work better at the module level to indicate to engineers where they need to focus.

Dynamic models are typically based on statistical distributions and tend to work better "in the large" on projects—when you need to estimate when or if the project will fail. One type of model encompasses the entire life cycle and utilizes Rayleigh distributions. Other models start with the testing and deployment process and use exponential distributions.

Reliability growth models are dynamic models that focus on data from the formal testing phase. The rationale is that the defect arrival rate during testing is expected to be a good indicator of the product's reliability, which is valid if the testing mirrors the expected usage (see Section 8.9.4). These models are used at the end of the cycle when finding and fixing bugs is the norm, the stability is increasing, and, hopefully, so is the reliability. The exponential and the S-curve reliability growth models seem to hold up best with experiential data.

"Time" is critical with dynamic models. It can be either execution time (CPU), testing time, or calendar time, but it needs to be consciously selected and well specified. For example, consider the following data for defects found in system test:

Week	1	2	3	4
Defects	10	5	3	2

This looks good. We are finding fewer defects each week, and it seems to be converging. But now consider the number of hours of tester time and number of hours of CPU time. This data tells a different story.

Week	1	2	3	4
Defects	10	5	3	2
Tester Hours	80	40	40	20
CPU Hours	100	20	50	30
Failure Intensity				
Per Week	10	5	3	2
Per Tester Hour	0.13	0.13	0.08	0.10
Per CPU Hour	0.10	0.25	0.06	0.07

Growth models can be based on either fault counts or MTTF. With fault count models, as previously discussed, the expectation is that the failure intensity will decrease over time. With MTTF models, the expectation is that the MTTF will increase over time as the reliability improves.

Some abbreviations and one key relationship may need clarification:

MTTF: Mean time to failure

MTBF: Mean time between failures

MTTR: Mean time to repair

MTBF = MTTR + MTTF

The most common failure model is the exponential distribution:

$$R(t) = e^{-\lambda t}$$

EXERCISE: If the MTTF is 10 days, what is the reliability function? What is the probability that it will not fail in the first five days?

Answer:

$$R(t) = e^{-\lambda t}$$
$$\lambda = 1/\text{MTTF} = 0.1$$
$$\text{Thus, } R(t) = e^{-0.1t}$$

$R(5)$ is the probability it will not fail in the first 5 days. $R(5) = e^{-0.5} = 0.606 = 60\%$.

There are many reliability distributions and models. Most become complicated quickly. Some take into account not only "find/fix" but also "break/fix" issues. There are many excellent references that go into these models in detail, such as Singpurwalla and Wilson [8], and we happily refer you to them. Our experience is that getting projects to use even the simplest reliability models has been a challenge, and the simpler, the better.

8.8.2 Predicting Number of Defects Remaining

There are numerous ways to predict the number of defects remaining after testing is complete, many of which we discussed in detail and for which we gave examples in Sections 7.4 and 7.5 of Chapter 7. There are some extremely simple ones. For example, one *extremely* simple method would be to base your defects delivered on your SEI level. That is, if you are SEI level 2 and *you know nothing else*, you could start off with the assumption that you will have 3.2 customer reported unique defects per KLOC and you will find 80 to 90% of the defects before shipment. A more complex method would be a projection based on Rayleigh curves.

Another method, which we have frequently mentioned, is using historical data. There are many ways to project from historical data. One is to use the defect removal efficiency (DRE) data. This is an extremely simple method and is recommended by Kan [1] for use on small projects. You need historical data from other projects. You could

- Select one or more similar, previous projects and gather the test effectiveness levels and the measures of variation (mean, SD, etc.).
- Gather the testing defect data for the current project and estimate the number of field defects based on the test effectiveness.
- If possible, express your prediction using interval estimates.

EXERCISE: Assume that you have three similar projects, and, in each, the ratios of problems found during system test versus first year in the field have been 1.5, 1.2, and 1.6. If you found 200 defects in system test, how many defects do you expect to find in the first year of your new project?

Answer: The mean of the ratios is 1.43 with a standard deviation of 0.21. Therefore, for the new project, if you wanted a 95% confidence level, you would use 2 SD, or ± 0.42.

$$\text{System test defects/expected first year defects} = 1.43$$
$$\text{Expected first year defects} = 200/1.43 = 140$$
$$\text{Top of range} = 200/1.01 = 192$$
$$\text{Bottom of range} = 200/1.85 = 108$$

Therefore, you can expect to find ~ 140 defects in the first year, with a range between ~ 110 and ~ 190 defects.

8.9 FAILURE ARRIVAL RATES

All of the reliability models attempt to predict the arrival rates of failures after shipment. The simplest method is to use the defect prediction techniques from Chapter 7 and assume that they follow a similar pattern after cutover. Sometimes this will work, but frequently, it will not. The issue is that failures are a function of (1) faults, (2) environment, and (3) system usage and mix.

Four techniques you can use to predict failure arrival rates are:

- Historical data from similar projects
- Engineering rules
- Musa's algorithm
- Operational testing

8.9.1 Predicting Failure Arrival Rates Using Historical Data

If you have historical data from similar system rollouts, you may be able to use it to predict the failure arrival rates. Look at the expected usage and rollout of the new system, and compare it with your other similar systems. If any fit, start with that

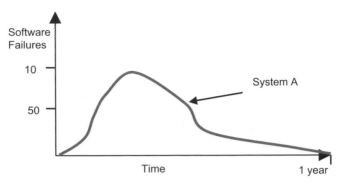

Figure 8.5. *Software failure arrival rates—system A.*

as a model. If more than one fits, you could use averages, standard deviations, or other techniques to determine a model. For example, suppose that you have system B, which is extremely similar to system A, and it is expected to have the same rollout and usage as A, except twice as fast. It is also expected to have 50% of the failures that A had. Then you take the curve for A and adjust the scales of both time and number of failures to match B as shown in Figures 8.5 and 8.6.

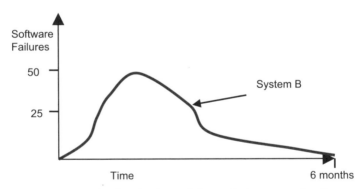

Figure 8.6. *Predicted software failure arrival rates—system B.*

8.9.2   Engineering Rules for MTTF

Care should be exercised in using the rules in this section. They are rough and based on limited empirical data.

Kan [1] has a rule for system software stating that roughly half of the remaining defects are found each year; that is, there is a "half-life" phenomenon.

Jones [9] published empirical data in 1991 relating defects per KLOC to MTTF, as shown in Figure 8.7. Note that this is completely from experience and observation: it has no theoretical basis. This assumes an exponential reliability curve after release.

For example, you predict ~ 7 defects per KLOC. Therefore, you could estimate the MTTF at ~ 2 hours, and the projected reliability equation would be $R(t) = e^{-t/2} \pm 50\%$.

Defects per KLOC	MTTF	
> 30	< 2 min	
20-30	4 to 15 min	
10 to 20	5 to 60 min	
5 to 10	1 to 4 hours	
2 to 5	4 to 24 hours	
1 to 2	24-160 hours	
< 1	indefinite	

Figure 8.7. *Predicted failure rate based on defect density.*

8.9.3 Musa's Algorithm

Musa's algorithm is based on determining the probability that a defective line of code will be executed and that the defect will cause a fault. He suggests to use it as a starting point in predicting failure arrival rates. It is to be used at the start of system test. This algorithm makes us a little nervous, because it looks likes magic, and it is not widely used.[4] Nevertheless, we present it to you because: (1) there is a pressing need to be able to predict failures from faults, (2) the variance on Musa's empirical data is low ($\pm$a factor of 2.7), and (3) it may work for you.

Musa's model takes as input the predicted number of remaining faults, the size of the program, the processor speed, and a probability that a given faulty line of code will cause a failure. This probability can be from past history or you can use the default, which is $4.2*10^{-7}$ (we told you this looked like magic). The output is an expected initial failure rate, based on CPU time. Let:

λ_0 = projected initial failure rate

W = number of faults

I = number of object code instructions

R = process speed in instructions per second

K = failures per fault executed, which can either be derived from other similar projects ($K=\lambda I/RW$) or be the "magic constant," $4.2*10^{-7}$

Then $\lambda_0 = RKW/I$. Note that K in this equation is calculated from previous projects or using the constant, and R, W, and I are from this project. Here's an example. Assume that you have a 100K source code program, and your projected delivered density is 1.5 defects per KLOC. The expansion ratio of source code to object code is 1 to 4. You are running on a 100MIP machine.

---

[4]On the other hand, we are reminded of Arthur C. Clarke's 1961 quotation: "Any sufficiently advanced technology is indistinguishable from magic."

From past experience, you've calculated K to be $1*10^{-7}$. What is the initial projected failure intensity?

$$W = 1.5*100 = 150$$
$$I = 4*100\,K = 400\,K = 4*10^5$$
$$R = 100\,\text{MIPS} = 10^8$$
$$K = 10^{-7}$$

Then

$$\lambda_0 = RKW/I = 10^8 * 10^{-7} * 150/(4*10^5) = 3.75*10^{-3}$$

This means you would project:

Initial failure intensity $= 0.00375$ failures/CPU sec or 0.225 failure/CPU min
Initial MTTF $= 1/\lambda_0 = 266.7$ CPU sec (or 4.44 CPU min)
Initial reliability equation $= R = e^{-0.225t}$

Note that λ_0 is linearly dependent on all input variables and that a change in the order of magnitude of any of them will change λ_0 by an order of magnitude as well.

Musa's algorithm was initially developed to predict the initial failure intensity for system test, where it is most readily applied. Nevertheless, it can be used to predict initial failure intensities in operation if no better information is available.

8.9.4 Operational Profile Testing

Operational profile testing runs the system as close as possible to the expected field environment and usage, and uses the results of that testing to predict the failure rate in the field. It is the preferred method for predicting field failure intensities.

The best testers are always trying to break the system, and they tend to find defects[5] at a relatively constant rate, which may not be useful for reliability prediction [10] as shown in Figure 8.8. System testing finds defects, and reliability estimation (or operational) testing predicts the system's stability and reliability.

Recall that the reliability of a software product depends on the environment in which it executes and how it is used. Therefore, in order to be able to estimate the reliability of software, it must be tested as it would be used in the field.

The *operational profile* is a quantitative characterization of how the software will be used in the field. A *profile* is a set of independent possibilities called *elements* and their associated probability of occurrence. J. Musa developed the concept of the operational profile and much of its technology and practice.

Figure 8.9 contains a simple operational profile for an ATM machine based on use cases. In this example, there is a 53% probability that the interaction will be a cash withdrawal.

---

[5]Hopefully, the impact of the defects found decreases as testing progresses.

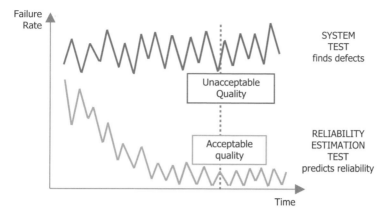

Figure 8.8. Testing failure rates.

Operational profile testing is a "fast-track" way to estimate the arrival rate of defects after shipment with greater validity, that is, to use the data from test to predict the reliability in operation. You test based on a profile of usage that is similar to what is expected in actual operation, and you use the failure intensity data to project the failure intensity for actual operation.

Creating an operational profile involves one or more of the following five steps:

1. Specify the *customer profile.*
2. Establish the *user profile.*
3. Define the *system-mode profile.*
4. Determine the *functional profile.*
5. Determine the *operational profile* itself.

In our ATM example, *customers* might be a bank customer or a bank employee. *User profile* is a refinement of customers such as business account customers or personal account customers for bank customer. *System-mode profile* specifies different

Use Case	Occurrence Probability
Cash Withdrawal	0.53
Checking Deposit	0.15
Savings Deposit	0.14
Funds Transfer	0.08
Balance Inquiry	0.06
Restock	0.02
Collect Deposits	0.02
Total	1.00

Figure 8.9. Operational profile example.

Use Case	Occurrence Probability	Predicted Failure Rate	Average Duration
Cash Withdrawal	0.53	0.001	10
Checking Deposit	0.15	0.002	10
Savings Deposit	0.14	0.002	20
Funds Transfer	0.08	0.003	30
Balance Inquiry	0.06	0.003	5
Restock	0.02	0.003	30
Collect Deposits	0.02	0.003	30
Total	1		135

Figure 8.10. Failure rate data example.

modes of access such as direct access (at a machine), or online transaction. The *functional profile* is the user scenarios or use cases. One might be deposit funds, which could have the *elements* of checking deposit and savings deposit. The *operational profile* has the probabilities of occurrence associated with the elements.

Once you have the operational profile, its probabilities guide your testing.[6] The testing should be focused on the most likely operations. Strict operational profile testing uses the same frequencies in testing as predicted in operation [2].

Using the test results, even without the strict operational frequencies, you can determine the failure rate for each element by using the expected duration with the profile to predict the initial reliability during system rollout. That is, given an operational profile with i elements, the initial failure rate is

$$\text{Initial Failure Rate} = \sum_i \big[\text{Occurrence Probability}(i)$$

$$* \text{Predicted Failure Rate}(i) * \text{Average Duration}(i)\big]/T$$

where

$$T = \sum_i \text{Occurrence Probability}(i) * \text{Average Duration}(i)$$

Let us try using the data in Figure 8.10 to predict the initial failure rate. Doing the arithmetic,

$$T = 13.5$$
$$\text{Initial Failure Rate} = 0.03/13.5 = 0.002$$

---

[6]If possible, use operational profiles with performance and stress testing as well as reliability testing.

Note that this failure rate is the *initial* failure rate. As fixes are applied, it should improve.

The quality and validity of the predictions are based primarily on the quality and validity of the profile created.

8.9.5 Predicting Reliability Summary

Predicting the reliability of a system from defects can be a daunting and difficult task. We've given you a variety of methods to use. The operational profile testing is by far the most reliable and trustworthy method and we highly recommend it.

8.10 BUT WHEN DO I SHIP?

Software reliability increases as a function of testing time, as defects are found and fixed. The art is to understand *what* curve you are on, and *where* you are on that curve.

The release criteria is typically that the quality must exceed a certain, predefined level, as measured by the number of open trouble reports (by severity class), completion of the acceptance test and the number of defects found, and/or the expected remaining defects (or defect density).

But the question always is: When do you release the software? The answer theoretically is easy—when it meets the release criteria, and when the cost of not releasing it exceeds the cost of releasing. Figuring out when that point occurs is more challenging and varies for each project. Remember that some of the variables include missing market windows, the cost for fixing defects found in the field, and the cost of finding additional defects in testing.

8.11 SYSTEM CONFIGURATIONS: PROBABILITY AND RELIABILITY

The traditional method of calculating reliability of a system is to decompose it into its components and subsystems, all of which have their own reliability, and to use probability theory and combinatorics to calculate the overall system reliability.

Let us examine the two basic configurations of subsystems, series and parallel, as shown in Figure 8.11. These two configurations are the basic building blocks for many more complicated architectures.

For components in series, all modules must function correctly for the result to be correct. If your system had a database engine, middleware, and an application, all of which had to work successfully for the system to work, a series model would be appropriate.

Looking at our series figure, the probability P of success of the whole is the probability of success of A and of B and of Z (assuming that they are independent events). Therefore, the reliability at time t is the product of the reliabilities of all the

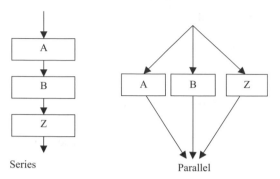

Figure 8.11. Subsystem configurations.

components at time t. For our picture, $R(\text{Series}, t) = R(A, t) * R(B, t) * R(Z, t)$, or generically,

$$R(\text{Series}, t) = \prod_i R_i(t)$$

For components in parallel, at least one module must function correctly for the result to be correct. If your system had three processors, any of which could handle the system load, then this parallel model would be appropriate to model the hardware. The probability of failure would be the probability that A, B, and Z all fail. The probability of A failing during time t is 1 minus the probability of A succeeding. Therefore, the probability of our parallel configuration failing by time t is

$$F(t) = [1 - R(A, t)] * [1 - R(B, t)] * [1, R(Z, t)]$$

and the probability of it not failing is

$$R(t) = 1 - F(t)$$

Generically, when you have a parallel configuration, which works if any of the components work,

$$R(\text{Parallel}, t) = 1 - \prod_i [1 - R_i(t)]^7$$

For example, in a series configuration, if A is reliable 80% of time, B is reliable 90% of the time, and Z is reliable 10% of the time, then the reliability of the system is $0.8 * 0.9 * 0.1 = 7.2\%$.

In a parallel configuration, with the same reliabilities, the reliability of the system is $1 - (1 - 0.8) * (1 - 0.9) * (1 - 0.1) = 1 - 0.2 * 0.1 * 0.9 = 1 - 0.018 = 98.2\%$.

---

[7]Note that the formula for parallel combination of subsystems requires all subsystems to be independent. If they have common-mode failure, it is invalid. Please refer to [2], p. 218 for further details.

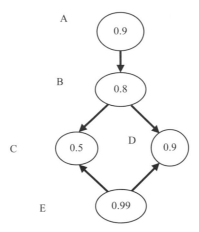

Figure 8.12. *Example configuration.*

EXERCISE: If the reliability for time t for each node is as shown in Figure 8.12, what is the reliability of the overall system?

Answer:

$$\text{Reliability of System} = R(A)*R(B)*R(C, D)*R(E)$$
$$R(C, D) = 1 - [1 - R(C)]*[1 - R(D)]$$
$$R(\text{System}) = 0.9*0.8*[1 - (0.5*0.1)]*0.99$$
$$= 0.72*0.95*0.99 = 0.68 = 68\%$$

8.12 ANSWERS TO INITIAL QUESTION

The initial question was:

> You've educated your boss that removing 99% of all the defects is probably an unreasonable goal, and he agrees. But (happily) he remains extremely committed to quality. Next, he says to you: "I want 99.99% reliability for the first 6 months in operation." You are still in the architecture phase of your project. What do you say and do?

Our advice is that you begin the discussion on the cost of reliability and understand the true reason for the 99.99% requirement. Determine if it is a based on economic justification, a gut feeling, or a safety requirement. In all likelihood, you will determine that a lower number may be the actual true requirement.

Do an architectural analysis of the system to determine what the reliability requirements are for all the components, including the software. Ensure that all are possible; if not, rearchitecture and/or adjust the requirement.

For the software, predict the reliability of the system in operation, using reliability modeling and operational profiling. Do not ship until the operational profiling testing (AKA, reliability testing) predicts that the resulting reliability will meet the reliability requirements.

8.13 SUMMARY

In this chapter we have given an introduction to software reliability measurement and prediction. We've examined reliability models, how to predict the reliability, failure classes, and failure intensity. If you understand and can practice these concepts, you probably know more than 90% of the people practicing software engineering today. If, on the other hand, you are building systems in which ultra-high reliability is required (e.g., life and death), and you need to be one of the experts, we highly recommend the various texts by Shooman [6], Musa [2] and others for additional in-depth study.

PROBLEMS

8.1 Define failure severity classes for Google.

8.2 What is the purpose of operational profile testing?

8.3 What are three ways in which to predict the reliability of a system?

8.4 Given a reliability function of $R(t) = e^{-0.1t}$ (e.g., $\lambda = 0.1$), what is the probability that the system will fail between day 2 and day 5 (approximately)? Show the formula and your work.

8.5 Given a reliability function of $R(t) = e^{-0.5t}$, what is the mean time to failure?

8.6 Assume a reliability growth distribution. If the probability of an outage for the first 10 hours of a system is 5%, what is the reliability function?

8.7 Over a one year time period, if each component has 0.99 reliability, how many components in series can you have and still have ≥ 0.95 reliability? ≥ 0.90?

8.8 Consider the configurations in Figure 8.11. If all of the reliabilities for one year were 0.99, what are the system reliabilities?

8.9 You have a 1M line source code program, and your projected delivered density is 0.5 defect per KLOC. The expansion rate of source code to object code is 1 to 10. You are running on a 2GIP machine. From past experience, you have calculated K to be $1 * 10^{-7}$. What is the projected initial failure rate?

8.10 Reliability and availability are both important, but the requirements will vary by system. Name a system where reliability is more important that availability and vice versa.

8.11 You predict that you will have an initial MTTF of 10 days. Your boss decides to put it on hardware that is twice as fast but has the same reliability. The usage will stay the same even though the hardware is more powerful. What will be the new MTTF?

8.12 You have the defect data as shown below. Are you ready to ship? Why or why not?

Week	1	2	3	4
Defects	20	5	2	0

8.13 What would be the block diagram for a system with one larger server and with middleware, GUI, and three backend database processors, each of which can access all of the data on the disk array?

8.14 Determine the reliability function and the reliability for $t = 6$ days for the series configuration and the parallel configurations in Figure 8.13 assuming that:

MTTF(A) = 5 days

MTTF(B) = 10 days

MTTF(Z) = 100 days

and a random arrival rate of faults, that is, it is an exponential distribution.

8.15 Based on engineering rules rather than theory, if the MTTF of your system is ~24 hours, what can you say about the number of defects per KLOC?

8.16 Why is it difficult to predict the failure rate in operation?

8.17 True or False: Static reliability models are the most useful during integration testing.

PROJECT

8.1 For the theater tickets system:
  (a) Define failures and severity classes.
  (b) Propose a failure intensity objective (MTTF) for the overall system. Explain your reasoning.

100 CPU Hours	1	2	3	4	5	6	7	8	9
Defects Found	13	36	22	48	50	45	41	35	32

Figure 8.13. *Testing results.*

(c) You determine that the MTTF for your hardware is 6 months, and for the software, it is 2 months. What is the MTTF for the entire system (assume it only has hardware and software as above)?

(d) Define an operational profile for the theater tickets project.

(e) Ignoring (c) above, you do operational testing and come up with the data shown in Figure 8.13, based on execution time. You go into operation after 900 CPU hours of testing. What do you predict as the number of defects you will see in the first 200 CPU hours of execution in the field? After that, how many defects do you expect to see in the next 800 hours? Assume faults are found and fixed immediately.

REFERENCES

[1]   S. Kan, *Metrics and Models in Software Quality Engineering*, Addison-Wesley, Boston, 2001.

[2]   J. Musa, *Software Reliability Engineering: More Reliable Software Faster and Cheaper—Second Edition*, Author House, 2004.

[3]   E. Marcus and H. Stern, *Blueprints for High Availability*, Wiley, New York, 2000.

[4]   L. Bernstein, "Software fault tolerance," in *Advances in Computers, Volume 58* (edited by Marvin V. Zelkowitz), Academic Press, San Diego, CA, 2003.

[5]   N. Fenton and S. Pfleeger, *Software Metrics: A Rigorous & Practical Approach*, PWS Publishing Company, Boston, 1997, pp. 364–368.

[6]   M. L. Shooman, *Reliabiity of Computer Systems and Networks*, Wiley, Hoboken, NJ, 2002, p. 437.

[7]   S. Chulani, "Modeling software defect introduction and removal: COQUALMO," Univ. of Southern California Center for Software Engineering Technical Report USC-CSE-99-570, 1999.

[8]   N. Singpurwalla and S. Wilson, *Statistical Methods of Software Engineering: Reliability and Risk*, Springer, New York, 1999.

[9]   T. C. Jones, *Applied Software Measurement: Assuring Productivity and Quality*, McGraw-Hill, New York, 1991, p. 282.

[10]   H. Levendel, Presentation at Stevens Reliability Seminar, 2003.

9

Response Time and Availability

The future belongs to he who knows how to wait.
—*Old Russian Proverb*

The opposite is true when it comes to designing systems.

Today, users expect systems to be there when they want them and to respond immediately. Availability and response time metrics measure these characteristics.

User response time is a "latency" metric. Although there are other latency metrics, such as the time it takes to update external systems, we are going to focus on response time. It is the most prevalent and all of the concepts are the same.

There are three types of analysis used for response time and availability metrics:

- Analytical performance modeling using mathematical models
- Simulation modeling using tools and based on the characterization of components
- Performance measurement using specialized tools and based on direct observation of the system

For simple systems, mathematical models are used. But as the systems become more complex, their overall behaviors become difficult to model. Consequently, measurement and instrumentation (i.e., measurability) become extremely important.

Software Measurement and Estimation, by Linda M. Laird and M. Carol Brennan
Copyright © 2006 John Wiley & Sons, Inc.

9.1 RESPONSE TIME MEASUREMENTS

Response time is the *interval* between a user's request and the system's response. A simple diagram of response time is shown in Figure 9.1. This diagram is ambiguous. What is the real start event? When the user first begins typing the request, or when the "submit" button is clicked? The more detailed diagram shown in Figure 9.2 specifies two potential response times—both starting when the user hits the submit button, but one finishing when the system starts to respond and the other when the system finishes responding. The typical measurement is Response Time 1, although in some circumstances, such as for longer running interactions, Response Time 2 is used.

Response time is measured in elapsed time: you need to specify both a start and stop event. It is frequently reported or specified with a minimum, maximum, and average or as a statistical distribution. The best measure of a system's response time during real operations is a "percentile" metric. The 95-percentile metric indicates that 95% of the transactions have a response time at or less than that number.

Consider the following specifications for response time:

1. The response time must be ≤8 seconds.
2. The response time as measured from the user submit to the system starts response must be ≤8 seconds.
3. The response time as measured from the user submit to the system starts response must be:
   (a) Maximum ≤30 seconds
   (b) Average ≤6 seconds
4. The response time as measured from the user submit to the system starts response must be:
   (a) 95 percentile ≤8 seconds
   (b) 100 percentile ≤30 seconds

Which specification do you like the best, regardless of the actual numbers? Can you see how the fourth is preferred? It is the clearest and the most informative, to both users and developers.

Seven seconds is the magic number for response time in transaction and web-based systems. Even in the systems we built in the 1980s and 1990s, the response time requirement was always less than or equal to 7 seconds, based on early usability research [1] and our own field studies with users. Response times longer than 7 seconds cause user irritation and/or boredom. Today's online users have the

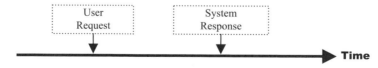

Figure 9.1. Response time model 1.

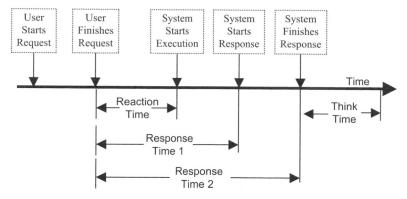

Figure 9.2. *Response time model 2.*

same or even lower thresholds. Simple interactions are expected to have response times of 2 seconds or less. For long running interactions, percent-done indicators are required [2]; otherwise, site abandonment (versus dissatisfaction) tends to occur between 11 and 16 seconds [3]. For incremental display transactions, useful content needs to load within 2 seconds and needs to complete within 20–30 seconds [4].

You typically measure and analyze your system's response time via tools that execute a set of representative transactions and measure the response times, under varying system loads (Figure 9.3). There are also companies that will measure (and benchmark) your live website and system.

The 7 second number is *system* response time. For systems, you need to recognize that as a developer you may only have control over the application response time and need to understand your application's response time requirement within the context of the larger system. "Transactional latencies," which include network, server, and middleware, tend to average between 0.5 and 1.5 seconds [3].

When modeling the overall performance and load of your system, do not forget about the "think time" shown in Figure 9.2. This is the time it takes for a human to

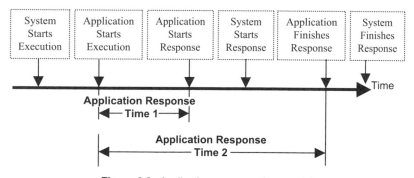

Figure 9.3. *Application response time model.*

respond to the system. Short think times can increase the load on the system; long think times can decrease the load on the system.

EXERCISE: You know that the transactional latency of your system is 1 second. You also know that the application response time can vary from 2 to 10 seconds. You are concerned about response time. What should you do?

Answer: Your response time is going to vary between 3 and 11 seconds. Look back at the guidelines. For simple interactions, it should be 2 seconds. Over 7 seconds is not good. You need to understand the rough distribution of the application response times. Assuming you do have simple interactions, you probably need to implement something to start the displays quickly (<2 seconds). If the probability of a response time of 8 through 11 seconds is low, you may choose to ignore it. On the other hand, if you expect a reasonable percentage, then you need to either: (1) redesign to improve the total response time to under 7 seconds; (2) determine a way to identify longer running interactions and use a percent complete indicator; or (3) use your "quick display" capability for all transactions.

9.2 AVAILABILITY

Your boss, who continues to have great intentions, tells you that your new system should have "five nines" availability. You know "five nines" means 99.999% availability. Without doing any calculations or looking at the charts, do you know if that is reasonable or not? Do you know how many hours of downtime per year that allows? Guess—and then look at Figure 9.4.

Surprised? It is not much time.

Availability is one of the most important measures of a system for the users. It is the measure of the probability the system will be up. We define it as Availability = MTTF/(MTTR + MTTF). This is just uptime/(uptime + downtime).

System Availability %	Downtime per System per Year
99.999	5.3 minutes
99.99	52.6 minutes
99.95	4.4 hours
99.9	8.8 hours
99.8	17.5 hours
99.5	43.8 hours
99	87.6 hours
98.5	131.4 hours
97.5	219 hours

Figure 9.4. *Availability and downtime.*

Figure 9.4 shows the correspondence between system availability and downtime per year. "Five nines" availability equates to a total of 5.3 minutes of downtime per year, which is extremely difficult and expensive to achieve. The cost of availability increases exponentially with each additional 9. Online vendors who weigh the cost of improving from 99.9% to 99.99% typically find that it is not worth the additional 8 hours of availability per year. Even if the software and hardware can achieve it, typical operations and processes within a data center are apt to cause more downtime than 53 minutes per year.

Here are some examples.

- If the system goes down once a week for 5 hours, what is the availability?

$$\text{Number of hours per week} = 7 * 24 = 168$$
$$\text{Availability} = (168 - 5)/168 = 0.97 = 97\%$$

- If the typical time between failures is 48 hours, and the typical time the system is down is 10 minutes, what is the availability?

$$\text{Availability} = \text{MTBF}/(\text{MTBF} + \text{MTTR}) = 48/[48 + (10/60)] = 0.996$$
$$= 99.6\%$$

EXERCISE: In 2001, IDC compared the availability of three different server platforms for ERP systems (such as SAP or Oracle), which were 99.98%, 99.67%, and 99.9% for an average of 99.85%. Your system's requirement is to have downtime less than 10 hours per year. What does the availability of your software need to be? Assume that the server platforms include disk, network, CPU...everything except the software.

Answer:

System Availability $\geq$ 99.88% *(10 hours per year)*

System Availability = Software Availability * Server Platform Availability

With average server availability, the Software Availability = 99.88/99.85, which is greater than 1, which is impossible. With the best platform, Software Availability = 99.88/99.9 = 99.98% available, which is 1.2 hours per year. Said another way, if you can only have 10 hours of outage, and the hardware takes X hours, your software can only be done $10 - X$.

Availability is primarily a user metric. It is how the users see the system, not how IT sees the system. IT organizations tend to look at the availability from the inside out, that is, looking at the individual components (servers, networks). Availability needs to be viewed from the outside in, as the users see the systems.

9.2.1 Availability Factors

The two factors that impact availability are:

Frequency of outages (MTTF)
Duration of outage (MTTR)

that is, how often the system goes down, and how long it takes to bring it back up. To improve availability, you need to work both the number and duration of the outages. Remember that if the MTTR approaches 0 in duration, the availability approaches 100% even if the MTTF is once per hour.

The length of the outage is impacted by a number of factors, which are frequently not considered by software development teams.

- *System Complexity*: Complicated systems take longer to start and restart, which makes the outages longer.
- *Problem Severity*: Usually, the more severe the problem, the more time it takes to fully resolve and restore the system, including lost data or lost work.
- *Support Personnel Availability*: If the outage occurs after hours and support personnel are required, the length of outage includes the time it takes to find the on-call personnel, get them online (either via a secured network or phys- ically at the data center), and allow them to diagnose and fix the problem.
- *Other Miscellaneous Factors*: There can be a variety of these, such as a third party supplier who can't fix the part quickly enough, or potentially, you cannot take the system offline to fix your application because other applications are running on the server.

Here are some examples.

- If the typical time between failures is 48 hours, and the typical time the system is down is 10 minutes, what is the availability if it takes 2 hours to get the right person to get the system back up?
- Availability $= 48/[48 + (2 + 10/60)] = 0.957 = 95.7\%$ versus 99.6% without the 2 hours to get the right person. Note how good performance drops to average or poor performance because you cannot get support person- nel instantaneously.
- Your system averages 10 outages every 100 hours. Ninety percent of the outages are 5 minutes each and 10% of the outages are 2 hours each. Your availability is poor—97.75%. You analyze the long outages and determine that they have a complex and lengthy recovery process. You also determine that you can improve the error handling process for these outages so that the recovery is simplified and the outage duration will be reduced to 15 minutes. What would be the impact of the improvement on availability? Overall

outage duration for 100 hours is reduced from 2.75 hours to 1 hour. The availability would increase to 99.00%.

9.2.2 Outage Scope

To improve system availability, you want to reduce both the scope and severity of the outages. One of the best fault-tolerant design concepts is that of "degraded mode," that is, designing your system so that it continues to process and function as a system even when some individual parts may be unavailable. For example, you could partition the database, perhaps by state, so that even if a part of the database is corrupted and needs to be restored (such as not having access to any of the customer databases for customers in New Jersey), the rest of the system continues to function.

9.2.3 Complexities in Measuring Availability

Measuring availability may seem pretty simple, but let's try an example that illustrates some of the complexities. How would you measure availability for a banking system in which the server and networks are up 100%, except for scheduled maintenance, which is from 2 a.m. to 3 a.m. on Sunday mornings, and $\sim$50% of the ATM machines fail $\sim$1 per month, and it takes a day to fix each one? We have complexities of scheduled versus unscheduled downtime, and system versus end terminal availability.

There are two different criteria for availability, based on how we want to count scheduled and planned outages. For continuous availability, the system or application is to be available 7×24 with no outages [5]. For high availability, the system or application is to be available during the committed hours of availability with no unplanned or unscheduled outages. The continuous availability definition is much stricter than the high availability definition. As an example, consider if during a month, there were 9 hours of outage due to a hard disk crash and 15 hours due to preventive maintenance. The achieved availability would be

$$\text{Continuous Availability} = (720 - 15 - 9)/720 = 96.7\%$$
$$\text{High Availability} = (720 - 15 - 9)/(720 - 15) = 98.7\%$$

But what about our ATM example? How should we count the availability of the individual clients? A typical way of reporting would be to separate out the "system" availability (meaning servers and network) and the end-client availability. From the user and business viewpoint, the end-client availability is what really matters. For this example,

System Availability:

$$\text{Continuous Availability} = 716/720 = 0.9944 = 99.44\%$$
$$\text{High Availability} = 100\%$$

Average End-Client Availability:

$$\text{Continuous Availability} = [720 - (24 * 0.5)]/720 * (\text{System-CA})$$
$$= 0.9833 * 0.9944 = 0.9778 = 97.78\%$$
$$\text{High Availability} = [720 - (24 * 0.5)/720] * (\text{System-HA})$$
$$= 0.9833 * 1 = 98.33\%$$

Degraded mode operations also complicate the availability calculations. A typical reporting method is to be explicit and report the portions that are fully operational and partially degraded, such as

For the past month, 99% availability except for degraded mode for 10 hours, which impacted 4% of the system.

Alternatively, you can define an "Effective Availability" metric, which takes into account the degraded mode, such as

$$\text{Effective Availability} = (710/720) * 0.99 + (10/720) * (0.04 * 0 + 0.96 * 1)^{\dagger}$$
$$= 0.976 + 0.013 = 0.989 = 98.9\%$$

9.2.4 Software Rejuvenation

There are a variety of techniques to improve the availability of software, such as fault tolerance, save/restore parallelism, "safe libraries," active fault detection, isolation and partitioning (for degraded modes), increased boot speeds, and concurrent release and fix upgrades. One fault-tolerant technique that we feel warrants more attention is *software rejuvenation*, which has been used successfully in Lucent, IBM, and Sun products (and probably others). Software rejuvenation cleans up the internal state of the system to prevent subsequent failures or performance degradation.

Software rejuvenation is based on two observations:

1. Software ages in operation, much like hardware. But instead of wearing out as hardware does, the software can be refreshed, or rejuvenated, by restoring it to its initial state.
2. The primary causes of failures in the field are latent and (pseudo)nondeterministic faults that are difficult to reproduce. They are caused by external event timing, aging, or other unforeseen events. Frequently, these failures can be cleared by rerunning the process [6].

---

†In this equation, the last factor means that for the 10 (out of 720) hours, 4% of the system was unavailability (0) and 96 was available (1.0).

Rejuvenation works when the software reliability decreases over time. This is not the reliability growth model, which assumes reliability increases over time due to bug fixes.

9.2.4.1 *Software Aging*   Software aging is the deterioration in the availability of system resources, data corruption, or numerical error accumulation. Potential fault conditions gradually accumulate over time, leading to either performance degradation or transient failures, or both.

Some of the frequent culprits of aging are memory leaks, unreleased file locks, hanging threads, data corruption, storage space fragmentation, and accumulation of round-off errors. We all know systems subject to aging, such as the Patriot Missile System (round-off errors), Windows 95 (many issues), and even the 2004 Mars Rover (data file overwrites).

9.2.4.2 *Classification of Faults*   It can help our thinking if we classify faults as follows:

- *Bohrbugs*: Faults that should be found in testing that represent design/coding/ requirement errors.
- *Heisenbugs*: Temporary internal faults, intermittent bugs, difficult to find and reproduce, caused by permanent design errors. Examples include failures caused by race conditions and defects in exception handling and overload handling.
- *Senilitybugs*: Faults caused by software aging and appearing during the ongoing execution of the system. Examples include memory leaks and unreleased file locks.

Today, with our improvements in software processes and testing, after a system stabilizes in the field, the predominant faults are Heisenbugs and Senilitybugs [7]. Heisenbugs can be handled through fault tolerance and fault management techniques. Senilitybugs can be prevented through software rejuvenation techniques.

9.2.4.3 *Software Rejuvenation Techniques*   Software rejuvenation is a proactive fault management technique aimed at cleaning up the system's internal state to prevent the occurrence of more severe crashes or failures in the future. The methods of software rejuvenation are:

- System restarts
- System cleanups (partial rejuvenation)
- Application/process restart (partial rejuvenation)
- Node/application failover (in a cluster system)

The concept of software rejuvenation was invented by Bernstein at Bell Labs in the 1970s, generalized by Kintala in the 1980s, and successfully implemented in Lucent Billing and Switching Systems in the 1990s.

System restarts have been called the sledgehammer approach to rejuvenation. Yet as Candea and Fox [7] point out, restarts (1) return the system to its initial state, which is usually the most tested and most reliable; (2) are a high-confidence restoration technique; and (3) are a known and tested procedure.

Restarts for rejuvenation can occur either on a regularly scheduled basis (such as once every night at 2 a.m.) or as needed, triggered by the monitoring of resource exhaustion or performance degradation. Controlled and scheduled reboots have the advantages over crashes of shorter recovery outages and occurring in more favorable time periods.

System cleanups are processes that execute in the background, which monitor the ongoing resource consumption and clean up the internal state. Releasing file locks, garbage collection, flushing operating system kernel tables, and killing zombie processes are all examples of system cleanups. This technique was used successfully in Lucent Switching Systems.

Application and process restarts are rejuvenations on a smaller scale. The architecture and design of the system must facilitate such restarts, such as the architecture described by Candea and Fox [7]. An example of the use of this technique is in the Apache Web Server, which has a controlling process and a handler process. The controlling process monitors the handler process, determines when it has consumed too many resources, then stops it and starts a new handler process [8].

Node or application failover is possible in cluster systems, when you have multiple machines working together. In a cluster, during lightly loaded times, you transfer the load from one of the machines and reboot it, rejuvenating the software on that machine without causing any loss of availability. IBM successfully combined this approach with application restarts [8].

9.2.4.4 *Impact of Rejuvenation on Availability*   The impact of rejuvenation on availability is difficult to model and highly dependent on the implementation. One question is how frequently you should rejuvenate and should you rejuvenate based on a schedule or system triggers (e.g., monitoring the status of resources).

For clustered systems, IBM's analytical models for a single spare showed a 25% improvement in availability when the rejuvenations were done on a regularly scheduled basis, and a 60% improvement when the rejuvenations were triggered by monitoring resource consumption. When they changed the model to dual sparing, such as in an 8/2 configuration (e.g., an 8 node cluster that can tolerate at most 2 node failures), it resulted in a 98% improvement with regularly (and frequently) scheduled rejuvenations and an 85% improvement for triggered rejuvenations [9].

EXERCISE: You have a system that works well for one week, then, inevitably, crashes. In fact, you measure the availability for the first week and it really is 100%. Once day 8 starts, it fails in 15 minutes. You decide to schedule a rejuvenation reboot every weekend at 2 a.m. The rejuvenation takes 6 minutes. Crash recoveries take 30 minutes. Compare the availability for the two scenarios.

Answer:

Rejuvenation scenario: Availability $= (7*24 - 0.1)/7*24 = 0.9994$

Crash scenario: Availability $= (7*24 + 0.25 - 0.5)/(7*24 + 0.25) = 0.9970$

If the rejuvenation took place during scheduled preventive maintenance:

$$\text{Availability} = 100\%$$

If the rejuvenation was "soft rejuvenation," that is, it was able to take place in background, causing no outage:

$$\text{Availability} = 100\%$$

EXERCISE: You are able to implement a soft rejuvenation in your system, which requires no downtime and changes the MTBF from 10 days to 100 days. Your MTTR after a crash is 1 hour. What impact did the soft rejuvenation have on the availability?

Answer:

$$\text{Availability Without Rejuvenation} = 10/(10 + 1/24) = 0.9958 = 99.58\%$$

$$\text{Availability with Soft Rejuvenation} = 100/(100 + 1/24) = 0.9995 = 99.95\%$$

$$\text{Impact} = 99.95 - 99.58 = 0.37\%$$

For most rejuvenation implementations, custom models and/or measurements will be required to predict and measure the rejuvenation's impact.

Fault injection is the typical method of testing the effectiveness of software rejuvenation, since you then know which faults you expect to cause failures, and you can verify if the rejuvenations prevent those failures.

9.3 SUMMARY

Response time and availability are key metrics for many systems. Performance on these measures can make the difference between users loving or hating a system and, in a few cases, businesses that thrive or struggle.

For response time, users have expectations of response time of 2 seconds or less for trivial transactions, of 7 seconds or less for average transactions, and percent-complete indicators for long-running transactions. Response time needs to be measured from the user perspective and includes application, system, and communications latencies.

By definition, there are only two factors that impact availability: outage frequency and outage duration. Both factors need to be considered in system design, since only through design (rather than testing and bug fixing) can high availability be achieved. Using today's technologies, we typically find the defects that can be found in system testing are caused by design, coding, and requirements errors. We typically do not find all of the faults related to external event timing, race conditions, unforeseen events, and system aging. Fault tolerance is required to handle these kinds of faults. Software rejuvenation, which involves either full or partial system restarts, is an under-utilized fault-tolerant technique that successfully handles most of these types of faults.

PROBLEMS

9.1 You design a beautiful website selling widgets. The initial page has streaming video and more . . . it actually is 1 MB of data. You launch your website, and although you have a good initial hit rate, you also have a high rate of abandonment. What is the reason? If many of your target customers use 128 KB lines, what is the maximum amount of data you should have on each page?

9.2 You average 10 outages per month, with an average restore time of 30 minutes. You have the three alternatives below. Which is the best to implement from an availability standpoint?
  • Improve your testing process, which you believe will cause an eventual reduction in outages by 2 per month.
  • Improve your boot speeds so that outages are 25 minutes instead of 30.
  • Implement rejuvenations once per day to reduce the outages by 4 per month, but each rejuvenation causes 1 minute of unavailability.

9.3 Describe a Heisenbug or Senilitybug you have had in your own code. What would have been the impact of rejuvenation on this bug?

9.4 Your system has:
  • 1 outage per month for preventive maintenance (PM) (6 hours per outage)
  • 1 outage every 6 months installing the new release (12 hours per outage)
  • 5 outages per week from defects (1 minute per outage)

Both the preventive maintenance and the release upgrades are scheduled in the off-hours of the system. The outages from defects occur in prime time. What is the availability, measured from the continuous and high-availability definitions? Which type of outage should you focus on to improve the continuous availability? The high availability?

9.5 Your system is required to have an availability of 99.8%. You have built it primarily from five commercial software components that each have a MTTF of 2 years. The MTTR of each is 2 hours. They are all required for the system to function. What is the availability of these components? What is the availability requirement for the code that you write?

PROJECT

9.1 Consider the theater ticket reservation system, with the architecture shown in Figure 9.5. You have built this system, and now you are responsible for the operation. Your customer is quite happy with the system, except for the availability and, occasionally, the response time. You've been in operation for 10 weeks. To date, the availability of the system components have been:

- Hardware: 99.9%—scheduled maintenance
- Software: 99.8 %—software problems
- External credit card verification and billing system: 99.0%—unscheduled, unplanned

The credit card system is required on only 30% of all transactions, and the implementation allows the other transactions and the system to work even if the credit card system is unavailable.

(a) Calculate the system's continuous availability percentage.

(b) What would be the change in availability if you implement a hot backup system to reduce the scheduled maintenance time by 90%?

(c) You know you need to improve the credit card vendor availability. You search hard to find another credit card system vendor but can only find one whose availability is much worse (80%). Still, you consider implementing it in addition to the first; that is, it is called if the first is unavailable. What would be the savings if you implemented this plan?

(d) If you implement both improvement plans, what is the projected availability of the system?

(e) How might you use the concept of degraded mode to further improve the effective availability?

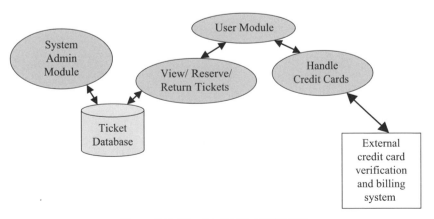

Figure 9.5. *Theater tickets architecture.*

(f) For the response time, the only problem seems to be that the credit card system responds either very quickly (<1 second) or very slowly (15–20 seconds). What should you do to improve your user satisfaction with the response time?

REFERENCES

[1] R. B. Miller, "Response time in man-computer conversational transactions," *Proceedings AFIPS Fall Joint Computer Conference*, **33**: 267–277 (1968).

[2] B. A. Myers, "The importance of percent-done progress indicators for computer–human interfaces," in *Proceedings ACM CHI'85 Conference*, San Francisco, CA, 14–18 April, 1985, pp. 11–17.

[3] Zona Research, The Need for Speed II, 2001.

[4] A. King, http://www.websiteoptimization.com/speed/1/. Accessed Mar. 20, 2005.

[5] F. Piedad and M. Hawkings, *High Availability*, Prentice Hall PTR, Upper Saddle River, NJ, 2001.

[6] J. Gray, "Why do computers stop and what can be done about it?" June 1985.

[7] G. Candea and A. Fox, "Designing for high availability and measurability," July 2001. Available from http://www.stanford.edu/~candea/papers/HA_measurability/HA_measurability.ps. Accessed Apr. 1, 2005.

[8] V. Castelli, R. Harper, P. Heidelberger, S. Hunter, K. Trivedi, K. Vaidyanathn, and W. Zeggert, "Proactive management of software aging," *IBM Systems Journal* **45**(2): 312–332 (2001).

[9] Y. Huang, C. Kintala, N. Kolettis, and N. D. Fulton, "Software rejuvenation: analysis, module and applications," *Proceedings of the 25th Symposium on Fault Tolerant Computer Systems*, Pasadena, CA, June 1995.

10

Measuring Progress

If you do not change direction, you may end up where you are heading.
—Lao Tzu

Are we there yet?
—Every kid to parents on a long car trip

How's the release going?
—Every software manager to every developer and tester

To ensure the success of any project,[1] it is important to know as the project progresses exactly where you are with respect to the project's objectives. Effectively monitoring progress allows course corrections and enables the project team to more effectively manage both internal and external customer expectations. This is especially critical in software projects given the creative and often exploratory nature of the work.

In this chapter, we provide a number of mechanisms and metrics that can be used to measure progress.[2] These are called *in-process metrics*. The five specific types

---

[1] And to help reduce your stress when the software release you are working on is having problems and your boss is in your office asking when you will be done . . . .

[2] We will not say any more about financial metrics in this chapter. In Chapter 12 we cover tracking progress toward the project's financial goals.

Software Measurement and Estimation, by Linda M. Laird and M. Carol Brennan
Copyright © 2006 John Wiley & Sons, Inc.

that are most applicable to software projects are:

1. Project milestones[3]
2. Code integration
3. Testing progress
4. Defect discovery and closure
5. Process effectiveness

The first type, project milestones, covers the life of the project including all phases and activities. In a software project, often the most time consuming and resource intensive phases are the code development and testing phases. For this reason, we have included in-process metric types 2 and 3 for more detailed discussion.[4] Building on what we discussed in Chapter 7, we talk about measuring defect discovery and closure as both a measure of progress and as an in-process predictor for software quality in the field. Finally, we discuss how process effectiveness influences our analysis of all these metrics and how we can define in-process metrics for this critical area.

10.1 PROJECT MILESTONES

In order to reach your goal of delivering software, the most important step in launching any project is to have a clearly defined project plan, which contains your strategy to meet your delivery goal.[5] That plan should be detailed enough to facilitate assessment of the progress of the project along the way. The best way is to include measurable milestones, which are tracked and reviewed throughout the life of the project. Common practice is to define milestones at two week intervals. The milestones you select, however, will depend on a number of factors including the following:

- Development methodology (i.e., each development methodology, be it waterfall, agile, spiral, or custom, will have its own work steps with its own timing)

---

[3]Calling "project milestones" an in-process metric is a bit of a misnomer. A milestone is not a metric, but rather a point in time when a project activity should occur. Measuring progress against milestones, however, can give a good view of the in-process progress being made. For that reason, we are taking poetic license and including a discussion of this critical monitoring mechanism here. We could create a true in-process metric from milestones if we wanted to though, such as percentage of milestones completed on schedule.

[4]It is essential to determine in-process metrics for all major phases of the development life cycle. Once you have determined the development model that you will be using, make sure your in-process metrics plan spans the entire cycle. For example, for earlier requirements and design phases in a waterfall model, you might select a metric on number of requirements and design reviews held.

[5]We recognize that there are research and exploratory projects as well as those with more well-defined requirements and constraints. Even with research projects, you need to have some idea where you want to go, even if it changes along the way. Project plans can and should be kept up to date with the changing needs and realities of the project.

- Project management methodology (the level of detail of what project managers call the Work Breakdown Structure will determine whether a daily, weekly, or monthly milestone definition makes sense)
- Project risk level (the higher the risk, the more closely/frequently you need to monitor progress)
- Experience and maturity of the team (less experienced teams may need more frequent and perhaps more detailed monitoring to allow for timely correction of any missteps)
- Comfort level and managerial style of the management team (e.g., is there a micromanager in the bunch?)

With those considerations in mind, the best way to define the milestones is to act **SMART**. In other words, define milestones that are

- **S**pecific (they are clearly defined),
- **M**easurable (you can tell if/when they are achieved),
- **A**chievable (it is reasonable to expect that they can be achieved),
- **R**elevant (they directly affect the achievement of project objectives), and
- **T**ime based (they fit in specific spots on the project time line).

Let us look at an example. Assuming we are going to follow a waterfall development model, we would want to define milestones in the major development life cycle areas of Requirements, Architecture, Design, Coding, Integration, Testing, and Cutover. Looking at the Requirements area, we might include milestones as shown in Table 10.1.

TABLE 10.1   Requirements Phase Milestones

Milestone	Due Date
Draft requirements available for review	6/1/06
Internal requirement review held for development/ testing staff	6/8/06
Requirements updated and delivered to customer for concurrence	6/15/06
Customer concurrence obtained	6/25/06
Final requirements published and put under formal change control	6/30/06

Let us look at these milestones and ensure they are SMART.

- Specific: We would add to each milestone the owner[6] to increase the specificity of that milestone.

---

[6]Having a specific person responsible for each activity and result is crucial. A successful manager we know used to say, "One job, one neck." It may sound harsh, but it works.

- Measurable: Each one has a measurable/desirable event associated with it. It must be clear whether or not each milestone was actually met. For example, was the draft published? Was the review meeting actually held?
- Achievable: If we have based our intervals on like-project history, previous projects with this customer, a clear understanding of both resource allocation and this project's needs, then we can view these milestones as achievable.
- Relevant: The clear understanding of what we are agreeing to build by both the internal team and the customer is absolutely critical to achieving successful project delivery and ultimate customer satisfaction.
- Time based: We have defined an actual date for each milestone.

One thing to keep in mind when you look at development phases is that the longer the phase, the more intermediate milestones you want to define. It is just common sense that you do not want to leave large chunks of time without progress visibility.

There are many project management tools[7] that allow you to capture the complete set of milestones you define. Typically, they will produce a number of views of the schedule including Gantt chart format. Figure 10.1 provides an extract from one such project milestone chart.

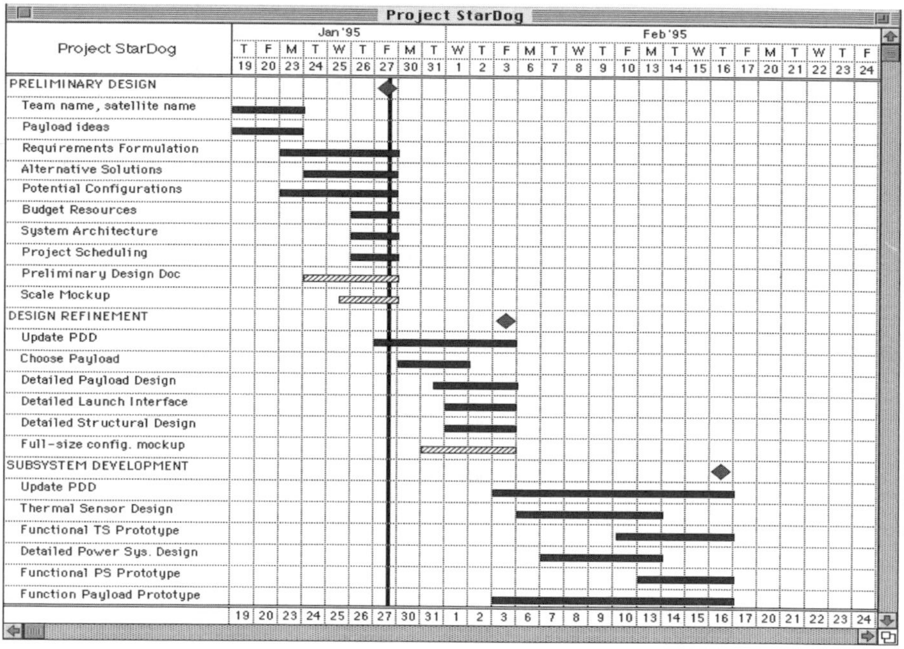

Figure 10.1. Gantt chart.

One advantage of defining SMART milestones is that they can be used as "gates" for our software project. Gates are simply specific points in the project with specific

[7]Microsoft Project and Sciforma PS8 are two such tools.

criteria that must be achieved in order to move on. Frequently, they are a set of key milestones. Establishing gates from milestones is one way of increasing the visibility and focus on intermediate progress that is critical to ultimate project completion and success. Often failure to meet a gate will trigger reassignment of resources to ensure the gate is quickly met while delaying the start of subsequent activities to avoid costly rework. Some examples of possible milestone gates are:

- Business case reviewed and approved by senior management: we will need to know it is OK to spend money on this project before we do.
- Software design reviewed and approved by development team: we will want to know the big picture before we start writing the code.
- Code reviews passed for all critical code: we will want to have as many defects found and corrected via this technique before beginning potentially expensive formal testing of the code.
- Formal test plan fully executed and target level of success achieved: we will need to make sure the software will meet customer and contractual expectations before we deliver it.

Whether used as gates or not, SMART milestones will be the foundation for effective in-process software project monitoring.

10.2 CODE INTEGRATION

Code integration is the phase of the software life cycle where the actual coding, unit testing, and integration of code into system libraries destined for formal system testing takes place. For most software projects, code integration is not one single event but rather a series of integration events as more and more features become ready for inclusion in the code base. With each integration step, the functionality of the system moves closer to full feature capability. Each integration step also, however, introduces potentially additional defects, both in the newly delivered code and the previously integrated code. Defects require software changes and thereby additional code creation and integration. Given the criticality of this fundamental activity, we will want to have reliable visibility into our progress during this phase.

In less mature organizations, you might see something called "percent complete" as the in-process metric used for the code integration phase (as well as for other phases). Depending on how this is defined and calculated, this metric can be very misleading. At worst, if it is based on a subjective assessment by developers, you (and the developers themselves) can very easily be misled as to the real status. Without hard measurement, what will it mean to say "coding is 80% complete"? Any milestones based on this metric will certainly not be SMART given the absence of a true "M." At best, if this metric is based on comparing measured work effort to estimated work effort, percent complete milestones may be Measurable by using this metric, but they may not be highly Relevant to our code

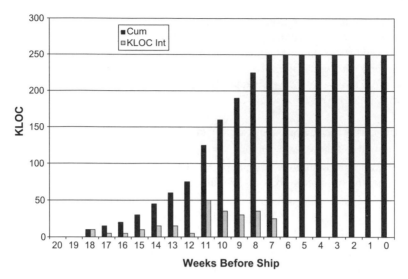

Figure 10.2. Code integration.

integration goals. Capturing work effort will tell us a great deal about what we have spent from a budget perspective, but it will tell us nothing about the actual code produced or coding progress made.

With that in mind, we want a measurement based on what we can observe about the code being created. The measurement we have chosen is the *lines of code* (typically KLOC) *turned over to integration*, or the *code integration metric* [1]. This is a count of the actual number of lines of code that have been delivered from unit testing to the integration libraries and now require formal change requests for any code updates. To understand whether the value of this metric at any point in time reflects good or bad progress, we will need to understand the acceptable value for it over time. We will call this acceptable value the expected integration pattern. For most organizations and software projects, the typical cumulative code integration pattern takes the shape of an S-curve. See Figure 10.2 for how this S-curve might look.

Most organizations will have patterns of both successful and unsuccessful code integrations. The particular pattern may vary with development methodology used, development platform, and/or experience of the development team. It is worth noting that the earlier integration occurs, the lower the risk is to the project. Early integration gives more time to adequately test a stable system. Figure 10.3 shows the code integration pattern for two different projects.

You can see from the picture that Project 1 will be less risky from a code stability perspective given that complete integration occurs earlier in the schedule.

To effectively use the code integration metric for your project, you will need to:

1. Select a successful code integration pattern that best matches your project's particulars. You might use one from a completed similar project or, perhaps, from a successfully delivered earlier release of your own product.

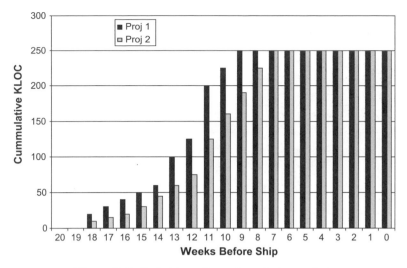

Figure 10.3. Code integration patterns for two projects.

2. Establish, based on the selected pattern, the expected code integration plan for your project.[8] This gives you the objective for this metric over time.
3. Track actual code integration progress during the coding phase and compare to the plan's expected values.
4. Take appropriate action when actuals deviate from the plan.[9]

Use of a code integration metric would provide the "M" for a SMART milestone of code integration complete for the coding phase of the development schedule.

10.3 TESTING PROGRESS

Formal testing is one of the most easily observed and measured stages of the development life cycle. Assessing progress will be based on the test plan that is established before testing begins. Test plans may vary in terms of detail and format, but must always cover what tests will be run during the testing phase. During the actual testing we can clearly observe how many test cases have been executed and how many have passed (i.e., gotten the intended results). This gives us two metrics that we can track:

1. Number of test cases executed over time (by day or week, depending on the project)

---

[8]An added benefit of looking at possible code integration patterns early in the planning stages is that you will get a better sense whether the development plan being considered is actually achievable.

[9]As with many metrics, there may be a range of acceptable values for the code integration metric at any point in time. Action would then need to be taken when actual performance was outside the upper or lower control limits that define the acceptable range.

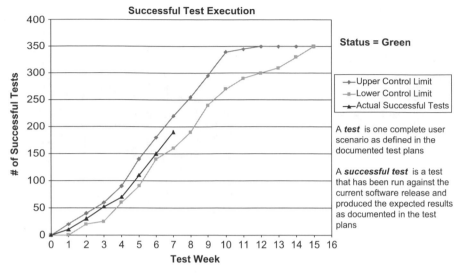

Figure 10.4. *Testing progress chart.*

2. Number of test cases that have successfully passed over time (using the same interval as above)

The test plan should provide the objectives for these metrics. We can then compare our actual data to objectives to determine whether or not our progress is on track. Figure 10.4 provides an example of how the second metric, test cases passed, could be tracked.

Note that we have identified the control range of acceptable values. We would have in all likelihood established that range based on previous performance of some like project (perhaps even an earlier release of the same product). Actual performance outside this range would require action. We could plot the number of test cases executed metric either on the same chart or a separate chart. These two in-process testing metrics provide the "M" for SMART testing milestones such as "50% of test cases executed" and "50% of test cases passed."

10.4 DEFECTS DISCOVERY AND CLOSURE

As we saw in Chapter 7, one of the most basic and telling measurable items in software is a defect. Recall that a defect is a deviation of the code from its requirements. The measurement of defect discovery (sometimes called "arrival") and closure ("departure") prior to software delivery to the customer provides some of the most powerful in-process metrics, shedding light on both quality and schedule progress.

10.4.1   Defect Discovery

Chapter 7 provided us with several methods of predicting our defect discovery pattern (e.g., a Rayleigh curve). This expected pattern can be used to establish or validate project schedules and resource allocation.[10] We can also base in-process metrics on this prediction. For example, if we predicted a particular Rayleigh pattern for the project with an associated S-curve during formal testing, we would track our actual performance (i.e., our defect discovery) against these patterns. If we see our performance is outside the control bounds for these curves, we would know that further analysis and, in all likelihood, corrective action were required. For example, seeing a peak in the Rayleigh discovery curve that is lower and earlier than our prediction would potentially be good news, while a higher than expected peak or one that happens later in the schedule could mean trouble.

Let us look at an example that makes use of historical data (from a similar project) and an established code integration plan to define a defect discovery plan.

Historical data: Our defect insertion rate has been 1 defect per KLOC.[11] Our defect discovery typically follows a pattern of 30% in week 1 after code turnover, 35% in week 2, 20% in week 3, 10% in week 4, and 5% in week 5.

Assume we have determined our code integration plan as shown in Figure 10.5. With the above information, we can now construct a defect discovery

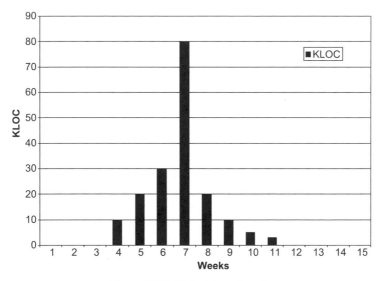

Figure 10.5. Code integration plan.

[10]Finding and correcting defects is one of the most time and budget consuming parts of any software project. Schedules and budgets will be created based on some expectation of the level of defect discovery and correction that will be seen on this project. Using Raleigh curves can provide a clear structure and basis for making those estimates.

[11]We have chosen 1 defect per KLOC to make the math easier. A more realistic defect rate would be higher.

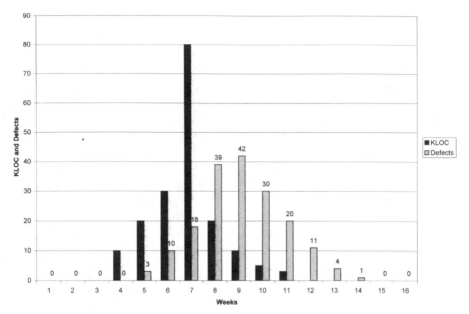

Figure 10.6. *Code integration plan and defect discovery plan.*

plan [2].[12] Our defect injection history of one injection defect per KLOC tells us that we expect to have 10 defects in the first 10 KLOC turned over, 20 defects in the second turnover, and so on. We also know that we expect to discover 35% of those first 10 defects (i.e., 3 defects) in the first week after that code is turned over, 35% (let us round that to 4 defects) in the second week after that first 10 KLOC is turned over, and so on. We will discover 30% of the 20 defects (6 defects) in the second code set in the first week after that code turnover, and so on. We can map that discovery plan on our code integration graph (see Figure 10.6) to get a complete view.

We created these plans based upon historical averages. It is easy to improve it significantly by adding in control limits, based upon standard deviations, which we highly recommend. Once we have our code discovery plan (with or without control limits), we would track our actuals against it and investigate any significant deviations from plan. We would also adjust our defect discovery expectations if/when changes to the code integration plan were made.

10.4.2   Defect Closure

We also saw in Chapter 7 that looking at defect closure, not just discovery, is important as well. Keeping track of in-process measurements of defect closure gives us

---

[12]This is a simplified discovery plan that makes the arithmetic easier while still illustrating the concept. Actual plans tend to span longer time periods and be more complex.

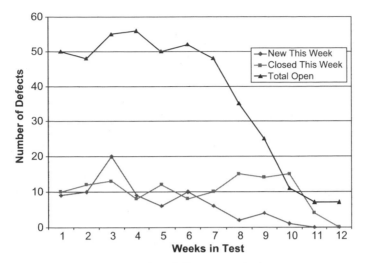

Figure 10.7. *Defect status chart.*

both a view of the effectiveness of the "development engine" in repairing code and an important measurement in the quality of the code itself at any point in time. Let us take another look at a defect status chart. Figure 10.7 shows us, by week in formal testing, how many defects have been newly opened, how many have been closed, and how many total defects remain open.

As we progress through the latter part of the testing cycle, we should be closing defects faster than we are opening new ones. In other words, our development engine should be able to effectively turn around fixes, reducing the backlog[13] of open defects and driving the quality of the code to ship-readiness. Indeed, Figure 10.7 is a chart that shows the hoped for trends.

Often, there will be a threshold set for the size and makeup of any defect backlog that must be reached before the software is deemed ready for shipment to the customer. This may be in terms of a defect removal efficiency (DRE) metric coupled with acceptable level of backlog defect severity. For example, defect ship criteria might include the following:

- Defect removal efficiency, based on actual defect discovery pattern, of 90% achieved
- No high-severity defects remaining in the backlog

The threshold for ship quality should be set at the start of the project with customer intended usage and quality expectations in mind. As you can imagine, the quality threshold for a life-critical software application (e.g., space shuttle software,

---

[13]Backlog is the number of defects that remain open (i.e., unfixed) at any point in time.

patient monitoring software) is much more stringent than for software intended for automation of back-office business functions.[14]

You can combine the actual defect discovery curve with the actual closure capability of the development engine (i.e., how many defects can be closed by the assigned staff per day) to see when you will reach the required quality threshold for shipment to the customer. If that date is beyond the committed ship date, then adjustments to either project resources (i.e., put more "defect fixers" on the project) or customer expectations (i.e., delaying shipment or shipping with lower quality) should be pursued.

Let us see how this might work by building on our earlier example. We have our code integration plan and defect discovery plan as shown in Figure 10.6. We then need an estimate for "fix productivity," say, 5 defects closed per week per programmer assigned to defect fixing.[15] If we know how many programmers (or percent of our programmer's time) we are assigning to fixing defects, we can project how our defect backlog will decline over time. To complete our example, let us say that we have 6 programmers and the percent of their time each week devoted to bug fixing will be 20% of all 6 for two weeks beginning 2 full weeks after the first code turnover (that will be week 7), 50% for the next 2 weeks, 80% for the next 2 weeks, and 100% for the remaining weeks. This would mean that our "development engine" could fix 6 defects the second week after code turnover (20% of 6 programmers = 1.2 "fix programmers"; 1.2 fix programmers can fix 6 defects in that week), 6 defects the third week, and so on. On any given week, the backlog is simply the total discovered defects minus the total fixed defects. We have shown all of this data in Figure 10.8.

We can see that if our actual performance stays close to this projection, we will have made all fixes and have a zero backlog by week 16 of the project. As with any of our projections, we will want to compare our actual performance each week and make adjustments as needed when our performance differs or any of our assumptions (like available programmer time or defects discovered) changes.

10.5 PROCESS EFFECTIVENESS

There is an additional area that can greatly affect how we interpret the in-process metrics we have already mentioned. That area is process effectiveness. When we are deciding on like projects for both initial planning and in-process comparison, there is an underlying expectation about how effectively our development processes will be executed. These expectations will be reflected in the patterns and objectives we set for our metrics. If we know at the start of the project that the effectiveness of

---

[14]In other words, *quality* is not an absolute concept. Quality is in the eye of the beholder, namely, the customer. Make sure you understand what you sold your customer and the associated expectations you set for quality levels.

[15]Again we have chosen a number to simplify the example. In practice you would want to choose a number that reflects the historical performance of your team or one from an appropriate benchmark.

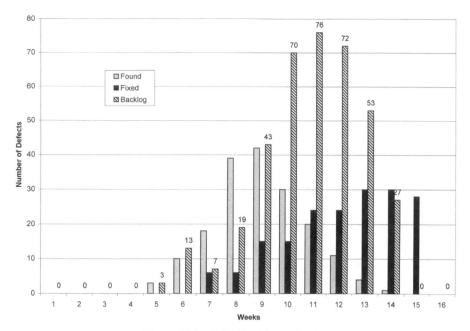

Figure 10.8. *Defect backlog projection.*

any of our processes will deviate from our comparison project(s), we can adjust our plans and metrics accordingly. Let us take our defect removal efficiency (DRE) metric as an example. DRE is based on our defect discovery pattern. That measure encompasses all defect discovery processes. In this example, if we are introducing a new mechanized tool to aid in code inspection, we can reasonably expect the inspection process to be more effective. We would need to alter our expectations about defect discovery accordingly. In other words, the defect injection rate is not expected to change, but the ability to discover defects earlier will have improved. This would result in differences in our defect discovery curve.

There can certainly be deviations in the effectiveness of our process execution that we will not be able to predict beforehand. It is beneficial, therefore, to introduce in-process *process effectiveness* metrics that can be used in conjunction with our other metrics. These will allow us to better understand when corrective action needs to be taken. One example would be an inspection-effectiveness metric.[16] We could define this to be

$$(\text{Inspection Hours})/(\text{Inspection Object Size})$$

where Inspection Hours = total number of staff hours spent in inspection and Inspection Object Size = KLOC for code, function points for requirements and designs.

---

[16]We might more accurately call this metric "inspection intensity." It is, however, one reasonable proxy for how effectively the inspection process was executed.

Based on history or like projects, we would have an objective for this metric that would equate to well-executed inspections (i.e., it would reflect reasonable diligence in inspection and support the selected defect discovery Rayleigh curve).

We could then use this metric in conjunction with our defect discovery metric to determine whether or not we are still "on plan." Let us look at several scenarios.

Scenario 1: Defect rate is lower than expected, but our code inspection effectiveness is meeting or beating the objective. An appropriate reaction would be: "Steady as she goes . . . software quality may be better than expected. . .no action needed at this time."

Scenario 2: Defect rate is lower than expected and we see that our code inspection effectiveness is also below objective. An appropriate reaction would be: "Defects are probably slipping through . . . let us take action by reinspecting or beefing up subsequent defect detection efforts . . . adjustment of resources needed."

Scenario 3: Defects are higher than expected and we see that our code inspection effectiveness is beating the objective. An appropriate reaction would be: "We are probably finding defects earlier due to better inspections . . . code quality is probably OK . . . keep an eye on subsequent phases to verify."

Scenario 4: Defects are higher than expected and we see that our inspection effectiveness is below the objective. An appropriate reaction would be: "Alert! . . . code quality is suspect . . . launch remedial quality efforts immediately . . . revisit schedule and budget."[17]

As the above scenarios illustrate, complementing our product and project in-process metrics with process effectiveness metrics will lead to a clearer understanding of project progress and better decisions on the need for corrective action. Effectiveness measures (beyond DRE) should be defined for all major processes in your chosen development model. For example, an effectiveness metric for a Unit Test or Component Test process might be code coverage (percentage of total code paths exercised by the tests). An effectiveness metric for system test could be requirements coverage or tests/KLOC or test/FP. Whatever the process, define a metric that will reflect how effectively that process is being executed.

10.6 SUMMARY

Software projects are inherently risky endeavors. Being able to accurately gauge your progress along the way is critical to successful completion. In this chapter we have provided five recommendations for in-process metrics:

1. Define SMART milestones covering the entire development life cycle.
2. Establish a code integration metric and a target code integration pattern.

[17]"Developers, be ready for some serious micromanagement . . . ."

3. Establish testing metrics and objectives.
4. Define your expected defect discovery and closure patterns and monitor your defect backlog.
5. Establish process effectiveness measures and objectives for all major phases of the life cycle.

Once you have done the above, track all actual results, compare to objectives, and take action as needed when objectives are not met.

PROBLEMS

10.1 Define possible milestones for the coding/unit testing phase of a waterfall development project.

10.2 Assume your project has 100 KLOC. You will turn it over in 3 builds each one month apart. Your development team tells you they will turn 20% of the code over in build 1, then 30%, then 50%. Define a code integration plan. Historically, once the code is turned over you find defects at the rate of 30% the first month, then 40% in each of the next two months. You have predicted an inserted defect density of 10 per KLOC. What is your expected defect discovery curve?

10.3 Define a process effectiveness metric for the requirements phase of a project.

10.4 Given the defect backlog projection in Figure 10.9, when will the software be ready to ship?

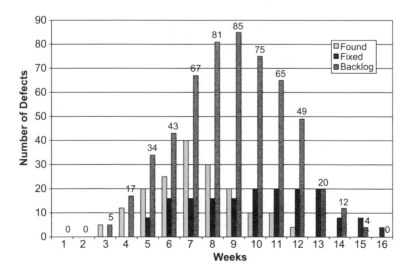

Figure 10.9. *Defect backlog projection for Problem 10.4.*

PROJECT

10.1   For the theater tickets project:

(a) Create a trouble report (TR) arrival based on:
- 10 K lines of code
- The following integration plan:

Week	1	2	3	4	5	6	7	8
Turnover (KLOC)	0	0.1	0.3	0.4	0.2	2.2	2.5	4.3

- You expect defect arrival to be algorithmically: 10%, 80%, 10% per week after each turnover.
- You expect to find 10 defects per KLOC before you ship.

(b) Create a backlog plan.
- Expectation is that each programmer can fix 2 defects per staff week if they work full time—10 programmers are on the job.
- Plan on 10% of the programmers fixing defects through week 8. After that, 100%.
- When will the backlog be cleared out?

(c) Create a second backlog plan.
- Plan on 10% fixing until week 6, when 50% start to fix troubles, then 100% after the final turnover.
- When will the backlog be cleared out?

REFERENCES

[1]   S. H. Khan, *Metrics and Models in Software Quality Engineering*, 2nd ed., Addison-Wesley, Boston, 2003, pp. 242–253.

11

Outsourcing

United, there is little we cannot do in a host of cooperative ventures.
—John F. Kennedy, Inaugural Address, September 20, 1961

11.1 THE "O" WORD

These days the word "outsourcing" can be used in a variety of contexts. Many times, it is given a diabolical connotation (see Figure 11.1) as if it is some kind of plague that must be avoided but the infection from which we cannot escape.

According to *Outsourcing Journal* [1], "the META Group's Technology Research Services predicts the offshore outsourcing market will continue to grow nearly 20% annually through 2008. By that time META estimates the average enterprise will outsource 60% of its application work offshore." Outsourcing is clearly a business strategy that is playing an increasing role in the software industry.

A recent study conducted by the management consulting firm DiamondCluster International sheds some additional light on the success of this increasingly used business strategy. The DiamondCluster 2005 Global IT Outsourcing Study [2] reported that

- 74% of the buyers surveyed expect their use of IT outsourcing to continue to increase in the coming year.

While at the same time:

- Buyer satisfaction with respect to offshore outsourcing fell dramatically from 79% in 2004 to 62% in 2005.
- The number of abnormally terminated outsourcing relationships more than doubled to 51% in 2005 versus 21% in the previous year.
- Buyers remained skeptical about outsourcing mission-critical services with the greatest demand anticipated in the application maintenance and support area.

Software Measurement and Estimation, by Linda M. Laird and M. Carol Brennan
Copyright © 2006 John Wiley & Sons, Inc.

GRAND AVENUE   **BY STEVE BREEN**

Figure 11.1. *Extreme outsourcing (Grand Avenue: © United Feature Syndicate, Inc.)*

With a key problem area being,

- *Many buyers still do not have effective metrics and measures in place to gauge the success of their outsourcing initiatives.*

Clearly, we need to learn from industry experience to avoid common pitfalls and better ensure our outsourcing engagements are successful.

In this chapter, we talk about outsourcing first in a generic sense and then identify particular incarnations that you might encounter in software engineering. Hopefully, this will put outsourcing in its rightful business context. We then, of course, talk about the key role metrics can play in successfully managing the various types of outsourcing.

11.2   DEFINING OUTSOURCING

Outsourcing is really nothing more than using resources external to your business to accomplish some portion of your software project. In the most generic sense, we might better call it third party utilization and management. We have used the word "outsourcing" as the title for this chapter to capture your attention, but we could just as easily have titled this chapter "Supplier Management." In that context we could include everything from the inclusion of prepackaged, mature, market-proven software or hardware in our software project to the inclusion of newly written, customized software as an integrated part of our software product. Some software activities that are typical outsourcing candidates include the following:

- Developing/supplying platform-level code
- Manufacturing/supplying hardware

- Providing/maintaining development/test environments
- Developing/supplying application level code for inclusion in the product
- Providing customer service/hot-line support to customers post delivery
- Maintaining production code post delivery
- Providing business continuity (disaster recovery) services

More generically, we could simply say we might select an outside supplier to provide:

- A technology or skill set not readily available in house
- Any service we define to be outside our core competency
- Any service or product that can be provided more cost effectively and/or more rapidly by the supplier than can be provided in-house

The true intent of outsourcing is to allow any business to best meet the goals of both its customers and shareholders for timely, cost-effective delivery of software that performs as expected and brings the power of new technologies to the market. The most important part in the decision to outsource is making the determination that doing so will better enable you to meet your goal, whatever that may be.[1] Perhaps someone has a new technology or product on which you can build, saving you the time and money of reinvention. Perhaps someone has skilled resources available which you can utilize more quickly or inexpensively than you could if you had to hire or train them.

Most simply stated, use of third party resources is the result of informed business decision making and becomes just another activity of the software project and must, therefore, be managed and monitored as we would other activities. By now we know that this is most effectively done with the aid of quantifiable metrics.

OUTSOURCING BUSINESS CASE CONSIDERATIONS

When making the business case for outsourcing, you will need to quantify the benefits and costs. We would like to highlight a few typical categories for both.

Typical benefits from outsourcing include the following:

- *Corporate Focus*: For a company to compete successfully, it needs to elect the areas that will give it a competitive advantage and develop competencies in those areas. This is typically called your *corporate core competencies*. Strategically, you do not outsource your core competencies. Similarly, you do not want to waste corporate attention and talent on activities that are

---

[1]See Box on Business Case Considerations for additional insights on making the business case for outsourcing.

commodities or will give you no strategic advantage, even though they may be important to you. For example, consider desktop support. Good support is crucial to a high-performance development organization, but it does not mean you need to do it yourself.

- *Cost Avoidance*: Lower labor rate, resource flexibility (as business needs change), avoidance of capital, training, and hiring costs, improved productivity (if supplier has demonstrably higher productivity, often true in a "non-core-competency" area), reduced cost of poor quality (if supplier has demonstrably better quality results).

- *Improved Time to Market*: Faster new technology inclusion and/or faster project completion resulting in an accelerated and/or augmented revenue stream.

- *Higher Customer Satisfaction*: Due to any projected increases in quality or timeliness of deliveries, which could translate into additional revenue.

On the cost side, it will be essential to ensure all costs are considered. Too often, we have seen a simple comparison of in-house versus supplier labor rates as the key financial "decision" measure. Better business decisions can be made and more realistic expectations set if we ensure we have included all cost factors in our outsourcing proposal. Typical cost categories include the following:

- *Labor*: What will the "new wage rate × number of staff" equation yield? On the "benefits" side, we will need to be clear on whether we are striving to reallocate skilled resources or to actually reduce staff to achieve bottom line savings. If the latter is our goal, we must take into consideration all applicable staff reduction policies with respect to notification windows and severance costs.

- *Oversight*: How will we manage this partnership? Will we need to have a dedicated "supplier manager"? Will they or we need an on-site presence? How will we measure the success of the relationship and the success of projects within that relationship (i.e., what metrics will be used, how will they be collected, how often will they be monitored and by whom)? The DiamondCluster study [2] indicates that 68% of buyers report that metrics reviews are performed monthly or more frequently, 21% review metrics quarterly, and the remainder of buyers review metrics semi-annually, annually, or as-needed.

- *Documentation and Training*: What documentation and/or training will need to be created and provided to ensure sufficient knowledge transfer occurs between us and the supplier? If we are handing off application code to a supplier to maintain, will existing documentation (e.g., manuals, design documents, commented code) be enough? Will we need to "reverse engineer" an overarching system design document if one does not exist? If we are going to include a supplier's "widget" in our code, will we need to allot time and budget to receive training? We may also need to include cultural training if we are outsourcing offshore.

- *Infrastructure*: What hardware platform(s), system software (and licenses), networking connections, office/lab space, and so on would we have to establish for this partnership? What security measures for communication and code transmission must be established? For an existing relationship, much of this may already be in place, but if not these are real costs that must be taken into account.

- *Travel*: Who will need to travel to/from the supplier's site and how often? Visits may be needed for various types of reviews, training, and/or oversight. For example, DiamondCluster reports [2] that 42% of buyers surveyed performed quarterly on-site visits to their supplier's facilities.

- *Reduced Productivity*: If we are transferring code production, testing, and/or maintenance of an existing product to a supplier, we can expect reduced productivity for some amount of time while that supplier gains expertise on the software. Staff turnover rates can also impact productivity, so we will need to understand our supplier's staffing market. We could use internal or industry benchmarks on productivity as a starting point and "discount" the rate based on our project's characteristic (e.g., well-documented design, code, and/or test suites) and our supplier's documented characteristics (e.g., high staff turnover).

- *Reduced Quality*: If we are transferring code production, testing, and/or maintenance of an existing product to a supplier, we can expect reduced quality levels for some amount of time while that supplier gains expertise on the software. We could use internal or industry benchmarks as a starting point for defect estimation (see Chapters 7 and 13) and adjust expectations based on demonstrated supplier capabilities.

11.3 RISK MANAGEMENT AND OUTSOURCING

The "once-removed" nature of any outsourced activity can increase risk to the project and so special attention must be given to managing this risk. Understanding for our particular circumstance what level of risk we have will help us choose the right path for our outsourcing activity, one that is aligned to project goals and has the appropriate level of management and metrics.[2]

---

[2]We want to define the "Goldilocks" plan: management processes, milestones, and metrics that are not too few (especially for high-risk efforts) and not too many (especially for small, low-risk efforts), but are "just right."

The level of risk for any outsourcing activity will be dependent on many factors including:

1. Supplier's financial stability
2. Supplier's track record for quality, on-time delivery, and service
3. Maturity level of the supplier's processes
4. Maturity of the supplier's service or product we intend to utilize
5. Clarity and effectiveness of communication with the supplier

The first two must pass our project/company's criteria for acceptability.[3] Often, publicly available information (e.g., Dun & Bradstreet rating/report[4]) tells us what we need to know on the financial front. Supplier provided data including customer references and product or service performance metrics (e.g., field fault history, percent on-time delivery, and average response time for customer calls) will get us over the second hurdle.

Process maturity helps us to understand whether past performance is any indicator of future results. The more mature the process, the more likely that the supplier's previous results (e.g., on-time delivery, quality levels) will be indicative of what we can expect from that supplier. Proof of certifications to industry standards such as ISO 9001 and CMMI[®] can provide assurances about process maturity and repeatability.

For service or product maturity, we might look at the length of time the supplier has been providing the service to projects like ours, total number of production months for the product, customer defect reporting history on the product, expected product life,[5] and so on. Obviously, the more mature the product or service is, the greater the assurance we have that it will perform as expected.

Communication with the supplier will be critical and none is more critical than communicating what our expectations are. In this regard, the contract[6] we eventually put in place will be the most important communications vehicle we have. As we have seen in previous chapters, quantifiable measures provide one manner of clear communication.

Evaluating the items listed above, quantitatively where possible, will give us a leg up on managing the risk associated with our outsourcing activity. Once the project has begun and our outsourcing partner(s) selected, we will need to manage the outsourced activities in concert with our internal activities. Establishing metrics specifically designed to help us ensure seamless integration of those

---

[3]For offshore outsourcing there will in all likelihood be a number of additional criteria for determining the acceptability of a possible supplier. These could include such things as the country's policy with respect to safeguarding intellectual property, the stability of the government, and the effectiveness of the local court system for adjudicating contract disputes.

[4]Dun & Bradstreet ratings and reports can help you assess the financial health and credit worthiness of a potential supplier. See www.dnb.com.

[5]Let us not forget to find out when the supplier plans to discontinue or stop support on the product/service and ensure that it dovetails with our own product life cycle and commitments.

[6]In some cases, the term Service Level Agreement (SLA) may be used to denote the formal agreement our project has with another organization. For our purposes, we will use the term "contract" to cover both.

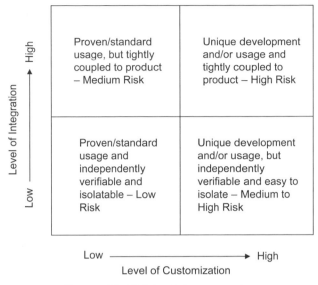

Figure 11.2. *Risk levels for outsourcing.*

activities will be the key to our success. One way that may help us in our thinking about the breadth and depth of the metrics to use is to look at the supplier activities in two specific dimensions:

1. Level of customization—How much new development specifically done for our project is needed?
2. Level of integration/dependence—How tightly coupled is the supplier's work to ours?

The higher the level of customization, the higher the risk, because the supplier's output has not been previously verified by other users. Likewise, the more we must integrate our software and/or activities with the supplier's, the higher the risk. This is particularly true when significant parts of software functionality cannot be demonstrated until software pieces from the supplier have been integrated with locally developed software. Figure 11.2 illustrates this concept.

Knowing where on this scale your usage of third party resources falls will help you determine how best to manage that activity to ensure your project's success. The greater the risk, the more you will want to define specific metrics to enable timely problem detection and resolution.

11.4 METRICS AND THE CONTRACT

The most powerful vehicle for ensuring third parties meet the expectations of our project is the contract[7] we establish with them. It is through the contract that we

---

[7]We will use the word "contract" to mean the agreement between us and our supplier regardless of the form that agreement takes (verbal or written, blessed by lawyers or simply sealed sealed with a handshake,

can clearly establish what we need from the supplier, how we will expect the supplier to communicate with our team on progress toward those expectations, and the incentives and/or penalties[8] that will apply to that supplier's performance. In essence, the contract serves as one of our risk mitigation strategies for the risky business of relying on organization outside our direct control (further discussion of risk management can be found in Chapter 12).

A contract is more effective when we use quantitative measures to describe our expectations. For example, think about the differences between the following two potential contract entries. Let us assume we are going to include newly developed code from the Software R Us Company to perform Function A for our product. Further assume that Function A software can be independently demonstrated without integration into our code.

> *Contract Example 1*: Software R Us shall deliver software that performs Function A six (6) months from the signing date of this contract.

> *Contract Example 2*: Six (6) months from the signing date of this contract, Software R Us will deliver software that performs Function A as demonstrated by a 95% successfully passed rate of the functional test plan. The functional test plan will cover 100% of requirements in Addendum A of this contract.

In the second example, we have selected a metric, percent test cases passed, that will be used to evaluate the functional acceptability of the software. We also clearly communicated and codified that metric for this supplier in the contract. We would certainly go on to include our expectations for delivery of software fixes, when 100% functionality it expected to be achieved, and clearly state what the penalty is for failure to perform, but this first metric is a good start. (Notice the use of the SMART metric technique.)

In general, you want metrics that allow you to monitor three[9] main areas of your supplier's efforts:

1. *Progress*: Are all schedule commitments on track to be met? Metrics to choose from in this area are similar ones to used for internal project schedule monitoring. The difference may be in the level of visibility the supplier allows into its business. Examples include percent of effort completed, percent of modules completed and/or inspected, and unit or multiunit testing progress (percent test cases executed and passed).

---

email order form or voluminous tome). It is most effective, however, to clearly document in writing our expectations.

[8]Penalties often take the form of monetary payments for some type of failure to perform to expectations. It can often be effective, however, especially for long-term partnerships, for some levels of missed performance to trigger senior-level, frequent project reviews and root-cause analysis and corrective action planning to drive results back to the expected levels.

[9]Depending on the type of work being outsourced and the type of contract put in place, you may also need metrics in two additional areas: productivity and financial performance. For example, for development services, where requirements are not already defined, you may end up establishing a function point developed per staff metric for scoping and pricing purposes. For ongoing maintenance services, there may be a function point per staff metric used for pricing or benchmark comparisons. For contract types other than fixed priced, tracking actual costs against budgets would be appropriate.

2. *Quality*: Are quality targets going to be met? Have they been met? Metrics in this area could include technical performance measures (e.g., transaction throughput or user response time), number of open defects, mean time to failure, and level of fault on fix.

3. *Responsiveness*: Are delivery of on-demand services and fixes to problems being handled in accordance with your project's needs? Metrics on responsiveness include time (average, maximum) to restoration (getting us moving forward even if it is with a temporary work around) and time to permanent fix delivery.

The extent of the metrics you need and the amount of data the supplier will give you will depend on the project characteristics. Let us look at two extreme examples using the risk level characteristics shown in Figure 11.2.

Example 1 (lower left quadrant of Figure 11.2): Off-the-shelf, software package with clearly understood and market-proven functionality and quality. Integration of the supplier's software with our software is clearly defined and well understood (virtually plug and play). Obtaining the software package is a matter of placing an order and obtaining a license. The supplier routinely handles order shipment and licensing for a large customer base and provides a standard customer service support agreement. In this case, the risk of managing this supplier for our project is very low. It is on the "standard, vendor management" end of the scale. No real metric for progress or quality needs to be established. Inclusion of order dates and expected arrival dates would be in our project plan. We would want to ensure that the support commitments (both for product life and problem resolution) are sufficient to enable us to meet the support commitment we make to our customers. Metrics on number of problems and time to problem resolution could be used to track responsiveness for this vendor if that were needed.

Example 2 (upper right quadrant of Figure 11.2): Custom-developed software that will be closely integrated into our own software under development. We are developing in parallel and will need to integrate the code before any multimodule or product testing can occur. In this case we want a project plan that includes numerous "touch points" with the supplier, such as joint design sessions (particularly interface design) and perhaps even code reviews. The metrics should be chosen to complement whatever project plan is developed, but should cover all three areas (progress, quality, and responsiveness). For example, if joint code inspections are in the plan, then we could have metrics on percent of code reviews complete (progress), number of defects found in those reviews (quality), and mean time to deliver updated code following the review (responsiveness). If early touch points were not agreed to (which increases the risk to our project), then we might have to rely on simply a percent complete metric from the supplier. We might build in early turnovers of their software, integrate it with early versions of ours, and run verification tests yielding quality (number of defects found) and responsiveness (time to fix, fault on fix) metrics.

11.5 SUMMARY

Outsourcing is a growing trend in the software industry. Planning and monitoring project activities that we choose to outsource are critical components of any successful software project. As stated in the DiamondCluster study [2]: "*Buyers need to dedicate more time and energy to monitoring and measuring performance in order to identify and remediate issues before they escalate and jeopardize the entire relationship.*"

The bottom line is that you will want to understand what level of risk you are taking on by the particular type of outsourcing you use. Based on that risk level, you can then define a metrics program that supports your project plan and allows you to establish effective contracts and relationships with your suppliers.

For those of you who are interested in further study, [3] provides additional interesting information on outsourcing.

PROBLEMS

11.1 You are a small middleware company for embedded software. You need a website for customer support. Should you outsource this work or do it yourself? Why or why not?

11.2 Other than a reduced labor rate, what are three reasons you might outsource a project?

11.3 You need to build a new system for 100 FPs. You have three developers in-house ready to go. They are experts in C++. They want to use VBScript for the project. It will take them 1 month to be up to speed on VBScript. You need to have the new system online in 4 months. Every month delay will cost you $25K in lost revenue. Which alternative would you choose from those listed below, and why? Which is the cheapest? Which is the fastest? Which is the most risky? Consider the different benefit and cost factors. You can put your developers on other jobs if they are not selected for this project. Make reasonable assumptions as needed.

   (a) Build it in-house using C++, which your development team knows very well.

   (b) Build it in-house using VBScript.

   (c) Contract with a hot new company that promises to meet the date with quality for $250K. A colleague of yours contracted with them previously and was pleased with the result. This company will only meet the date if you can sign the contract within 2 weeks.

   (d) Contract with a stable development company who promises to meet the date with quality for $350K. This company has an excellent track record and has built many similar systems.

PROJECTS

11.1 For the theater tickets project:

   (a) Consider the external supplier of the credit card system.

      What risk quadrant would it be in?

      What metrics would be reasonable for a contract?

   (b) Assume you are considering outsourcing the development of a new module, which would email subscribers to announce new productions and specials.

      What risk quadrant would it be in?

      What metrics would be reasonable for a contract?

   (c) Assume you are now the outsourcer rather than the outsourcee for the new development. What metrics would you now think would be reasonable for a contract?

11.2 If you work on a project, speak with your boss about what work is being outsourced in your company. If you are not working, find out what IT work is being outsourced at your college. For one project, find out the following:

   (a) What metrics are being used to manage it.

   (b) How well it is going.

   (c) How much overhead is required to manage the outsourced project.

REFERENCES

[1] B. E. Rosenthal (editor), "META predicts offshoring will continue to grow at 20 percent clip through 2008," *Outsourcing Journal*, December 2004. Available from www.outsourcing-journal.com.

[2] DiamondCluster International, "2005 Global IT Outsourcing Study." Available from www.diamondcluster.com.

[3] T. C. Jones (2000). *Software Assessments, Benchmarks, and Best Practices*, Addison-Wesley Longman, Boston, Chap. 8. www.offshore-software.org.

12

Financial Measures for the Software Engineer

Money, money, money, money, MONEY
—For the Love of Money, The *OJays* [1]

12.1 IT'S ALL ABOUT THE GREEN

It may seem out of place to include a chapter on financial measures in a software engineering textbook, but no matter what the software project, even if you are purely focused on technical issues, someone who is important to you cares greatly about value—value to the customer and value to the business. The common denominator most often used to measure value is money. Business is about money: getting it, making it, and using it in a way that maximizes its growth. Even the best technical ideas require a sound business case to attract investment money. Nonprofit organizations must also ensure they are using their money to maximum effect.

As a software professional, you will be exposed to financial measures in a variety of ways, such as:

- Selection of projects to undertake: Which is a better use of limited resources?
- Determination of project/product pricing: What must we charge to give us the greatest probability of achieving the desired profit margin?
- Estimation of costs, expected revenue (external projects), expected savings (internal projects): How do we capture all project factors in the common denominator of dollars?

Software Measurement and Estimation, by Linda M. Laird and M. Carol Brennan
Copyright © 2006 John Wiley & Sons, Inc.

- Monitoring of progress, in financial terms, of a software project: How do we ensure we're on track to meet the financial goals of the project?

As a software engineer, you do not need to be an expert on financial measures. There will be financially trained people (project controllers, organizational financial managers, and the business' Chief Financial Officer) associated with your projects and products. It will be extremely beneficial to you, and improve your credibility with them, if you understand what the key financial measures are and what they mean. Financial metric knowledge will help you become a more valued and active participant in project decision making, since you understand more fully the financial impact of those decisions on your company. Additionally, should you find yourself with project management responsibility, you will be accountable for ensuring budgets and profitability goals are met, so you will need to understand the financial measures. In this chapter we present the most common financial concepts and measures used on software projects.

12.2 FINANCIAL CONCEPTS

Let us start out with three basic concepts to guide your financial thinking.

Profitability Is the Goal: We want our project to be worth doing. Quite simply, we want the revenue and/or savings that result from the project to outweigh the costs of the project (and we mean ALL the costs) and be comparatively the best choice among project alternatives.

Pessimism Is Good: There are always risks associated with software development and uncertainty associated with possible revenue/savings. Understanding and quantifying what are often called "rainy day" scenarios is important to ensure good decisions are made.

Financial Experts Are Your Allies: Your skills are in software engineering. Those skills required years of training and experience to acquire. The same can be said of financial professionals and their skills. You need to know enough to speak the language of your financial experts, but they are the experts. They will ensure you ask and answer the right questions and help you drive your project to meet its financial objectives.

With that in mind, let us now start building our financial vocabulary. Let us do this in the context of the two major scenarios in which a software engineer might find him/herself: building the case for a project launch and managing an active software project to successful completion.

12.3 BUILDING THE BUSINESS CASE

It is a wonderful testament to our inventiveness that there are always more ideas for software projects than there are dollars to spend on them. One of the most important decisions businesses make is where to invest their money. When pitching an idea for a new software project, a business case will have to be created and approved. Each company will have its own unique way of reviewing and approving business cases. There may be target levels for certain financial measures such as Return on Investment, Payback Period, or other measures important to that company. In all cases, it will be necessary to understand fully the costs involved in bringing the project to successful conclusion and to understand the benefits (revenue or savings) that are expected to be achieved. There is no single, right way to do this. For that reason, we will provide definitions and guidance on the most frequently used terms and methods. You will then need to bring to bear those that are appropriate to the business environment in which you work.

12.3.1 Understanding Costs

One portion of the business case for a project is a delineation of expected costs. All costs must be included. This means everything: salaries, travel, hardware, software, tools, and overhead. We will need to know when these costs will be incurred in order to understand how they will build over time. Optimally, costs should be delineated by month as this is typically how project progress will be monitored. Often, as a starting point, costs will be looked at as a whole (i.e., for the entire life of the project) and then spread across the estimated project lifetime. The more closely the monthly estimates reflect the proposed project work schedule and external expenditures, the more easily we will be able to monitor the project ongoing. Let us now look in more detail at what some of the typical costs might be.

12.3.1.1 Salaries With software development, the largest portion of the cost is often the labor cost. Using the techniques mentioned in earlier chapters, you will need to estimate how much staff time it will take to successfully complete the project. This estimate will eventually need to be translated into dollar costs. Often, estimates and the resulting budgets are established in terms of staff hours. When this is done it is critical to ensure the "multiplier" used to convert hours to dollars is reflective of the staff mix that will be used on the project. There are typically a variety of staff classifications (and therefore pay grades) involved in any project. The project manager needs to be sure these differing salary costs have been included appropriately. Often this will be done using a "blended rate" as a single multiplier. If this is done, the project manager must ensure that as the staff mix changes over the life of the project, the ongoing staff profile meets the blended-rate assumption.

12.3.1.2 Overhead Costs Overheads are sometimes known as internal taxes. They are the cost of doing business that is spread over all projects in that business. The cost of corporate organizations such as Human Resources and Legal Services, the salaries for the senior managers, and the cost of the building facilities are all overheads that must be covered by the revenue generated by the business. The pro-rated cost appropriate to your software project must be included in your project costs at some point to get to the true bottom line profitability of the project. Overhead cost allocation is typically assigned to a project by corporate and/or business unit financial staff based on a predetermined allocation scheme. One typical method is to calculate the overheads as a percent markup on direct project salaries. Another is to allocate a percentage of the overheads in line with the percentage of total corporate revenues that the proposed project revenues reflect. Regardless of the method, overhead costs must be included on the cost side of the project's business case. If projects ignore these overhead costs, the projects themselves might look profitable while the entire company loses money day after day.

12.3.1.3 *Risk Costs*

According to the Quality Assurance Institute [2], one of the top ten challenges facing software project management is the lack of risk management, in particular, the lack of knowledge of how to quantify risks. We provide here some fundamentals of risk management and guidance for determining the associated risk management costs. This subject, however, is worthy of detailed study and in fact is the subject of numerous books and courses. Hopefully, the information here will whet your appetite for deeper study. Some additional reading material that you may find useful is given in References 4–8.

Risk management includes identifying, assessing, planning, and monitoring the risk triggers and mitigation plans associated with your software project.

Identifying Risk   There are many types of risks that can be associated with software development projects. There are business, contract, cost, schedule, technical, and customer satisfaction risks, known risks that, if not mitigated, could critically impact the success of a project. For example, one type of business risk is the risk of a change in market conditions such as the unexpected appearance of a competitor in the target market or an economic downturn in the target market. Technical risks include items such as the length of time it will take to get a new technology to work or the ability to meet a specific performance requirement. There can be cost and schedule risks associated with staff turnover, customer availability for needed collaboration, and downtime of the software development environment. There are many sources available that identify risks that may need to be considered for a particular project. For example, Barry Boehm's [3] top ten list of software project risk items (Table 12.1) provides a generic list of potential problem areas you may want to consider. The Project Management Institute's publications on Risk Management also identify typical project risk areas. It is also helpful to look at risks that similar completed projects (e.g., from within your company or from industry data within a project management tool database) encountered. It is often quite effective to get an interdisciplinary team (engineering, development, quality assurance, legal, etc.) together to brainstorm potential risks (and ultimately mitigation plans). In any case, the risks to your specific project should be delineated.

Assessing Risks   Each risk identified must be assessed to understand the likelihood of occurrence, the impact should it indeed occur, and what possible actions may exist to mitigate either the likelihood of occurrence or the extent of the

TABLE 12.1   Boehm's Top Ten Software Risk Items

1. Personnel shortfalls
2. Unrealistic schedules and budgets
3. Developing the wrong software function
4. Developing the wrong user interface
5. Gold-plating
6. Continuing stream of requirements changes
7. Shortfalls in externally performed tasks
8. Shortfalls in externally furnished components
9. Real-time performance shortfalls
10. Straining computer science capabilities

impact. For example, the risk may exist that the requirements may change after software coding has already begun. Should that happen, there could be significant cost associated with the resulting rework. There may, however, be actions that could be taken to reduce the exposure. Prototyping with the customer may be an option or more closely involving customers with requirements development and ensuring their participation contractually.

For each risk identified, the costs associated with the risk (assuming the risk event happens), its probability of occurrence, and the costs associated with potential risk mitigation strategies[1] should be estimated so that the project team can make an informed choice on whether and/or how to accept, avoid, or mitigate each risk.

It is also worth noting that the type of contract you enter into is a major factor in potential risk and therefore cost. A time and materials contract that is "pay as you go" has significantly lower risk to you as the developer than a multiyear, new software development, fixed price contract. The contract type, therefore, can be a potential risk avoidance/mitigation vehicle if we have a choice. If the contract type is a given, it will definitely affect the risks identified and their potential costs.

Planning for Risk   Now that the team has a clear view of potential risks and possible strategies for dealing with those risks, a plan of action can be determined. The costs associated with that action plan can then be summarized and included in the total project cost. The total cost associated with risk (including mitigation) on software projects can be anywhere from 1% of total other direct costs to over 100%.

There are a number of ways the risk plan[2] can be quantified. One possibility is to first view the risks qualitatively in terms of their probability, impact, and ability to mitigate and then assign a high, medium, or low risk categorization.[3] The qualitative risk to the project as a whole can then be assigned based on engineering judgment

---

[1]Risk mitigation strategies can run the gamut from requiring no real additional cost (e.g., strengthen terms and conditions in the contract) to being prohibitively expensive (e.g., create a duplicate test environment). So, you may end up mitigating some risks, accepting others (i.e., including the full impact should it happen), and potentially, passing still others on to the end customer (via the contract).

[2]Whenever we use the term "risk plan" we will include risk mitigation activities as part of that plan.

[3]The Project Management Institute provides probabilistic methods in risk quantification in the Risk Management portion of its Project Management Body of Knowledge (PMBOK). Go to www.pmi.org for more information.

TABLE 12.2 Qualitative to Quantitative Risk Mapping

Risk Item	Probability of Occurrence	Impact	Risk Assessment
Loss of key resource	20%	High	Medium
More than 25% requirements growth after design starts	40%	High	High
Development environment unavailability > 10%	10%	Moderate	Low
New technology delivered to project late	10%	High	Medium
Overall qualitative risk			Medium (= 20% risk factor)
Total risk cost			$500K ∗ 20% = $100,000

and/or some defined weighting scheme. Once this overall qualitative assessment is done, some industry, company, or project "standard" could be applied. For example, perhaps the company as a whole assigns a 5% (of estimated direct project costs) risk factor to low-risk projects, a 20% factor to medium-risk projects, and a 40% factor to high-risk projects. Once other direct costs are estimated, the risk factor would be applied and added to the total project cost. Table 12.2 provides an example (assuming total direct project costs were $500,000) of this method.

A second way of representing the risk plan is to specifically quantify each risk in terms of its estimated cost of occurrence, probability, and estimated cost of mitigation. An example of this type of strategy is shown in Table 12.3.

In this example, the cost to be included in the project budget for the risk plan is $62,600. Note that if we did nothing to mitigate the risks, the total risk cost would be $230,600.

There are many methods from which to choose for quantifying risk. Your team should select one that best meets the needs of your project and business. Whatever method is selected, getting to a quantitative view of risk is the essential task.

Monitoring Risk   The risks associated with a project change over time. Some never occur and when their time passes they can be eliminated from the costs going forward. Some occur and their costs are indeed incurred by the project and show up in our actual cost tracking. New risks can appear as well and impact our estimates on how much it will cost and what actions must be taken going forward. The bottom line is that the risk plan must be regularly reviewed and updated.

12.3.1.4 *Capital Versus Expense*   When looking at the costs of a project there are two broad categories of dollars spent—capital dollars and expense dollars. These types of dollars are treated differently from an accounting standpoint. Capital dollars can be thought of as investment money. This money is spent on

TABLE 12.3 Quantified Risk Plan

Risk Item	Cost of Occurrence	Probability of Occurrence	Cost of Risk Acceptance	Mitigation Action	Cost of Mitigation	Probability After Mitigation	Total Cost
Loss of key resource	1 month delay in overall development = 20 days × 30 staff × ($640 per staff day) = $384,000	20%	$384,000 × 20% = $76,800	Train backup in this area	10 days × 2 staff = $12,800	0%	$12,800
Required hardware delivered late	1 week delay in overall development = $96,000	30%	$96,000 × 30% = $28,800	Place delivery penalty in subcontract	None	5%	$4,800
Contractual throughput measure not achieved	Penalty clause in contract invoked = $500,000	25%	$125,000	Instrument code for early measurement and correction	$20,000	5%	$20,000 + ($500,000 × 5%) = $45,000
Total			$230,600		$32,800		$62,600

assets[4] whose expected value is derived over multiple years. Buying a piece of equipment for a business can be viewed as spending capital dollars. From an accounting standpoint, this cost is spread over the useful years of the equipment. Expense dollars are those that are spent and whose value is consumed within the year. An employee's salary is an expense. The purchase of printer paper or the payment of a utility bill is also an expense. Expenses, from an accounting perspective, are taken in the year spent. It is important to understand which project costs fall into which category for two reasons:

1. There are typically separate budgets for capital and expense dollars. To understand the viability of the project, you will need to know how much will come from each. There is at times some limited flexibility in choice of budget. For example, you might decide to lease computing equipment (an expense) for a project rather than purchase (a capital budget item) the same equipment.
2. The costs and value associated with capital are accrued over time and therefore must be treated differently in any business case than in-year expenses.

Let us take a brief look at some concepts unique to capital budgets: service life, depreciation, and salvage value.

Service life is just what it sounds like, the length of time the tangible asset is expected to provide value. There will usually be a "generally acceptable" service life for common pieces of equipment. For example, a PC or printer is typically assigned a service life of three years while a server is more commonly assigned a five-year service life. You will need to know what the acceptable service lives are for your particular company.

Depreciation is the amount of a tangible capital asset's value that is "used up" each year. This yearly depreciation is taken as an in-year expense.[5] Let us look at an example. Assume we purchase a computer for $50,000 and we assign to it a service life of five years. It would then be reasonable to depreciate this asset over the five-year life of the asset. We would, therefore, take a depreciation expense of $10,000 (1/5th of the purchase price) for this year and each of the following four years rather than taking the full $50,000 as an expense this year.

Salvage value is that residual value we can extract from a capital asset after its assigned service life. There may be salvage value, for example, if we can sell this older asset or can derive some other useful service from it after it is fully depreciated. If there is salvage value for the asset, this could be taken into account when determining how to calculate depreciation expense.

---

[4]We often think of spending capital dollars on tangible assets, such as a building or a large software product. There are times, however, when purchase of a tangible asset might be considered an expense. For example, the purchase of one desk might be treated as an expense rather than a capital purchase. Most companies set a threshold for such purchases to be considered capital.

[5]You may also hear the term amortization. Amortization is the spreading of costs over time for an *intangible* asset, such as patents, goodwill, trademarks, and prepaid insurance policies.

In our example, if we knew that we could derive $5000 of value from the computer after the first five years, we would calculate our five-year depreciation on $45,000 rather than the full purchase price of $50,000. That would give us in-year expenses for each of the first five years of $9000 and a residual expense of $5000 that would need to be accounted for in year 6.

More commonly, the full cost of a capital asset is depreciated. If any income is realized from the salvage value of a depreciated asset, it is then shown as "other income—sale of asset" in the corporation's financials. As with other forms of estimation, trying to predict the value of an asset several years in the future is an inexact endeavor at best.

Typically, capital depreciation costs are done on an organizational or corporate basis rather than per project. This means that depreciation expenses would then become part of the overhead costs allocated to each project.

12.3.2 Understanding Benefits

The "other side" of the business case looks at the benefits expected from the project. For externally sold software, this would take the form of projected sales revenue. You will want to look at this year over year. For example, let us say you are proposing the development of a new software product. If the price established for the product is $50,000 and you anticipate limited introduction followed by gradual market penetration, you would view the benefits over three years as shown in Table 12.4.

This indicates that our three-year projected revenue for this software product is $1,550,000.

For software developed for internal use, this would take the form of expected savings or expected revenue impact. Some typical expected savings might include:

- Reduced labor costs—for example, a given job can be done in less time or completely eliminated
- Reduced error costs—for example, this could be translated into less waste and/or reduced error recovery costs
- Reduced material usage—for example, less paper or publishing costs incurred

For example, perhaps we wish to introduce new software that will allow the person who uses it to save an estimated 2 hours per day. We could calculate

TABLE 12.4 Projected Revenue

Sales Region	Year 1	Year 2	Year 3
North	2 sales @ $50,000 each = $100,000	6 sales = $300,000	10 sales = $500,000
South	2 sales = $100,000	4 sales = $200,000	7 sales = $350,000
Total	$200,000	$500,000	$850,000

TABLE 12.5 Projected Savings

Target Staff (Average Rate = $20/h)	Year 1	Year 2
Department A—30	30 staff × 2 h × 240 days × $20/h = $288,000	$288,000
All other departments—120	0	120 × 2 × 240 × $20 = $1,152,000
Total	$288,000	$1,440,000

projected savings by taking the average hourly rate for those technicians who would be using the software and multiplying that by the number of staff hours saved. Table 12.5 shows how this might look if we target, say, one department for use in the first year and the rest of the departments in year 2. Assume there are 240 productive days per year.

With this type of project, the projected savings will in all likelihood not be realized as actual dollars to the bottom line. More likely, it will be seen in increased productivity for the staff. Even so, this is a reasonable way to quantify the value of the project.

Recall that we said we do not want to be overly optimistic with regard to potential savings or revenues. Temper your enthusiasm on revenues by getting a realistic view of the size of your target market and the strength of your competitors in that market. Typically, product managers work with sales and marketing colleagues to determine reasonable projections. For internal savings, make sure you remember that introduction of new systems/processes have a learning curve and are not immediately introduced at 100% effectiveness. Make sure to spell out all of your assumptions and any "adjustment" factors that you may use in calculating benefits. In our example above we could have introduced adjustments for the learning curve by, for example, estimating only 50% effectiveness of use of the new software for the first month of any introduction (that would mean only 1 hour saved by the staff in the first month of year 1 and in the first month on year 2 for all but the original department). Table 12.6 shows this revised, more realistic perspective.

TABLE 12.6 Projected Savings (Including Learning Curve)

Target Staff (Average Rate = $20/h)	Year 1	Year 2
Department A—30	(30 staff × 1 h × 20 days × $20/h) + (30 staff × 2 h × 220 days × $20/h) = $276,000	30 staff × 2 h × 240 days × $20/h = $288,000
All other departments—120		(120 × 1 h × 20 × $20/h) + (120 × 2 × 220 × $20) = $1,104,000
Total	$276,000	$1,392,000

12.3.3 Business Case Metrics

Once we have both the cost and benefit sides of the business case, we can determine those financial measures that are deemed important for business case authorization. Some typical measures include Return on Investment, Payback Period, and Cost/Benefit Ratio. There are also two financial reports that can be created from the business case information that are also commonly used: Profit/Loss (or Income) Statement and Cash Flow. You will typically see these reports on either a company-wide basis, a product basis, or a project basis. In this text, we use them to reflect the software project under consideration. Let us look at each of these items.

12.3.3.1 *Return on Investment*   Return on Investment, ROI, is one of several measures that may be used in business cases to compare different investment opportunities. ROI is calculated as follows:

$$ROI = Net\ Benefits/Investment$$
$$Net\ Benefits = Benefits - Costs$$

Let us look at an example. Assume we have a project that will require $100,000 the first year with an additional $10,000 of incremental cost required in each subsequent year. Further assume that we have calculated the benefit of this project to be $50,000 each year. We could then calculate a cumulative ROI for this project by year as follows:

$$ROI\ Year\ 1 = \frac{(Net\ Benefit\ Year\ 1)}{Investment}$$

$$= \frac{(\$50,000 - \$100,000)}{\$100,000} = -50\%$$

$$ROI\ Year\ 2 = \frac{(Net\ Benefit\ Year\ 2,\ cumulative)}{Investment}$$

$$= \frac{(\$50,000 + \$50,000 - \$100,000 - \$10,000)}{(\$100,000 + \$10,000)} = -9\%$$

$$ROI\ Year\ 3 = \frac{\left(\begin{array}{c}\$50,000 + \$50,000 + \$50,000 \\ -\$100,000 - \$10,000 - \$10,000\end{array}\right)}{(\$100,000 + \$10,000 + \$10,000)} = 25\%$$

$$ROI\ Year\ 4 = \frac{\$70,000}{\$130,000} = 54\%$$

$$ROI\ Year\ 5 = \frac{\$110,000}{\$140,000} = 79\%$$

$$ROI\ Year\ 6 = \frac{\$150,000}{\$150,000} = 100\%$$

As with most metrics, ROI will not be the sole metric looked at when deciding on investment opportunities. It does, however, provide a view of the magnitude and timing of expected benefits and costs. Companies may have ROI thresholds for projects to be considered for approval (e.g., a positive ROI must be achieved by year 3).

With ROI, bigger is better.

12.3.3.2 Payback Period The Payback Period for any project is the length of time it will take to recover your investment, that is, to hit the break-even point. What we are looking for is that point where the net benefits equal the net costs. Once you have passed this point, you are finally making a profit on your investment. For a simple example, if you have a $50,000, one-time investment that will pay you $25,000 every year, the payback period is two years. You can calculate this for both internal and external projects. The only difference would be whether the benefits line reflects sales revenues or some form of internal savings. Figure 12.1 illustrates graphically what the break-even point and payback periods look like.

For an external product sale example, let us look at the following. Assume you have a fixed cost of $25 and that each product unit costs you $10 to build. In other words, Total Cost = $25 + $10 * (# of units). You can sell each product unit for $15. In other words, Total Benefit (in this case, Revenue) = $15 * (# of units). You can now determine the number of product units that you must sell to break even. Remember, the break-even point is where total benefit equals total cost.

$$15 * (\text{\# of units}) = \$25 + \$10 * (\text{\# of units})$$
$$\$5 * (\text{\# of units}) = \$25$$
$$\text{\# of units} = 5 \text{ at the break-even point}$$

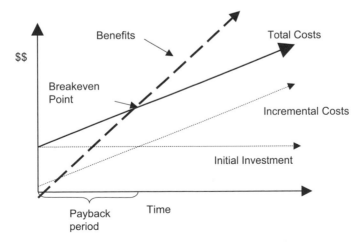

Figure 12.1. *Break-even point and payback period.*

Relating this back to ROI, at the break-even point the ROI would be 0%. Like ROI, companies may have set a payback period threshold for projects to be approved.

With payback periods, shorter is better. This is especially true for high-risk projects.

12.3.3.3 Cost/Benefit Ratio

12.3.3.3 Cost/Benefit Ratio Another financial measure that is often used to evaluate and compare investment opportunities is the Cost/Benefit Ratio. With this term we are going to introduce the concepts of Present Value (PV) and Future Worth (FW). By introducing PV and FW we are trying to assign a value today to future cash flows. This allows us to account for the growth today's money can achieve based on the going interest rates. If we define the interest rate to be i and the number of interest periods to be N, our formula for Future Worth is

$$FW(N) = PV * (1 + i)^N$$

this means, conversely,

$$PV = FW/(1 + i)^N$$

With that terminology in our vocabulary, we can now talk about Cost/Benefit Ratio (CBR).

$$CBR = PV \text{ (Total Costs/Total Benefits)}$$

In other words, we are looking at the ratio of total cost to benefits over the life of the project and stating it in today's value. Let us try an easy example. Assume total costs of \$500,000 are incurred in the first year. If benefits of \$1M are achieved over two years and the cost of money (the interest rate) is 5%, then

$$i = 0.05 \quad \text{and} \quad N = 2$$
$$PV \text{ (costs)} = 0.5M$$
$$FW \text{ (benefits)} = \$1M$$
$$PV \text{ (benefits)} = \$1M/(1 + 0.05)^2 = \$0.907M$$
$$CBR = \$0.5M/\$0.907M = 0.55$$

With CBR, smaller is better.

Figure 12.2 illustrates the importance of understanding PV or perhaps the importance of involving the real financial experts during business case creation.

Figure 12.2. *The importance of financial experts. (DILBERT: © Scott Adams/Dist. by United Feature Syndicate, Inc.).*

12.3.3.4 *Profit and Loss Statement*

A Profit and Loss (or Income) Statement looks at the revenues and expenses of the given project over time. It provides a total view of the project's profitability over time. It will include all cost and benefit data that you have estimated for the project and show the resulting project profit (often called Contribution Margin). Figure 12.3 provides a sample Profit and Loss (P&L) Statement. (In this example, we have included depreciation expenses in the overhead allocation for this project.)

Figure 12.3 reflects only the summary of the totals for the project. The categories of cost shown in a P&L Statement can be any that are appropriate for the particular project and can be at the level of detail deemed appropriate. For example, if there will be specific purchases of third party software that will be used in our product (and delivered to the customer), that could be a separate category. Perhaps you

CARLASOFT CO
MONEY MACHINE PROJECT PROPOSED P&L

Project Budget

	Hours	Dollars
Revenue		2,338,875
Salaries	10,395	779,625
Fringe benefits		155,925
Subcontract costs		75,000
Travel		75,000
Packaging & Delivery		6,000
Telephone		15,000
Miscellaneous		4,500
Gross Margin		1,227,825
Overhead allocation		233,895
Contribution Margin		993,930

Figure 12.3. *Profit and Loss (P&L) Statement.*

CARLASOFT CO
MONEY MACHINE PROJECT PROPOSED P&L

	Proposed Budget	
	Hours	**Dollars**
Revenue		2,338,875
Salaries	9,395	704,625
Fringe Benefits		155,925
Subcontract Costs		55,000
Purchase of UBUYIT software		15,000
Lease of Talk2Me test equipment		5,000
Travel		75,000
Packaging & Delivery		6,000
Telephone		15,000
Management Reserve		75,000
Miscellaneous		4,500
Gross Margin		1,227,825
Overhead Allocation		233,895
Contribution Margin		993,930

Figure 12.4. Detailed P&L Statement.

have made a decision to lease some specific equipment for interface validation during the test cycle. You could then include that cost explicitly in the P&L. Risk costs, often called Management Reserve, could be a separate item although often they are translated into equivalent staff hours and included in the salaries line item. Figure 12.4 provides an example of a more detailed P&L Statement.

A projected P&L will typically be created for project proposals. If the project is approved, the projected (or modified) P&L will become the commitment against which the project's progress will be tracked. During periodic reviews of an ongoing software project, the P&L Statement showing budgets (i.e., agreements made at the start of the project based on the estimates) and actuals to date is often the key talking point.

12.3.3.5 Cash Flow Cash Flow Statements simply show how the money is actually coming in (from revenues) and flowing out (to cover costs). Obviously a business needs to ultimately have a positive cash flow to be viable. At the project proposal stage, a projected cash flow reflecting the proposed project schedule for expense and revenue will typically be created. Figure 12.5 provides a typical Cash Flow Statement.

The Cash Flow Statement in Figure 12.5 shows the customer providing an initial upfront payment at the start of the project and then three subsequent payments over the life of the project. It also shows payment occurring thirty days after bills are rendered. As you can see, you will need to know the proposed payment schedule in order to do the Cash Flow Statement. Payment schedules are typically created in conjunction with the sales force and take into account client credit ratings and previous payment histories as well as the type of contract established (e.g., time and materials, cost plus, etc.).

**CARLASOFT CO
MONEY MACHINE PROJECT
PROJECT CASH FLOW STATEMENT**

Month	Outflows	Inflows	Net Cash
Apr-04	146,172	467,775	321,603
May-04	97,448		224,155
Jun-04	97,448		126,707
Jul-04	97,448		29,259
Aug-04	97,448		(68,189)
Sep-04	97,448		(165,637)
Oct-04	97,448	701,663	438,578
Nov-04	97,448		341,130
Dec-04	97,448		243,682
Jan-05	97,448		146,234
Feb-05	97,448		48,786
Mar-05	97,448		(48,662)
Apr-05	97,448	701,663	555,553
May-05	97,448		458,105
Jun-05	48,724		409,381
Jul-05		467,775	877,156

Figure 12.5. *Cash Flow Statement.*

12.3.3.6 Expected Value As indicated earlier, the projected benefits from any project must be tempered with a bit of pessimism. But how much is the right amount? One technique often used to establish a reasonable view of a project for comparison purposes is to calculate the expected value based on several views of the possible outcome. For our purposes we will look at three views: optimistic, projected, and pessimistic. By assigning probabilities to these three views, we can calculate an expected value for each project under consideration.

Expected Value (EV) = %Probability * Optimistic View + % Probability
$$* \text{Projected View} + \% \text{ Probability} * \text{Pessimistic View}$$

When probabilities are not easily estimated, yon can use a 1-4-1 ratio for a standard distribution:

Expected Value (EV) = (Optimistic + 4 * Projected + Pessimistic)/6

As an example, let us look at a project that is projected to save $300,000 each year for three years. Perhaps you believe there is an upside potential for realizing $500,000 in year 3 should an expected competitor be delayed in bringing its product to market. At the same time, there is the downside potential for realizing only $200,000 in year 3 should that same competitor arrive earlier than announced.

For this example,

$$EV = (\$1,100,000 + 4 * \$900,000 + \$800,000)/6 = \$916,667$$

If we know that our competitor's market history is that it delivers early 5% of the time and late 40% of the time, we can use that information to better calibrate our expected value:

$$EV = 0.4 * \$1,100,000 + 0.55 * \$900,000 + 0.05 * \$800,000 = \$975,000$$

This can be done for alternative projects as another factor in deciding which project to launch.

You can use the projected cost data along with projected revenues to calculate EVs for ROIs or CBRs for the projects as well.

12.4   LIVING THE BUSINESS CASE

Once the project is approved and launched, it will be critical to monitor progress to ensure that the financial goals laid out in the business case are actually achieved. The most important tasks in this regard are:

1. Tracking actual costs as they occur and comparing these to the business plan
2. Revisiting and updating risk costs regularly (adding new risks if needed, removing risks when the risk window has passed)
3. Quickly identifying any deviations from the plan, working with the project manager and financial experts to understand underlying problems and taking corrective action

Figure 12.6 shows one way a P&L Statement might be used to track progress. As you can see from Figure 12.6, project management would be looking at actual expenditures and revenues by month and year-to-date, our updated expectations of how much more is needed (Estimate to Complete, or ETC), how much the final total costs will be (Estimate at Completion, or EAC), and how the latter compares to our approved budget. Fortunately for the project manager of the project reflected in Figure 12.6, it looks like the project will be more profitable than expected. Had it been the reverse, some action planning to get costs back in line would be required.

12.5   SUMMARY

Software engineers must be aware of all the goals of the software projects with which they are involved. This includes the financial goals for profitability and business case realization. Key items we have addressed in this chapter are provided in Table 12.7.

CARLASOFT CO
MONEY MACHINE PROJECT ESTIMATE AT COMPLETION (EAC)
AS OF 3/31/05

| | Current Month | | | | Job-to Date | | | | | | | | Project Budget | |
| | Actual | | Budget | | Actual | | Budget | | Estimate to Complete | | Estimate at Completion | | | |
	Hours	Dollars	Hours	Dollars	Hours	Dollars	Hours	Dollars	Hours	Dollars	Hours	Dollars	Hours	Dollars
Revenue		75,000		155,925		1,912,500		1,871,100		405,000		2,338,875		2,338,875
Salaries	500	25,000	693	51,975	8,500	637,500	8,316	623,700	1,800	135,000	10,300	772,500	10,395	779,625
Fringe benefits		5,000		10,395		127,500		124,740		27,000		124,740		155,925
Subcontract costs		10,000		5,000		50,000		60,000		20,000		70,000		75,000
Travel		3,000		5,000		45,000		60,000		10,000		55,000		75,000
Packaging & Delivery		500		400		5,000		4,800		1,400		6,400		6,000
Telephone		600		1,000		12,500		12,000		3,500		16,000		15,000
Misc.		200		300		3,500		3,600		1,200		4,700		4,500
Gross Margin		30,700		81,855		1,031,500		982,260		206,900		1,289,535		1,227,825
Overhead allocation		15,593		15,593		187,116		187,116		46,779		233,895		233,895
Contribution Margin		15,107		66,262		844,384		795,144		160,121		1,055,640		993,930

Figure 12.6. Project estimate at completion.

225

TABLE 12.7 Summary of Key Items

Term	Definition	Highlight
Overhead Costs	"Internal taxes"; organizational, cost-of-doing-business spread over all projects	Include in project financials to understand true profitability
Risk Management	Identifying, assessing, planning and monitoring risk triggers and mitigation plans for the project	Quantify the risk costs and include in project expenses
Capital Expense	The cost of an asset whose useful life spans more than one year	Depreciate the asset over its service life; often included in Overhead Costs
Return on Investment (ROI)	A measure of benefits derived over time from an investment	Bigger is better
Payback Period	Length of time it takes to recover an investment	Shorter is better
Present Value (PV)	The value assigned today to future cash flows	Allows common point of comparison for competing investment opportunities
Cost/Benefit Ratio (CBR)	The ratio of total costs to benefits over the life of a project, stated in today's value	Smaller is better
P&L Statement	Profit & Loss or Income Statement; summary of total project revenues and expenses	Summarize for life of project and include as many detailed line items as you need
Cash Flow	Shows inflow and outflow of cash over time	Show for life of project to ensure health of business
Expected Value (EV)	A view of value that helps temper optimism and pessimism	Absent unique modifiers, a standard distribution [(Optimistic + 4 × Probable + Pessimistic)/6] can be used
Estimate to Complete (ETC)	In-process estimate of what the remaining cost to reach completion is at any given point in time	During the life of any project you will need to regularly re-estimate what it will take to complete the remaining work
Estimate at Completion (EAC)	In-process estimate of what the final costs will be when we reach completion of the project	During the life of any project you will need to regularly revisit your estimates for total project costs

Your understanding of business case creation, including quantification of costs and benefits and basic financial reports such as P&L and Cash Flow Statements will allow you to actively participate in the informed decision making and strong project management required to make your project a financial success.

PROBLEMS

12.1   Identify whether the following are capital costs or expense costs:
   (**a**) Payment of salaries
   (**b**) Purchase of an office building
   (**c**) Acquisition of a new payroll system
   (**d**) Purchase of copier paper
   (**e**) Purchase of computer hardware
   (**f**) Payment of utility bills

12.2   Name some typical overhead costs.

12.3   What financial report shows business profitability over time?

12.4   Assume you invest $50,000.
   (**a**) What is your ROI if this investment yields $200,000 in one year?
   (**b**) What is your ROI if this investment yields $200,000 in five years?
   (**c**) When is the break-even point for our five-year example?
   (**d**) What is the Cost/Benefit Ratio for our five-year example assuming the cost of money is 4%?
   (**e**) Compare this CBR for our five-year example with a project that requires a $100,000 investment in year 1 and yields $300,000 in six years? Which is better?

12.5   You are putting together a business case for providing a new feature for your product. You believe that offering that feature will bring increased revenues of $50,000 in the coming year based on existing customer feedback. Your colleague in sales believes that the revenue increase will be closer to $150,000 because the new feature could draw in new customers. Your colleague in market research believes there is a small possibility that your chief competitor will beat you to market with a similar feature and thereby dampen your revenue increase to only $30,000. What value for revenue benefits should you use in your business case?

12.6   What steps should you take to manage your project financials once the project has been launched?

12.7   Your financial people tell you your project is losing money. You look at the data that shows all of the salaries, benefits, building space, and computing resources you have used. You look at the sales data. You calculate that your project is making a 10% profit. Where is the disconnect?

12.8 You know that you have some big risks in your development program, especially in the specification of one algorithm, which requires extensive mathematics and will then be implemented using an AI (artificial intelligence) engine. Your team is chomping at the bit to do this work. They estimate it will take 12 staff months. You think this is an optimistic view and that it could easily be 18 or even 24 staff months. You decide to use your risk management techniques and quantitatively analyze the situation to determine what to do. You determine you could bring in experts to help out, and you think that will work, but it might not.

You come up with the following risk factor:

> Risk: Overrunning schedule by 6 staff months.
> Probability: 75%
> Additional cost to project (other than the 6 staff months): $200K
> Mitigation Plan: Bring in experts to help out
> Additional cost for experts: $100 K
> Residual risk: 30%

Your fully loaded staff costs are $25K per month. Should you bring in outside experts or not? Only consider the factors given to you in the problem.

PROJECTS

12.1 If you are working, for your project (or another one in your organization), find out what exists on risk planning. Is it quantitative? If not, suggest how it might be improved. If you are not working, create a quantitative risk plan for your theatre ticket project.

12.2 Theater Tickets Availability Alternative Analysis: Financially analyze the alternatives for improving availability of theater tickets. (The first four questions are from the project in Chapter 9.)

Use the block diagram below for this project.

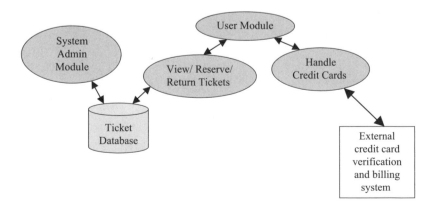

You are also responsible for the operation of the entire system. Your customer is quite happy with the system, except for the availability. The customer loses $10,000 in profits for each hour the system is unavailable. You have been in operation for 10 weeks. To date, the availability of the system components have been:

Hardware: 99.9%—scheduled maintenance

Software: 99.8 %—software problems

External Credit Card Verification and Billing System: 99.0%—unscheduled, unplanned

The credit card system is only required on 30% of all transactions, and the implementation allows the other transactions and the system to work even if the credit card system is unavailable.

(a) Calculate the system's continuous availability in percent.

(b) What would be the change in availability if you implement a hot backup system to reduce the schedule maintenance time by 90%?

(c) You know you need to improve the credit card vendor availability. You search hard to find another credit card system vendor but can only find one whose availability is much worse (80%). Still, you consider implementing it in addition to the first; that is, it is called if the first is unavailable. What would be the projected availability if you implemented this plan?

(d) If you implement both improvement plans, what is the projected availability of the system?

(e) Assume that the cost of money is 2% per month, and you start implementing both improvements immediately. For the hot backup, it will:

- Take 6 months
- Cost $50K (all expense is for servers and development.) (Cost in is month 1.)
- Have an ongoing cost of $10K per month for months 2 through 6

For the second credit card system:

- The development effort is 3 staff months at $12K per staff month.
- It will take three months for the project.
- You need to pay the verification software company $5K per month for the service.
- No additional hardware is required.

For each improvement

What is the cost (over a year)?

What is the benefit?

What is the ROI after one year? After two years?

What is the CB after one year? After two years?

REFERENCES

[1]   "For the Love of Money," words and music by Kenneth Gamble, Leon Huff and Anthony Jackson, ©1974 (renewed) Warner-Tamerlane Publishing. All rights reserved, used by permission.

[2]   Quality Assurance Institute, "The top ten challenges of software project management," www.qaiusa.com.

[3]   B. Boehm, "Risk management—assessing project risk," *Software Tech News 2-2.* www.softwaretechnews.com/technews2-2.

[4]   R. Kazman and D. Port, "Risk management for IT security," *Information Technology Management*, University of Hawaii.

[5]   Project Management Institute, There are courses in Risk Management offered through the Institute.

[6]   Thompson and Thompson Corporation, "What is a Profit and Loss Statement?" www. t-tlaw.net.

[7]   www.solutionmatrix.com; "Return on investment: What is ROI analysis?"

[8]   www.en.wikipedia.org; "Return on investment."

13

Benchmarking

You're the top! You're the Louvre Museum
—**You're the Top, Cole Porter [1]**

13.1   WHAT IS BENCHMARKING?

According to the dictionary,[1] a benchmark is a standard by which something can be measured or judged. To effectively use benchmarking in software engineering, you will need to:

1. Define the goal of the benchmarking exercise.
2. Identify the area/metric that you would like to benchmark.
3. Identify and obtain the standard benchmark that will be used.
4. Collect/calculate the actual data for the chosen metric for your project (or document the current process for process benchmarking).
5. Take action, as indicated by your goal, based on the difference between your actual results and the benchmark.

Let us look at each of these activities.

---

[1]*The American Heritage College Dictionary*, 3rd edition, Houghton Mifflin Company, Boston, 1997.

Software Measurement and Estimation, by Linda M. Laird and M. Carol Brennan
Copyright © 2006 John Wiley & Sons, Inc.

13.2 WHY BENCHMARK?

It is important to first determine why you would want to benchmark something. Some typical reasons for benchmarking in software include the following:

- To drive process improvement
- To drive better financial or quality results
- To differentiate one's company, product, service, organization, or self from the competition
- To validate a claim or belief about relative performance
- To determine compensation (i.e., "pay for performance")

It is always, as the definition indicates, to be able to compare the item in hand to some recognized, desirable standard so that action can be taken. Benchmarking will cost time and money, so the goal of any benchmarking effort must be clear. Benchmarking is a way to look outside yourself, your organization, and/or your project to more objectively assess your current state and your actual results and to learn from proven standards and high-performing organizations.

13.3 WHAT TO BENCHMARK

Virtually anything can be benchmarked: strategies, processes, and any software metrics you can define. For example, if the goal is to achieve higher levels of software product quality, we may choose to benchmark a field fault density metric. If the goal is to drive development costs down, we may choose to benchmark one or more development process metrics such as defect removal efficiency or level of mechanization in software testing. If we wish to differentiate our company from the competition based on our ability to better meet client needs, we might choose to benchmark a customer satisfaction measure. You can use the techniques such as the GQM^2 approach from chapter 2 to determine the actual metrics to be benchmarked.

The questions to consider when choosing what to benchmark are the following:

- How does this item relate to our goal? The relationship can be direct or indirect but must clearly tie in to the stated goal.
- Can a valid benchmark be obtained and at what cost?
- Can actual performance data be obtained and at what cost?
- Will comparing actuals to benchmark enable action?

In other words, you are looking for a metric that correlates well with your goal, for which a standard benchmark and actual performance data can be affordably obtained, and which will enable an action plan when actuals are compared to the benchmark.

You will also want to be clear about the level of performance that you want to benchmark. For example, do you want to know best-in-class levels? World-class levels? Average or competitive levels? Alternatively, you may be benchmarking against a specific or collection of specific organizations/competitors.

13.4 IDENTIFYING AND OBTAINING A BENCHMARK

Deciding on what benchmark to use is critical. You may decide to use an internal benchmark of a project or organization that is performing to desired levels. You may decide to look for an external benchmark in the identified area. Whichever is used, the source of the benchmark must be documented and the definition(s)/algorithm(s) on which the benchmark is based clearly understood. (For example, does a system size measured in KLOC include comments?)

If you choose to look externally, it may be possible to use an easily obtainable and widely recognized benchmark (the lyrics to the Cole Porter song [1] mentioned at the start of this chapter contain many examples of widely accepted best-in-class benchmarks). Often, in software development, benchmark data can be purchased either directly (e.g., Rubin's World Wide Benchmarking Report, ISBSG's Software Metrics Compendium[2]) or as part of a reference database in a development tool (e.g., COCOMO). For process benchmarking, numerous standards exist and can be used as a benchmark (e.g., ISO 9000, CMMI, TL 9000). The closer the area matches your project specifics, the more relevant your ultimate comparisons will be. Many benchmarking and project sizing tools will ask you for numerous project characteristics (e.g., programming language, staff expertise levels, technology base, and development methodology) in order to find the most appropriate comparison.

You may decide to launch or participate in a specific benchmarking study. You can select a particular target organization/company that fits the bill and conduct a study of their relevant operations and metrics. Effective design of a benchmarking questionnaire is a skill. The right questions must be asked and the definitions of the data to be collected must be clearly communicated to the target respondents. If you are going to launch a benchmarking study, get appropriate training or expert help. This should ensure that the data collected will actually provide a valid comparison for your project. Be aware that many companies, however, are hesitant to share their internal processes and data directly. In that case, it may be possible to find benchmarking studies that contain the desired targets but sanitize and amalgamate the data. Typically, when you provide your data to such a survey you will be entitled to the summary findings.

13.5 COLLECTING ACTUAL DATA

Whatever it is that you are benchmarking, you will need to collect the same data for your own project, software, or organization. It will be important to make sure that

---

[2]ISBSG is the International Software Benchmarking Standards Group of the International Function Point User Group (IFPUG). Information about both the IFPUG and ISBSG and their available products can be found at www.ifpug.org.

your data is defined in the same way (or as near as possible) as the benchmarking data. If some small differences exist, they must be noted and the possible effect of those differences taken into account during reporting and action planning. As we mentioned in earlier chapters, be clear on the level of precision that you need. Frequently, a ballpark range is all that is needed to drive action.

13.6 TAKING ACTION

Remember that the reason for benchmarking is to take action.

Once you have both the benchmarking and project data, you can determine what actions are needed to reach your stated goal. Typically, performing below benchmark data will trigger some form of root cause analysis[3] to determine the specific areas that need attention. For example, if the goal is to achieve best-in-class levels of product quality and we find that our field fault density is well below the industry best-in-class benchmark, we will need to determine the causes of our product's field faults. We will need to drill down to find the largest problem areas. Perhaps our field fault data will tell us that we have one particularly problematic module. With that known, we might launch a detailed inspection of that code.

Benchmarking can be used for goal setting and trends can be shown over time to demonstrate progress toward goals. Be aware, however, that any particular benchmark will change over time. Keep up to date on those changes so that goals can be adjusted accordingly. What was best-in-class today may simply reflect average performance a few years down the road.

13.7 CURRENT BENCHMARKS

In earlier chapters, we discussed a number of metrics that are commonly used in software engineering and frequently have provided both benchmarks and engineering rules for those metrics. Finding appropriate benchmarking data on each for use by your project team can be quite a treasure hunt. Some useful sources include IEEE, Software Productivity Research (www.spr.com), META Group (www.metagroup.com), the International Software Benchmarking Standards Group (www.isbsg.org), the Software Engineering Institute (www.sei.cmu.edu), and the Project Management Institute (www.pmi.org) to name a few. Table 13.1 provides a sampling of some of the currently published software benchmarking data. Notice the benchmark publication dates vary greatly and few are extremely current. To get current data targeted at your desired area will often require you to purchase it from a third party. So be clear on what you are looking for and spend those benchmarking dollars wisely.

---

[3]*Root cause analysis* (RCA) is a structured process designed to get at the underlying cause of a quality/performance problem. There are numerous techniques and tools available that support RCA. The American Society for Quality lists articles and books about RCA on its website: www.asq.org. A list of widely used software tools to support RCA can be found at www.rootcauselive.com.

TABLE 13.1 Public Benchmarks

Software Project Item	Benchmark	Date	Source
Staff turnover	U.S. companies: 9.9% (average)	2001	IEEE [2] (www.computer.org)
Postrelease defects	U.S. companies: 0.37/KLOC (average)	2001	IEEE [2] (www.computer.org)
Defect removal efficiency (DRE)	96% best-in-class	2000	T. Capers Jones, Software Productivity Research (SPR) [4]
Length of schedule (calendar months)	#FP raised to the 0.4 power	2000	T. Capers Jones, SPR [4]
Defect potential	#FP raised to the 1.25 power	2000	T. Capers Jones, SPR [4]
Number of test cases needed	#FP raised to the 1.20 power	2000	T. Capers Jones, SPR [4]
Project failure rate	For projects 10 K FPs	2000	T. Capers Jones, SPR [4]
	SEI Level 1 > 50%		
	SEI Level 3 < 10%		
	SEI Level 5 < 1%		
Cost/FP (unburdened)	U.S. average $1000	2000	T. Capers Jones, SPR [4]
	Best in class <$250		
Expected feature growth beyond first release of software	7%/year (average)	2000	T. Capers Jones, SPR [4]
Productivity	8–12 FP/staff month (average)	2000	T. Capers Jones, SPR [4]
	>50 FP/staff month (best in class)		

13.8 SUMMARY

Benchmarking is a method of obtaining a standard of performance for one or more of the metrics you use in your software project or organization. To effectively benchmark you will clearly define (1) the objective of the benchmarking effort, (2) the metric(s), related to that objective, that you will benchmark, and (3) the source of the benchmark data and your project data.

With your benchmarking plan in place, you will then (1) obtain the benchmark, (2) collect your project data, and, most importantly, (3) take action based on the comparison of your project's performance relative to the benchmark.

Your benchmarking efforts will enable you to set performance goals that are aligned with your business and project objectives and that will help drive improvement of your project's results.

Additional resources can be found in References 4–9.

PROBLEMS

13.1 List two reasons why you might want to benchmark software testing productivity in your organization.

13.2 Where can you obtain benchmark data?

13.3 How frequently do you need to revisit a benchmark you have collected?

13.4 Your boss tells you to expect a 2% growth in features for the next year for your system. You ask where the 2% came from. "Gut feeling" is the answer. What do you now say?

13.5 You compare your organization's productivity to world class and find you are 10% better than the standard. You dig deeper, and you find out the difference is because you count reused code as 100% new code. Now what do you do?

13.6 Your delivered defect density is 10 defects/KLOC. Should you focus your next release on quality improvement or feature development?

PROJECTS

13.1 For the theater tickets project, your CEO tells you to benchmark the performance of the company's website against its competitors. What benchmarks do you choose and why? What benchmark data do you know (from this text)? What other data can you find on the web?

13.2 You work in a company that develops software applications for the health care industry. You would like to have benchmarks for software quality and developer productivity. Identify available sources for such benchmarks and indicate what it will take to obtain them.

REFERENCES

[1] "You're the Top," words and music by Cole Porter, ©1934 (renewed), Warner Bros. Inc. All rights reserved, used by permission.

[2] H. Rubin, M. Johnson, and S. Iventosch, "The US software industry," *IEEE Software Online Magazine*. Available from www.computer.org/software/homepage/2002/01CountryReport.

[3] T. C. Jones, Software Productivity Research. "Software benchmarking: What works and what doesn't?," November 27, 2000. Available from www.cs.uml.edu/Boston-SPIN.

[4] International Software Benchmarking Standards Group (ISBSG) description, www.ifpug.org.

[5] T. C. Jones (2000). *Software Assessments, Benchmarks, and Best Practices*, Addison Wesley Longman, Boston.

[6] Longstreet Consulting, "Benchmarking best practices." Available from www.ifpug.com/benchmark.htm.

[7] Longstreet Consulting, "Software measurement." Available from www.ifpug.com/sm.htm.

[8] Longstreet Consulting. "Software productivity since 1970." Available from www.ifpug.com/Articles/history.htm.

[9] K. D. Maxwell, "Collecting data for comparability: benchmarking software development productivity," *IEEE Software Online Magazine* **18**(5), September/October 2001. Available from www.computer.org/software/archives.htm.

14

Presenting Metrics Effectively to Management

Man-age \man'-ij\, v., to exert control over.
—American Heritage Dictionary, Third Edition

A picture is worth a thousand words
—My mother

Whether you are a member of a software development team, the manager of one small group in a large software project, or the president of a software product company, you will want to base your decisions on timely and accurate information. The basic question that each manager must continuously be able to answer is: Are we on target and if not, why not and what can we do about it? What we choose to measure and *how we communicate* those measurements will directly determine our ability to effectively manage the risks inherent in software development and to successfully deliver software that meets the customer's needs.

In this chapter, we describe an approach that will enable the "conveyor of metrics" to meet this management challenge.[1] We call this approach "the 4 Ds" for effectively communicating metrics. The 4 Ds are:

Decide on the meaningful metrics based on the intended audience.

Draw an appropriate picture (graph, histogram, etc.) for each metric.

---

[1]Although we concentrate in this chapter on managers as customers for our metrics, you will find that the metrics charts created using the approach defined here will also enhance communication among all team members.

Collect related metrics into a **D**ashboard.

Provide the ability to **D**rill down on high-level metrics that indicate trouble.

Let us look in detail at how each of these steps can be effectively followed.

14.1 DECIDE ON THE METRICS

As we discussed extensively in Chapter 2 (What to Measure), when deciding on the metrics to be collected and presented, you must first and foremost know for whom the metrics are intended. The first-level test manager may need to know how each tester is progressing and in which features/areas of code defects are being found while the higher-level software project manager may simply need to know how the overall test plan is progressing as part of the larger project.

Once you have identified the audience, that is, the customer for the metrics, you will need to ensure you understand that customer's requirements for metrics data. Is the customer trying to manage resource allocation, as a first-level manager might, or is the customer looking for high-level confirmation that the project is "on track," as a vice president might? (Our GQM approach in Chapter 2 can be used to ensure a clear understanding of what's needed.) You are, in essence, creating a contract with each customer as to what will be presented and how often. It is useful to actually document these agreements in standard process descriptions or local project plans.

When deciding on the metrics to collect and report, it is important to know what can be collected given resource and mechanization levels (again, recall the GQM^2 discussion). Recognize that for each metric collected and reported, resources will be required. We need to find the right level of metric collection to have enough information to make informed decisions while not burdening the project with unnecessary metrics collection and reporting costs. Recall our accuracy versus precision discussion in Chapter 3: we typically want accuracy not precision when we are considering the cost/benefit equation for our metrics program. The most effective approach is to select data that can be a natural output of the development process (e.g., KLOC built to date, percent of budget spent, number of defects found, number of test cases successfully executed). Look at the data that can easily be extracted from any mechanization that is in place, such as build tools and test drivers. Consider mechanization of report generation. Often, making a small investment up front will ultimately save both time and money by facilitating better decision making throughout the life of the project.

As an example, let us identify our customer as the program manager of a project that includes software. A typical set of metrics for this program manager might be:

- *Schedule Performance*: To assess if the team is on track to deliver on time. This type of metric includes measures such as percentage of schedule completed, development-specific phase progress measures (e.g., requirements signed off on to date), and Schedule Performance Index (SPI).[2] If our project is using a project management tool such as Project Scheduler (PS8™) from Sciforma Corporation or Microsoft Project, then we will in all likelihood have a Work Breakdown Structure (WBS) containing all project activities and the associated effort (cost) for those activities. With that mechanization in place, SPI would be a good choice as the schedule performance metric.

- *Technical Product Performance*: To assess if the software is on track to meet the expected functionality. This type of metric includes measures such as number of open defects and specific performance demonstrated over time. If a key performance requirement is throughput and we have mechanized drivers to measure it on each controlled build of software, then tracking this measure over time would be good.

- *Financial Performance*: To assess if the project is on track to deliver the objectives for cost and profit. This type of metric includes measures such as percentage of cost budget spent, percentage of Management Reserve (i.e., risk dollars) spent, and Cost Performance Index (CPI).[3] As with SPI, if a WBS is in place, CPI would be a good choice.

- *Customer Satisfaction*: To assess if the project is meeting customer expectations for project and software performance. This type of metric includes measures such as customer survey scores, number of customer found defects, and the dreaded number of customer complaints to the company president. If we have a mechanized tracking system for customer reported defects, as most software companies do, then choosing defects reported as a barometer of customer satisfaction may be an efficient and effective choice.

The bottom line for this first "D" is: Agree on a small, manageable set of metrics that meets the needs of the project for timely, informed decision making and cost effectiveness.

14.2 DRAW THE PICTURE

Once we have defined the metric or metrics to be collected and presented, each metric must be conveyed in an effective manner. We will call this creating an *eloquent metric*.

---

[2]Schedule Performance Index (SPI) is formally defined in the Project Management Body of Knowledge, which is maintained by the Project Management Institute [1]. SPI = Budgeted Cost of Work Performed/ Budgeted Cost of Work Scheduled. This measure requires the creation of a Work Breakdown Structure (WBS) for the project and identification of the costs for each activity in the WBS.

[3]Cost Performance Index (CPI) is formally defined in the Project Management Body of Knowledge, which is maintained by the Project Management Institute. CPI = Budgeted Cost of Work Performed/ Actual Cost of Work Performed. This measure requires the creation of a Work Breakdown Structure (WBS) for the project and identification of the costs for each activity in the WBS.

el-o-quent: 1. Speaking or spoken beautifully and forcefully; said or saying something in a forceful, expressive, and persuasive way. 2. Expressing emotion clearly; expressing a feeling or thought clearly, memorably, or movingly.

To make a selected metric eloquent:

1. Define the metric—clearly indicate what the metric represents and how it is calculated.
2. Set the objective—show the desired target measurement for the metric.
3. Provide current status—show the current measure for the metric, clearly indicating relationship to objective.
4. Trend the metric over time.
5. Provide a benchmark, either industry average and/or best-in-class, if available.

All of these listed attributes should appear on a single chart for the given metric. Graphs, timelines, and histograms convey the intended message of the metric more powerfully than words or numbers in a table. Use accepted, common terminology for all labels and annotations or else provide a clear definition or an explicit algorithm for the terminology used. For example, if all team members and managers on our project are familiar with the term field fault density (FFD), and know exactly how it is calculated for our project, simply using that term on a chart will suffice. If we needed to convey the same data to someone outside the company (say, a customer), we would want to show that FFD is equal to the total number of customer reported defects against a specific software release divided by the size in new and changed KLOC for that release. If needed for clarity, the source of the data should also be identified.

Once clearly defined, we need to establish an objective for each metric and then display that objective clearly on the chart. The objective could be a single value or a range of acceptable values. Often, these objectives are based on historical performance or performance of a comparable entity.[4]

Now that we have the graph defined and the objective shown, we need to display the current status data at each reporting period. It should be obvious whether or not this performance is meeting objectives. This is often done with a "stop light" technique—color coding the data point or chart red for missed objectives, yellow for poorly trending metrics in danger of missing objectives, and green for values that meet objectives.

We plot the values of the given metrics at each measurement point (e.g., daily or weekly). Trending the metric over time allows for potentially degrading performance to be spotted and addressed.

If possible, identify what an industry average or best-in-class value of the particular metric would be (see Chapter 13—Benchmarking). This could be one taken from

---

[4]In Chapter 6 (Estimating Effort), we discussed models, techniques, and tools for estimating which can also be used to help set objectives for the other metrics you choose to collect and present.

industry or from a high performing organization within our own company. This is particularly helpful for driving continuous improvement and setting appropriate objectives.

As an example, let us take the scenario of a test manager presenting testing progress to a software release manager. The eloquent testing progress metric is shown in Figure 14.1.

Audience: Release manager.

Metric Selected: Number of successfully executed test cases.

Definition: A test case is one complete user scenario defined in the documented release test plan. Successful execution means the expected, documented outcome was achieved for that test scenario when run against the software. To ensure audience understanding of the terms used, we have included a brief definition on the chart.

Objective: Based on historical data for this software and team and given the estimated size of the release, a range of acceptable execution progress has been determined prior to the start of testing. This range is represented by the upper and lower control limits. These control limits reflect what will be considered acceptable variation that will still lead to successful project completion. Anything outside the expected performance requires analysis to determine what actions, if any, may be needed. We could choose red for the lower control bound to indicate that falling below requires immediate action—the team is behind plan. Similarly, the upper control limit could be shown as yellow to indicate that moving above that line should be examined and there is the potential for action. Moving above the upper control limit may be good news, because things are going better than anticipated, but it could

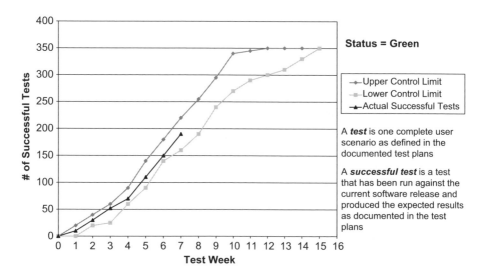

Figure 14.1. Successful test execution.

mean that the test plan is not exercising the software thoroughly enough (not getting at the defects) or testers are not doing thorough enough analysis (if analysis of results is manual).

Trending: For this example, the progress will be trended weekly until completion of the test program.

Benchmark: No real benchmark exists for this metric. However, the upper control limit does reflect what the best-case execution path is estimated to be.

Bottom line for the second "D": Use graphs, colors, and clear, concise definitions to quickly convey the good or bad news to management.

14.3 CREATE A DASHBOARD

To allow for related metrics to be viewed as a whole, the creation of a dashboard is very effective. It allows for easier "triangulation" of several metrics to the real conclusions that should be drawn from the data. To create a dashboard:

1. Identify metrics that will typically be looked at together to get the "full picture."
2. Follow "eloquent metrics" guidelines for each metric.
3. Combine those metric pictures together on a single page—typically 2 to 6 can fit reasonably on a page.

A simple dashboard for a test manager might include successful test execution and software defects found. These two are typically looked at together. Figure 14.2 shows this simple, test manager dashboard.

We could add other useful charts to the dashboard based on what we determine most effectively allows us to derive accurate information. For example, we might have progress of successful test execution by feature. We might also add a view of current status of defects found in test, such as how many are being fixed and how many have been fixed but not yet verified.

Depending on the type of dashboard you want to create, it may be helpful to look at one or more of the many commercially available dashboard tools that now exist.[5]

Bottom line for the third "D": If it takes two or three charts to derive the desired information, make it easy for the audience by putting them on a single dashboard.

14.4 DRILLING FOR INFORMATION

When a metric indicates something is "off track," we will want to be able to go under the covers and examine the components that make up that metric so that the correct

---

[5]A few dashboard provider websites we found include www.idashes.net, www.iexecutivedashboard.com, and www.distributive.com. You would need to determine for yourself what tool would best meet your particular needs.

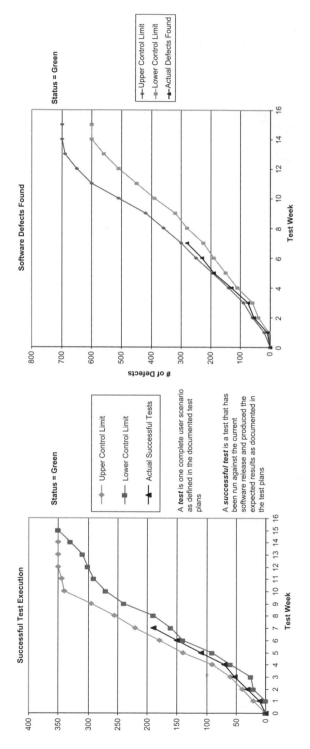

Figure 14.2. Test manager's dashboard.

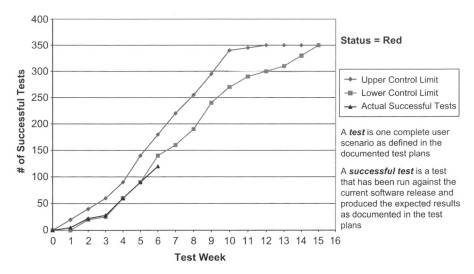

Figure 14.3. *Successful test execution.*

hot spot (i.e., root cause) can be identified and appropriate action taken. We must, therefore, be able to drill down from higher level metrics and be able to continue drilling until it is clear what area requires corrective action.

Figure 14.3 shows a test case execution chart with current performance below the lower control limit.

We are off plan and action needs to be taken. One of the typical reasons for the successful execution being in "the red zone" (i.e., below the lower control limit) is that the tests are uncovering a greater number of defects than originally expected. Alternatively, it could be that tester productivity is lower than planned or perhaps fixes to identified faults are being turned over more slowly than planned. Obviously, we need more data to determine the root cause. We might first look at the defect found chart (perhaps on a dashboard) for a more complete high-level picture. Figure 14.4 shows us what's happening with defect discovery.

Defects found are above the upper control limit, making the status RED for this metric as well. Greater than expected defects can indeed slow successful test execution, causing test progress to miss expectations. Seeing current status on the testing of each feature would be a helpful "drill down" on the off-plan test execution metric. Figure 14.5 provides this view.

This drill down shows that Feature 3 is the "problem feature," contributing to the slower than predicted progress on successful test execution. It also shows that it is due to "buggy" feature code. Possible action could include reinspection of the code and/or design.

If we had seen that this was simply a test execution problem (we would see this if the black[6] plus vertical stripe areas in any feature column did not reached

---

[6]As stated before, it would be most effective to use colors on our graphs. Green for successful, red for failed, and yellow for "to be run."

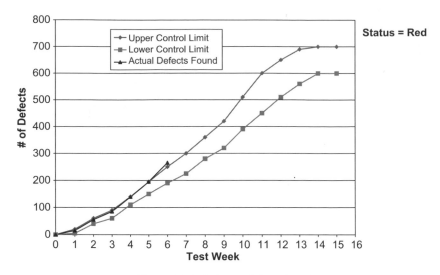

Figure 14.4. *Software defects found.*

the "star"), that would indicate that testing resources were the issue. Further drill downs could then be done to look at machine availability and individual tester progress.

Bottom line for the fourth "D": Keep drilling until the root cause is determined so that the correct action can be taken.

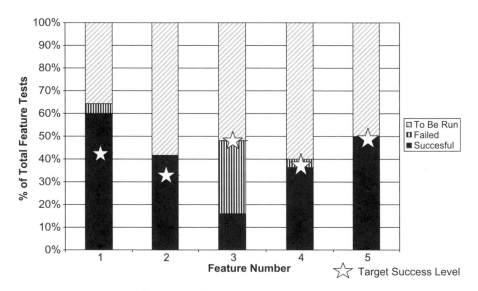

Figure 14.5. *Feature test progress—week 6.*

14.5 EXAMPLE FOR THE BIG CHEESE

Let us put it all together with one more example. In this example, we will look at a Quality Assurance Vice President.

As the high-level decision maker for quality assurance for a software company, the QA Vice President may want to know:

- Cost effectiveness of the QA organization
- Level of customer satisfaction
- Quality level of deliverables

For this example, we are going to use modified versions[7] of ones used by a real QA organization from a major software company.

For cost effectiveness, this organization chose to use a derived measure: cost to test/LOC, as shown in Figure 14.6.

This particular metric indicates the productivity of the QA testing organization but can be affected by the quality of the code entering test. We would,

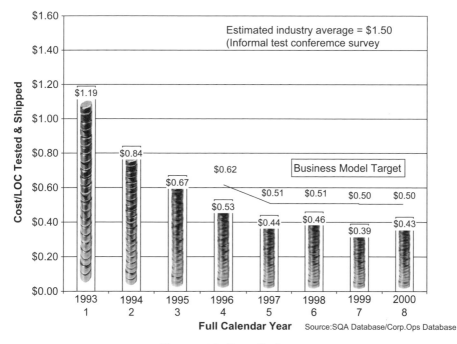

Figure 14.6. Cost effectiveness.

---

[7]Modifications were made to "sanitize" the data and make chart time frames compatible for the dashboard.

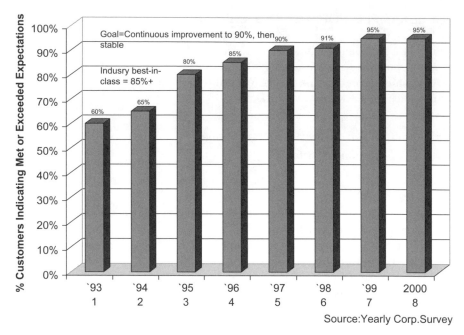

Figure 14.7. Customer satisfaction.

therefore, want to know if the incoming quality was stable over the same time period. We could look at defect removal ratios by phase and/or percentage of test cases passed first time to get at this ... and perhaps put those on the dashboard as well.

Note that a published benchmark was not available, but an informal verbal survey at a well-attended testing industry conference provided some useful insight. The organization's goal was based on a business model that took into consideration how many testers (at each pay grade) and how much mechanization were appropriate given the type of software product being tested (i.e., a new product, one being significantly enhanced, etc.).

Customer satisfaction for this particular company was measured by a yearly survey. Figure 14.7 shows how this metric trended over time.

For a product field quality metric, this company chose to measure field fault density. The measure is the number of customer faults against the entire software portfolio of current releases divided by the size of the portfolio in millions of lines of code. Figure 14.8 shows this metric.

These three charts would make a good start to a dashboard for the QA VP. Using GQM from Chapter 2, we could determine what other charts might be added to fully meet the "customer's" need.

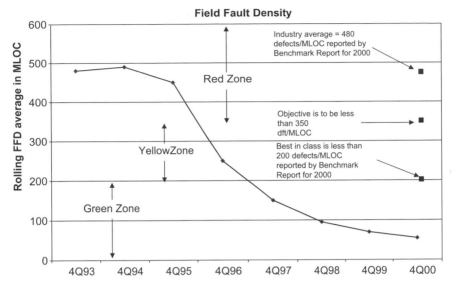

Figure 14.8. Field fault density.

14.6 EVOLVING METRICS

As we indicated in Chapter 2, it is important to evolve metrics programs over time. Just as the goals and demands of the business may change over time, the metrics used to manage that business must keep pace. For example, for many years a software product company used product-specific surveys to measure customer satisfaction. Given the survey method and poor initial customer satisfaction, this metric served the company well by driving continuous improvement for several years. Once the company achieved consistently high levels of customer satisfaction (levels greater than 85%), this metric was no longer meeting the business need for continuous improvement. The company then migrated its customer satisfaction survey to a total customer experience survey and measured the results against the customer's best-in-class experience. In other words, the company measured itself against a "virtual competitor." The new metrics allowed the company to focus on reducing the "gap" between its performance and the customer's best-in-class experience.

Metrics can become stale over time for other reasons as well. When metrics are presented to management, they have the added weight of reflecting on individual and/or organizational performance. For this reason, you must guard against people and organizations "learning how to play the numbers game." For example, one company focused for a time on specifically reducing customer reported defects of high severity level. Over time some teams started "reclassifying" defects from high to medium severity, while still working to respond to the customer in a timely manner. This would skew the "severe problem" metric, giving a false impression of both quality and customer satisfaction. This behavior precipitated a change to the metrics program to look at total number of defects and require that metric to trend down as well.

Evolution of a metrics program must be done carefully. Changing what is measured too frequently can weaken an organization's ability to make valid historical comparisons and clearly see trending over time. Change should be driven by the goals of the organization and the usefulness of the metrics in driving the organization toward those goals.

14.7   SUMMARY

To ensure effective and efficient communication of metrics to management, remember the following:

1. Know your audience. Tailor the number and level of the metrics to that audience.
2. Minimize the number of metrics. Keep the metrics to the fewest possible that convey the intended message, but be able to get under the covers if questions arise. Expand only when necessary for corrective action.
3. Ensure all metrics are *eloquent*. Eloquent metrics will ensure that each chart accurately conveys the intended information and can speak for itself if it "travels" without its author.[8]
4. Keep you metrics program fresh. Revisit your metrics program regularly to ensure that it is meeting the needs of the business and driving the intended behavior.

PROBLEMS

14.1   True or False: If you do a good job of defining your set of metrics, you should be able to give the same presentation to all of your management.

14.2   Why might you want to drill down on a particular metric?

14.3   How would you improve the metric in Figure 14.9 to make it "eloquent"?

---

[8]Metric charts have a tendency to reproduce and spread through a management team in a manner similar to a virus. Ensuring all metrics are eloquent will serve as your vaccination against a flood of requests from the "infected" parties to explain what the metrics really mean.

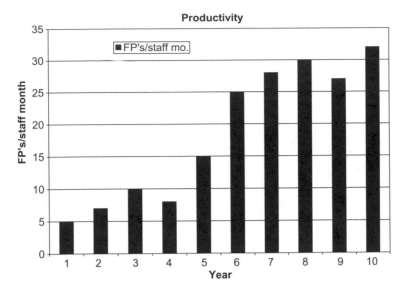

Figure 14.9. *Data for problem 14.3.*

PROJECT

14.1 You have been hired as the CIO of an online trading company. The systems have had availability issues and the customers are complaining. From what you have seen, your organization has tons of data, but not much information. Define and create the charts and dashboard you want to present to the CEO to show that you are on top of the situation.

REFERENCE

[1] Project Management Institute, *A Guide to the Project Management Body of Knowledge*, 3rd edition, 2004. Available from www.pmi.org.

Index

Albrect–Gaffney Model, 103–104
Actors, 96
AFP, 42
Agresti–Card–Glass Metric, 67–71
  Counting Rules, 69–70
  Engineering Rule, 71
  Example, 70–71
Algorithmic Models, 103–107
  Duration, 105
  Manual Models, 103–105
  Tools, 105–107
Arrival Rate Prediction Models,
  see Software Reliability
Availability Measurement, 170–178
  Availability Factors, 172–173
  Definition, 170
  Downtime Per Year, 170
  Measurement Complexities, 173–174
  Outage Scope, 173
  Rejuvenation, 174–177

Bailey–Basili Model, 103–104
Benchmarking, 231–237
Benefits in a business case, 216–217
Boehm Simple Model, 103–104

Bohrbugs, 175
Break-even point, 219
Business case
  For outsourcing, 199–201
  For software project launch, 209–224
  Realization of, 224

Capability Maturity Model Integration®,
  see Standards
Capital costs, 213–216, 226
Cash Flow, 217, 222–223, 226
CBR, *see* Cost Benefit Ratio
Chidamber and Kemerer Metric Suite,
  72–73
CMMI®, *see* Standards
COCOMO, 89, 94, 103–106, 132
Code integration, 182, 185–187
  Metric, 186–187
  Pattern, 186
  Plan, 187–189
Complexity, 52–78
  Computational, 74
  Conceptual, 73
  Cyclomatic Complexity, 58–63
  Halstead's Metrics, 63–64

Software Measurement and Estimation, by Linda M. Laird and M. Carol Brennan
Copyright © 2006 John Wiley & Sons, Inc.

Complexity (*Continued*)
   Information Flow Metrics, 65–67
   Module Size and Complexity, 56–57
   Objective, 54
   Object-Oriented Metrics, 71–73
   Structural Complexity Metrics, 55–73
   System Complexity Metrics, 67–71
   System Size and Complexity, 55–56
Cone of Uncertainty, 110–112
Continuous improvement, 242
Contract metrics, 203–206
COQUALMO, 132
COSMIC Full Function Points, 41
Cost Benefit Ratio, 217, 220–221, 226
Cost of Reliability, 147–148
Cost Performance Index, 240
Costs
   Overhead, 210–211, 226
   Risk, 211–213
   Salaries, 210
CPI, *see* Cost Performance Index
Creeping Requirements, 81, 93
Customer satisfaction, 240, 246–249
Cyclomatic Complexity Metric, 58–63
   Counting Rules, 58
   Cyclomatic Complexity Density, 61
   Engineering Rules, 60–61
   Essential Cyclomatic Complexity,
      61–63
   Examples, 53–60

Dashboard, 243–244, 247
Deciding on metrics, 239–240
Decision maker model, 10
Defect Density
   Benchmark Data, 133–135
   Definition, 120
Defect Density Benchmark Data
   133–135
   By Application Domain, 133
   By SEI Level, 134
   By Size in Function Points (1991), 134
   Latent Defects, 135
   Recommendations, 135
   US Averages (2000), 134–135
Defect Projection Techniques and
   Models, 123–133
   Dynamic Defect Models, 123–129
   Static Models, 129–133

Defect Removal Efficiency, 130–132,
   191–193
   Definition, 130
   DRE Matrix, 130–131
Defects, 118–143
   Arrival Rates, 120
   Backlog, 191–193
   Benchmark Data, 133–135
   Closure, 182, 188, 190–192
   Cost Effectiveness of Removal, 136
   Customer Reported Defect Patterns, 139
   Defect Density, 120, 133–135
   Discovery, 182, 188–190, 243–245
   Dynamics and Behaviors, 118–123
   Failures, 119–120
   Faults, 119–120
   Metrics, 11,188–192
   Simple Metric Example, 136–139
   Versus Code Production Rate, 121
   Versus Effort, 120
   Versus Module Complexity, 122
   Versus Staffing, 120–121
   Versus System Size, 122–123
Depreciation, 215
Design-to-code expansion ratio, 39
Doty Model, 103–104
DRE See Defect Removal Efficiency
Drilling down, 243–247
Duration, 11
Dynamic Defect Models, 123–133
   Customer Reported Defect Patterns,
      139–140
   Empirical Evidence, 128–129
   Exponential, 127–128
   Rayleigh, 124–127
   Recommendations, 129
   S-curve, 127–128

EAC, *see* Estimate at Completion
Effort, Estimating, 11, *see also* Estimating
   Effort
Eloquent metrics, 240–243
Engineering Rules
   Agresti–Card–Glass Metric, 71
   Creeping Requirements, 93
   Cyclomatic Complexity Metric, 60–61
   Defect Density, 135
   Defect Removal Costs, 136
   Response Time, 168–169

Estimation Uncertainty, 111–113
Function Points, 47–49, 92–93
Maintainability Index, 68
Reliability Prediction Techniques,
    156–157
Schedule, 92
Staffing, 93
Estimate at Completion, 224–226
Estimate to Complete, 224–226
Estimating Effort, 79–119
Estimation, 79–117, *see also* Estimating
    Effort
    Combining Estimates, 107–108
    Issues, 108–112
    Methodologies and Models, 79–106
    When to Estimate, 112–113
Estimation Issues
    Agile Methodology Results, 112
    Estimation Uncertainties, 109–112
    Estimation Uncertainty Engineering
        Rules, 111–112
    Inadequate Budgets, 108–110
    Limitations of Estimation, 109
    Overconfidence in Experts, 111
    Targets versus Estimates, 108–109
Estimation Methodologies and Models,
    79–106
    Algorithmic Models, 103–107
    Analogy, 88–91
    Benchmark Data, 85–88
    Current Performance, 80–81
    Custom Models, 101–103
    Delphi Methods, 84–85
    Engineering Rule—Creeping Features,
        93
    Engineering Rule—Effort, 93
    Engineering Rules—Staffing, 93
    Expert Opinion, 82–85
    EZ Estimation Model, 85
    Function Blocks, 84
    Maintainability Index, 67–69
    Proxy Points, 91–101
    System Decomposition, 83–84
    Work and Activity Decomposition,
        82–83
ETC, *see* Estimate to Complete
EV, *see* Expected Value
Evolving metrics, 12, 247–250
Expected Value, 223–224, 226

Expense costs, 213–216
Exponential Defect Models, 127–128
Exponential Distribution, 123, 149–152

$f(t)$, 149
$F(t)$, 151
Failure Intensity, 146
Failure Severity Classes, 145–146
Failure—Definition, 119–120
Fault Classification, 175
Fault—Definition, 119–120
Feature Points, 50–51
Financial
    Concepts, 209
    Measures, 208–230
    Performance, 240
    Software engineer involvement,
        208–209
Four D's, 238–246
Function Points, 40–51, 92
    Converting Function Points to Effort,
        47–48
    Converting Function Points to LOC, 47,
        See Gear Factors
    COSMIC, 93–94
    Counting Rules, 41–44
    Engineering Rules, 47–49, 92
    Example, 45–46
    Productivity Benchmark, 87–88
    Pros and Cons, 49–50
    Effort Estimation, 92–93
Future Worth, 220
FW, *see* Future Worth

Gearing Factors, 35–39
General System Characteristics, 43
Goal Question Metric approach, *see* GQM
GQM, 9–10, 239, 247
GQM^2, 11–12, 239

Halstead's Metrics, 63–64
Hawthorne Effect, 21
Heisenbugs, 175
Hope-based Planning, 81

IFPUG, 41
Income Statement, *see* Profit & Loss
    Statement
Index of Variation, 26

Information Flow Metrics, 65–67
  Counting Rules, 65
  Examples, 65–67
  Henry and Kafura version, 65
  IEEE 982.2 version, 65
In-process metrics, 181–196
Inspection-effectiveness metric, 193–194
International Function Point Users
    Group, 41
International Software Benchmarking
    Standards Group, 87
ISBSG, 87

Kemerer Model, 103–104

Language Productivity Factors, 35–39
Latency Metrics, 167
Lines of Code
  Productivity Benchmark, 85–87
  Counting Rules, 34–39
Lorenz–Kidd Method, 41

Maintainability Index, 67–69
  Counting Rules, 67–68
  Engineering Rules, 68
  Example, 68–69
Management reserve, 222, 240
Matson–Barrett–Meltichamp Model,
    103–104
McCabe's Cyclomatic Complexity See
    Cyclomatic Complexity Metric
Mean-Time-Between-Failures
    (MTBF), 119
Measurement Theory, 22–29
  Central Tendency, 25
  Measurement Error, 28–29
  Measurement Reliability, 27
  Measurement Validity, 27–28
  Variability, 25–26
Measurement Validity, 27–28
  Construct, 27
  Content, 28
  Criterions-Related, 27
Mechanism for metrics collection and
    reporting, 11–12
Metrics
  Accuracy, 30
  Limitations, 30
  Precision, 30

Milestones, 182–185
  As gates, 184–185
  SMART, 183–185, 188
Models, 16–21
  Diagrammatic, 18
  Of Software Development, 17–18
  Text, 16
  Algorithmic, 18
  Meta-Model, 20–21
  Of Response Time, 18
Motivation for studying estimation and
    metrics, 3–5
MTBF, 154
MTTF, 119, 149–150, 154, 170
MTTR, 154, 170

Object Points, 41, 94–95
Object-Oriented Design Metrics, 71–73
Outsourcing, 197–207
  Definition, 198–201
  Making the business case, 199–201
  Managing risk, 201–203
  Risk levels, 202–203
Overhead costs, *see* Costs

P&L Statement, *see* Profit & Loss
    Statement
Pantometric Paradigm, 19
Partial Rejuvenation, 175–176
Payback Period, 217, 219–220
Percent complete metric, 185
Power of Measurement, 21–22
Present Value, 220–226
Presenting metrics, 238–251
Process
  Adherence to, 7
  Effectiveness, 182, 192–194
Productivity, 11, 86, 88, 217
  By Application Domain, 86
  By Platform Type, 88
  LOC Benchmarks, 85–89
Profit & Loss Statement, 217, 221–222,
    226
Profitability, 7, 209
Progress
  Measuring, 181–196, 204, 224
  Testing, *see* Testing
Project management methodology, Affect
    on methodology, 183

Project milestones, *see* Milestones
Projects, 2, 13, 52, 77, 116, 142, 165–166, 179, 196, 251, 207, 228–229
Proxy Points, 41, *see also* Function Points, Feature Points, Use Case Points, Object Points
PV, *see* Present Value
pX Estimate, 111–113

Quality Surprises, 81
Quality, 7, 246–247, 204

R(*t*), 151–152
Random Distribution, 149, *see also* Exponential distribution
Random Error, 28–29
Range, 25
Rayleigh Defect Models, 124–127
Rayleigh Distribution, 123–127, *see also* What to measure
Rejuvenation See Software Rejuvenation
Reliability See Software Reliability
Response Time Measurement 167–170, 178
    Models, 168–170
    Recommended Response Times for Systems, 168–169
Responsiveness, 205
Return on Investment, 217–219
Risk
    Affect on milestones, 183
    Assessing, 211–212, 226
    Cost quantification, 211–213, 222, 240
    Identifying, 211–226
    Management for outsourcing, 201–203
    Monitoring, 213, 226
    Planning for, 212–213, 226
    Top ten software risks, 212
ROI, *see* Return on Investment

Salvage value of a capital asset, 215
Schedule Engineering Rule, 92
Schedule Performance Index, 240
Schedule performance, 239–240
S-Curves
    Defect Models, 127–128
    Distribution, 123
Senilitybugs, 175
Service life of capital, 215

Shalls, 39
Size, 7, 11, 34–53
    Functionality Measurements, 40–51
    Gearing Factors, 35–39
    Language Productivity Factors see Size, Gearing Factors
    Lines of Code (LOC), 34–39
    Non-Procedural Code, 39
    Physical Measurement, 34–40
    Refactored Code, 37
    Reused Code, 37
    Source Code Counting Checklist, 35–36
    Specifications and Design, 38
SMART milestones, 183–185, 188
Software Aging, 175
Software Engineering Institute (SEI), 35
Software Rejuvenation, 174–177
    Fault Classification, 175
    Impact on Availability, 176–177
    Software Aging, 175
    Techniques, 175–176
Software Reliability, 7, 144–166
    Cost of Reliability, 147–148
    Decision to Ship, 161
    Definition of Software Reliability, 144–145
    F(*t*), 151
    f(*t*), 149, 152
    Failure Arrival Rate Prediction Models, 155–161
    Failure Intensity, 146
    Failure Severity Classes, 145–146
    Models, 152–155
    Predicting Remaining Defects, 154–155
    Probability of Failure During a Time Interval, 150–151
    Probability of Failure by Time *T*, 151
    Software Reliability Prediction Techniques, 155–157
    System Configurations, 161–163
    Theory, 148–152
Software Reliability Prediction Techniques, 155–161
    Engineering Rules, 156–157
    Historical Data, 155–156
    Musa's Algorithm, 157–158
    Operational Profile Testing, 158–161
Source Code Counting Checklist, 35–36
Specification-to-Code Expansion Ratio, 39

SPI, *see* Schedule Performance Index
SPR Complexity Adjustment Factors, 44
Staffing Engineering Rule, 93
Standard Deviation, 26
Standards
   CMMI®, 4–6, 11, 202
   EIC 60880, 11
   ISO 9001, 202
   TL9000, 11
Standards driven metrics, 10–11
Static Defect Models
   Defect Removal Efficiency (DRE),
     130–132
   Insertion and Removal Model, 129–130
   Tools—COQUALMO, 132
Stop-light technique, 241
Strncat, 15, 59, 63, 66
Supplier management, *see* Outsourcing
System Complexity Measurement, 67–71
   Agresti–Card–Glass Metric, 69–71
   Maintainability Index, 67–69
System size, *see* Size
Systematic Error, 28–29

Technical product performance, 240
Testing
   Execution, 243–245
   Progress, 182, 187–188, 242–243
Time
   Affect on metrics, 12, 247–250
   Affect on reliability, 153–154
   Measuring, 5
Triangulation, 107

UCP, UUCP See Use Case Points
UFP, 42
Uniform Distribution, 148
Use Case, 96
Use Case Methodologies, 95
   Use Case Points, 96–101
   Using Function Points, 96
   Using LOC, 96
Use Case Points, 41, 96–101
   Calibration, 101
   Counting Rules, 96–98
   Effectiveness, 100–101
   Example, 98–100
Use Case Productivity Factor, 97, 101

VAF, 42
Variability
   Index of, 26
   Measures of, 25–26
   Range, 25
   Standard Deviation, 26
   Variance, 25
Variance, 103–104

Walston–Felix Model, 103–104
WBS, *see* Work Breakdown Structure
WebMo, 41
Weibull Curves, 124
What to measure, 7–14
Work Breakdown Structure, 240

λ, 149–152